More praise for *Competing Globally* . . .

"*Competing Globally* brings you to the real scene. It gives the right guidance for business . . . planting a seed for the future."
Professor Rahardi Ramelan, former Minister of Trade and Industry, Indonesia

"Very informative, practical, and invaluable. This book will be of great value to those who want to understand and deal with other cultures."
Dr. Ismail Osman, Chairman of the Board, Arab Contractors, Egypt

"*Competing Globally* contains lots of useful examples which will help American business people to succeed with Asians and many other peoples."
Shinichi Yamashita, Program Manager, Agilent Technologies, USA

"Very easy to read and lively. *Competing Globally* is pictorial, knowledge-based, and well-written."
Dr. Sununta Siengthat, Asian Institute of Technology, Thailand

"*Competing Globally* makes navigation of global business less hazardous."
Dr. Helena Hannonen, President, Global Management, USA

"I especially enjoyed the little quizzes in each chapter. They enabled me to perform informative self-assessments."
David Sheen, President DataMagic, USA

COMPETING GLOBALLY:

Mastering Multicultural Management and Negotiations

THE MCD SERIES
MANAGING CULTURAL DIFFERENCES

Competing Globally: Mastering Multicultural Management and Negotiations
Farid Elashmawi

Developing the Global Organization: Strategies for Human Resource Professionals
Robert T. Moran, Philip R. Harris, and William G. Stripp

Dynamics of Successful International Business Negotiations
William G. Stripp and Robert T. Moran

Intercultural Services: A Worldwide Buyer's Guide and Sourcebook
Gary Wederspahn

International Business Case Studies for the Multicultural Marketplace
Robert T. Moran, David O. Braaten, and John E. Walsh

International Directory of Multicultural Resources
Robert T. Moran and David O. Braaten

Managing Cultural Differences, Fifth Edition
Philip R. Harris and Robert T. Moran

Mentoring and Diversity
Belle Rose-Ragins, David Clutterbuck, and Lisa Matthewman

**Multicultural Management 2000: Essential Cultural Insights
for Global Business Success**
Farid Elashmawi and Philip R. Harris

**Succeeding in Business in Central and Eastern Europe: A Guide to Cultures,
Markets, and Practices**
Woodrow H. Sears and Audrone Tamulionyte-Lentz

Transcultural Leadership: Empowering the Diverse Workforce
George F. Simons, Carmen Vazquez, and Philip R. Harris

FORTHCOMING TITLES:

Eurodiversity: Cultural Considerations and Business Success in Western Europe
George Simons

NAFTA—Best Practices
Robert T. Moran and Jeff Abbott

COMPETING GLOBALLY:
Mastering Multicultural Management and Negotiations

FARID ELASHMAWI, Ph.D.

BUTTERWORTH
HEINEMANN

Boston   Oxford   Auckland   Johannesburg   Melbourne   New Delhi

⎰ A member of the Reed Elsevier group

Copyright © 2001 Farid Elashmawi

∞ Recognizing the importance of preserving what has been written, Butterworth–Heinemann prints its books on acid-free paper whenever possible.

Library of Congress Cataloging-in-Publication Data

Elashmawi, Farid.
  Competing globally: mastering multicultural management and negotiations / Farid Elashmawi.
    p. cm.—(Managing cultural differences series)
  Includes bibliographical references and index.
  ISBN 0-87719-371-1 (alk. paper)
    1. International business enterprises—Management. 2. International business enterprises—Management—Cross-cultural studies. 3. Intercultural communication. 4. Competition, International. I. Title. II. Series.

HD62.4 .E423 2001
658'.049—dc21

                                                          2001018458

British Library Cataloguing-in-Publication Data
A catalogue record for this book is available from the British Library.

The publisher offers special discounts on bulk orders of this book.
For information, please contact:
Manager of Special Sales
Butterworth–Heinemann
225 Wildwood Avenue
Woburn, MA 01801–2041
Tel: 781-904-2500
Fax: 781-904-2620

For information on all Butterworth–Heinemann publications available, contact our World Wide Web home page at: http://www.bh.com

10 9 8 7 6 5 4 3 2 1

Printed in the United States of America

Contents

1

Sailing Across Business Cultures 1
Negotiating Globally 2. Managing Globally 6. Mastering
Multicultural Meetings 7. Managing Multicultural Teams 9.
Conducting Training Across Culture 17. Summary 18.

2

Working One-on-One with Americans 19
Test Your Skills Dealing with Americans 20. American Cultural
Values 22. Meeting the Americans 25. Tips for Meeting
Americans 28. On the Phone with Americans 28. Tips On

3

4

Conducting Meetings and Presentations 88. Tips for Conducting
Meetings with Koreans 89. Enhancing Relationships with
Koreans 90. Persuading Koreans 92. Characteristics of
the Korean Negotiator 92. Contracting with Koreans 95.
The Korean Decision-Making Process 96. Encountering the
Korean Negotiators 97. Enhancing Your Negotiation Success
with Koreans 98. Working with Koreans 99. Training
Koreans 100. Tips for Training Koreans 100. Motivating
Koreans 101. Promotions within Korean Organizations 102.
Social Etiquette When Dealing with Koreans 102.
Summary 103.

5

6

7

8

9

Foreword

In an information age dominated by electronic communications and commerce, it is important to be reminded of people differences that can either guarantee success or ensure failure in business negotiations. *Competing Globally* does just that. It empowers managers and professionals in the cross-cultural arena. Its subtitle concisely states the objective of this publication, namely to assist you in mastering cross-cultural negotiations and management. Reading the nine chapters of this volume will enhance your ability to create cultural synergy, as well as your effectiveness with Americans, Arabs, Asians, and Europeans. Each chapter is pragmatic and readable, containing helpful tips and mini-cases for dealing with specific peoples, such as Koreans, Thais, Chinese, and Indonesians. Throughout, there are many questionnaires useful for self-evaluation and learning.

This text is a sequel to another successful work by the author on similar themes, *Multicultural Management 2000* (Houston, TX: Gulf Publishing Co., 1998). Both volumes by Dr. Farid Elashmawi are part of Gulf's *Managing Cultural Differences Series*. Elashmawi is himself a model of cross-cultural competence. Born in Egypt, but based in the United States, he serves a wide variety of international clients, especially in Asia and the Middle East, through his company, Global Success, which is located in San Jose, California. Though his doctorate is in engineering, his MBA degree facilitated his crossover into the field of business where he is a world-renowned consultant and trainer in transcultural management and negotiation. Thus, the insights he presents in this book are grounded on action research and experience, which may explain why his publications are so popular. Reading and applying the lessons of this book will undoubtedly advance your management skills in the global marketplace!

Philip R. Harris, Ph.D.
President, Harris International, Ltd.
LaJolla, California, USA

Series Preface

Culture is a fascinating concept. It has so many applications, whether between nations, organizations, or peoples. Communicating effectively across cultures, negotiating on a global scale, and conducting international business are always challenging. To thrive, and in many cases to survive, in the 21st century, individuals and institutions must incorporate cultural sensitivity and skills into their relations, strategies, and structures. Inability to deal with differences or diversity in human cultures is a sign of weakness and obsolescence in persons and groups. The new millennium has no tolerance for "ethnic cleansing," anti-Semitism, or any other form of religious, racial, or gender discrimination.

As originally conceived, our book, *Managing Cultural Differences*, was intended to increase human effectiveness with people who differ in cultural backgrounds. With the new century, our "flagship" sails into her fifth edition. We are particularly gratified that business organizations have not only found the book useful, but in academia, more than 200 universities worldwide have adopted our work as a textbook. But this pioneering publication has also spawned many "offspring," so the *Managing Cultural Differences Series* was launched and has subsequently grown into more than a dozen titles.

As series editors, we are pleased with these outstanding products. We trust that you will continue to find our literary efforts helpful as you seek to address transcultural challenges in our rapidly changing, highly interdependent communities!

Philip R. Harris, Ph.D.
LaJolla, California
Robert T. Moran, Ph.D.
Scottsdale, Arizona

Acknowledgments

I am grateful to my clients and partners with whom I have been directly or indirectly in contact while developing the material for this book. Those managers and friends have helped me learn to succeed with their own culture through the process of communicating, training, or even socializing after work with them. My appreciation to Professor Philip Harris, my mentor over the last several years, who has encouraged and guided me while developing the manuscript for this book.

My special thanks to my family, which has been highly tolerant and supportive during my frequent travel overseas: To my wife, Fatma; our sons, Amre and his wife Raania, and Esam and his wife Pessant; and our grandson, Yousef.

I acknowledge the valuable editorial work done by Tim Calk and Debbie Markley. My appreciation to Mr. Richard Coleman, Mr. Robert Cobez, and Professor Sununta Siengthai for reading chapters of the manuscript. Special thanks also go to my staff: Steve Scully, Laura Lawless, Sherine Nafie, and Jillian Appel for their extra effort and time spent in preparing the manuscripts for this book. Without the effort of the virtual and local team, this book would not be a reality.

F. E.

Introduction

During the last century, many Western nations and firms have successfully competed on a global scale through their use of new technological advances. Many other Eastern nations have recently managed to expand their global business through acquiring the West's basic technologies and by manufacturing products at reduced prices.

In the 21st Century, however, new technology and lower prices will no longer be the sole competitive edges. Western technology will be quickly acquired by other countries and lower prices will be attained through enhanced productivity and automation. As a result, a new competitive edge to successful global business is needed: *cultural competency.*

Cultural competency is what future global business managers will need to supplement both technological advances and price reductions. Competing globally through enhancing one's cultural competency is the goal of this book. It was written to help today's managers deal successfully across global business cultures.

Competing Globally will introduce you to the cultural norms of several national cultures and show you how to compete for business success in each country. Each chapter will help you master important business daily activities—including personal introductions; making overseas phone calls and written communication; recognizing nonverbal messages of diverse cultures; conducting business meetings, presentations, price persuasions, and negotiations; managing culturally diverse workers; and, finally, avoiding costly social taboos.

Most of the material in the book has been based on more than 15 years of personal experience in the global market, providing my training seminars on multicultural management and negotiation across cultures. I have spent about four years in and out of Japan coaching managers from major Japanese organizations, as well as learning from them. In Japan, I dealt with Sony, NEC, Hitachi, Fujitsu, and others. It took me another two years to understand the Korean system and how to succeed with them through dealing with organizations such as Samsung, DaeWoo, and Lucky Goldstar. I then sailed across Thailand, Malaysia, and Indonesia to enter these unique markets—training, coaching, and learning from the managers that I encountered. I have also dealt with major organizations in Thailand, such as NIDA Management Development, Thai Management Association, Shinawatra Group, and Phonelink.

In Malaysia, I encountered major organizations and trained managers from Petronas, Renong, and INTAN. In Indonesia, I spent three years coaching managers in Telkom, Indosat, Satelindo, and Telkomsel from the telecommunication industry. Entering the Chinese market from inside China, Hong Kong, Taiwan, and Singapore was the most difficult because of the time it took to build relationships and negotiate prices. However, it was a good learning experience for me and I hope I can present it for you to learn from. In my attempts, I did not succeed the first time, but through my learning from other cultures and my persistent persuasion in building relationships I succeeded in the long term. Through these efforts, I have earned the respect, business, money, and friendship of these peoples. Finally, I returned to Egypt to the Arab culture I was born into and spent my first 24 years in, to rediscover my culture and conduct business in that important market.

In Chapter 1, I will take you across the globe through several cultures to feel how frustrating it is if you are not familiar with the basics in understanding the culture you are dealing with. This will be presented through the story of many of our sales managers who go global without recognizing the value of understanding client cultures. In Chapter 2, you will learn how to meet Americans one-on-one and respond to their value for equality, freedom of choice, self-reliance, and directness. Through a series of personal stories and encounters, you will be able to succeed in competing with them in their own territory. I will give you my insight in living in America the last 25 years. Next, you will learn in Chapter 3 how to deal with the Japanese salaryman, who is the gatekeeper to many business opportunities in Japan, through a series of personal examples that I have faced. You will learn how to counter the Japanese team and to enjoy their sushi and Karaoke nights.

In Chapter 4, you will discover the Koreans and how to prepare to meet them on the business battleground to sustain success in this important market. The chapter will help you understand Korean managers and how to persuade them. In Chapter 5, I will help you to open the door to the fourth most populous nation, Indonesia, and discover its diversity and how to deal with the big Pak, the decision maker. In Chapter 6, I hope you will be cooled off from the Korean battle and from bowing to Indonesian Paks and enjoy the polite and harmonious Thais. In Chapter 7, I will attempt to give you an entry into the Arab cultures and how religion influences their daily activities and decision processes. In Chapter 8, we will discover the diversity of several European cultures, and discuss the differences in dealing with British, French, Italian, Dutch, German, and Swiss business cultures with specific tips on how to make it in each culture. Finally, in Chapter 9, we will return to Asia with a broad look at how to deal with the Chinese in the most populous nation in the world, and what you also need to deal successfully with other Chinese in Taiwan, Hong Kong, and Singapore.

I must admit that no book may ever exist that provides contrast in dealing with all the cultures in the world as we know it. However, the process developed in presenting the book materials, personal stories, tests for your skills, cultural contrasts, tips and taboos, and social etiquette will all help you master the process of negotiating and managing across cultures in general. I hope that the information in this book and the diversity of cultures presented will help you in your daily business encounters in the international community. Now sit back, relax, and fasten your seat belt as we sail together across global business cultures. Enjoy the sailing!

Sailing Across Business Cultures

*How would you present your business proposal
to a Malaysian client?
Who will decide on your proposal in Indonesia?
How do you negotiate prices with Koreans?
Where will you entertain your Japanese client?
How do you establish trust with your prospective
agent in Thailand?*

These questions are at the heart of global business success. Today's businesspeople need to master cross-cultural negotiation skills more than ever. In this chapter, through several cross-cultural encounters, you will find valuable tips and skills for dealing with clients, suppliers, partners, and employees from different cultures. We will read about the experiences of John Smith, an American salesman who shows some of the mishaps that can occur when traveling to secure business in Malaysia, Indonesia, Korea, Japan, and Thailand.

You will learn how Malaysians pass the buck, who makes decisions in Indonesia, how to deal with the boss in Korea, and who will end up paying for a $400 Sushi dinner with the Japanese. The chapter will then take you through several cases in negotiating globally, managing global operations, mastering multicultural meetings, negotiating work orders, managing multinational joint ventures, and conducting training sessions across cultures.

Negotiating Globally

Smith goes to Asia

John Smith, an American marketing manager, wondered about the probation note he had received from his boss after he returned from a four-week overseas sales trip throughout Asia. He worked for a wholesale distribution outlet that supplied its clients with high-quality clothing and garments based on licenses from top American brands. Due to his excellent sales performance in California last year, Smith had been assigned to head the company's international sales in Asia.

Hoping to capture numerous sales in one business trip, Smith had called numerous contacts in the countries he was to visit and had arranged meetings and presentations with them. He scheduled visits to Kuala Lumpur, Jakarta, Seoul, Tokyo, and Bangkok. Armed with numerous samples of his company's new product line, including evening gowns, lingerie, cosmetics, and luggage, a confident Smith sat in his business-class seat on a flight to Kuala Lumpur.

Passing the buck in Malaysia

On the morning of his arrival in Kuala Lumpur, Smith phoned his client, Abdul Magid, to confirm his appointment at 9 a.m. This company had been one of his big targets, and he hoped to capture their order quickly so that he could focus on other clients for the rest of his two-day visit. Unfortunately, he was told that his meeting was changed to an 11 o'clock lunch with the assistant manager, Noor Ismail. Although Smith had already planned a lunch appointment with other clients, he had no choice but to agree. He had to shuffle his meeting with another potential client.

Smith arrived at Ismail's office on time and quickly began discussing how much profit the Malaysian company could make from his new products. But Ismail was more interested in learning about Smith's company's credibility and past activities in Malaysia than in specific negotiation details.

After an hour into the meeting, when Smith was eager to know if the price offer was acceptable, Ismail said he had to meet with other suppliers and asked Smith if he would like to join other members of the company team for lunch. Smith wondered if Ismail was just passing the buck.

Smith soon recognized that he needed to show more flexibility when dealing with Malaysian organizations. Their desire to maintain harmony will be shown in their indirect refusal of an offer. They will entertain your offer with a polite smile. Smith, on the other hand, was used to a direct "yes" or "no" when dealing with his clients. The lunch with the assistants went well, but no purchasing contracts were finalized.

In order to gain the Malaysian company's business, Smith must maintain further contacts with his clients and continue prodding them for a definite response. To succeed with Malaysians, you must present your company's capabilities, management expertise, and Malaysian clients. You must then maintain on-going communication with them in order to highlight your product's features and market potential. Behind a day in his travel plans, Smith slowed down and began to understand the importance of building relationships with his Asian clients.

Planting seeds in Indonesia

A less confident Smith boarded his next flight to Jakarta. He had worked very hard over the previous three months to recruit his Indonesian marketing agent, who had arranged several marketing meetings and presentations with potentially lucrative companies.

Marketing to the Indonesian companies proved to be quite rigorous. Smith and his agent spent a full day with one prospective company, scheduling meetings with three of the important buyers. Each meeting consisted of an hour of waiting and 15 minutes of presentation. Smith tried to make a sale to each of the directors, but ended up simply giving away samples of his product line. Again, he was surprised that price negotiation did not begin. He thought his low prices would easily clinch the sale.

His agent cooled him off and mentioned that in Indonesia you have to make several visits to make sure that everyone involved in the sale approves of it, even before the official submission of the proposal. His agent was just planting the seeds that Smith would have to water with more samples.

On his last night in Indonesia, Smith's agent invited him and two other purchasing managers to dinner at Hotel Indonesia. He was now confident about the deal, and after three hours of dinner and discussion, the purchasing manager smiled politely and said, "*Insha Allah* (God Wishes), you may possibly receive our order." The purchasing manager and the agent then left and Smith found himself with a $200 bill on his account. No purchase order was made.

When dealing with Indonesians, you must identify key players in the game: a person to introduce you to the highest position in the company, another within the company who will recommend and lobby for your product, and a third who will influence the decision on your behalf. Unfortunately, Smith's agent did not have the connections he needed as yet.

Securing the boss's blessing in Korea

Boarding a flight to Seoul, Smith recalled his early negotiations with Koreans. For several weeks prior to the commencement of his overseas trip, Smith had spent much of his time negotiating a deal to distribute his product with a large Korean company. He had begun by contacting the company's sales vice president, whom he had met a few months earlier at a garment show. The vice president had referred him to a junior manager, with whom he negotiated prices.

At the end of the negotiations, which lasted until just a week prior to his trip, the junior manager confirmed the sales agreement. Smith had asked his company's legal staff to draw up a contract to carry with him. While he was on his trip, the marketing staff was to develop promotional materials for the Korean market.

Upon meeting the junior manager in Seoul, however, Smith was told that the vice president had not actually agreed upon the terms of the contract, claiming that another company was offering a similar product line at a reduced price. A done deal was not a done deal. The Korean manager was now asking for another 30% discount.

After a few more rounds of negotiation, which lasted two days, a contract was agreed upon, but only after Smith learned the valuable lesson that in Korea only the boss makes the final decision. Like the junior manager, each Korean worker simply tries to satisfy his immediate superior by executing orders in an unquestioning manner. This lesson, though, offered very little consolation: Smith felt that he would have been a better salesman to Koreans if he would have graduated from a military academy, not a business college.

Sushi with the Japanese salaryman

Boarding his flight to Tokyo, Smith recalled his first attempt to meet his Japanese clients. He had tried to sell his product line to a large corporation that a colleague had previously visited. The colleague gave him the name of a manager in the acquisitions department, a Mr. Suzuki. One month prior to leaving Singapore, Smith had prepared a marketing packet of his company's services and mailed them to Suzuki. Two weeks had passed with no response, so Smith telephoned Suzuki. The latter remembered the company and product, but said he might be too busy to meet when Smith was in Japan. He asked Smith to call him upon arriving in Tokyo.

Smith reached Suzuki's secretary when he called from his hotel and was informed that Suzuki would be too busy to hold a meeting. Smith wondered about the cold response. It seemed as if Suzuki wasn't even making an attempt to meet with him. Smith later learned that Suzuki was not a close acquaintance of the colleague. The two had simply met at a garment show. Suzuki declined to do business with him because the two did not have a close mutual acquaintance.

Failing to secure direct sales, Smith now fell back on his former Japanese agent, with whom he had been working for several months. Fortunately, his relationship with this contact was a strong one, and a meeting with another important buyer was secured.

When making his first presentation, which was to a group of high-ranking Japanese buyers, Smith found himself in a lengthy question-and-answer period. He was happy that the Japanese asked so many questions and carefully examined the samples, thinking it indicated he would secure a good order. Smith even noticed that the top sales VP had quite a smile on his face ten minutes into the talk. Smith thought this smile indicated an appreciation of his products.

Smith therefore talked with even more enthusiasm for the rest of the hour and made attempts to elicit feedback from the VP. After his presentation, however, no offers were made. Feeling pressured to close a sale, Smith invited the team to a sushi dinner, where he was also bombarded by many questions about the products' quality, his company's ability to meet production quotas, and order delivery time. At the end of the dinner, Smith still did not receive any orders.

Sitting in the taxi to the Imperial Hotel in Tokyo at 11:30 p.m., Smith now wondered if the $400 sushi bill would ever pay off. He wondered aloud to his agent why the company had not made an offer: "You should have seen the expression on the VP's face. He had enjoyed the dinner with a wide smile!" His agent then informed him that a smile can indicate not only an appreciation of what one is saying or doing, but can also indicate embarrassment. You must be patient as most Japanese host meetings with foreigners to ask further questions or to clarify an issue. They will then hold meetings among themselves and decide if they want to proceed to make you an offer.

Socializing with the Thais

Taking his last trip, Smith boarded a plane to Bangkok, as a Thai distributor there had faxed his office with a request to discuss purchasing an unspecified amount of the company's elegant wedding dresses. The Thai had learned of the company through a connection in America. Smith hoped to discuss matters quickly and leave with an agreed-upon deal.

The Thai met Smith at the airport, at which time the American supplied the Thai with several catalogues of his company's products. Upon receiving the catalogues, the client said that it would take him a couple days to show the catalogues to his superiors and others involved. They could then make final arrangements. Pleasantly surprised at this indication that a deal was very possible, Smith extended his two-day visit to a week and enjoyed himself at an expensive hotel in Bangkok.

His stay was not all fun and no work, however. His Thai connection often requested meetings with him, many of which had no apparent relationship to the looming deal. One day they met for lunch, another for dinner, and a couple times for drinks and entertainment. On a few occasions, though, he had turned down the agent's request for a meeting, opting instead to visit the city on his own. When he reiterated his desire to close the deal before he left Bangkok, he was shocked to hear that the Thais had yet to make up their mind on the product. Smith thought to himself, "Well, of course, they can't make up their mind on the dresses—they've spent all their time asking me about myself." What he should have realized is that those personal questions were the most important: Thais will only do business with people they trust. They expect the boss or salesperson to be generous in giving them free samples and to pay the entertainment bills. Smith should have taken every opportunity he was given to socialize with his Thai counterparts. Had he gotten to know them well and proven his generosity, he may have flown back home with a lucrative deal.

Managing Globally

The following cases demonstrate how cultural differences can impact managing multicultural teams in local or global joint ventures. As most organizations join together for financial and marketing purposes, ignoring the importance of enhancing one's skills in mastering multicultural meetings, presentations, and negotiations can lead to many businesses' failures.

Mastering Multicultural Meetings

As companies become increasingly global, clashes between managers of different cultures are occurring with greater and greater frequency. Many of these clashes could be avoided if people were simply more aware of how people from other cultures perceive them and how those cultures differ from one another.

Consider the case of Laura Fischer, the CEO of Global One, a multinational mobile communications company. She was recently appointed CEO both for her technical aptitude and for her multicultural management skills. Her first challenge was to chair the executive director's meeting, comprised of the American director of marketing, John Miller; the German operations manager, Hans Schmidt; the Japanese construction manager, Nato Suzuki; the Arab financial director, Mohammed Salleh; and the Chinese director of research and development, Li Chen. What a challenge!

After a brief introduction by each director to present the status of his division's objectives and activities, Fischer opened the floor to the directors' feedback. Schmidt immediately questioned the data that Suzuki presented and its sources. Suzuki responded briefly, but sensed an argument. Not wanting to break up the harmony with Schmidt, Suzuki suggested that the two of them meet later. In the meantime, Miller tried to defend Suzuki's position, at which point Miller and Schmidt got into a heated debate. Salleh tried to intervene, pointing out that everyone should listen to what each director had to say.

In order to proceed with the meeting, Fischer now had to utilize her multicultural expertise and draw on the other members of the team who had been listening more than participating. She again invited Suzuki to present his rationale, experiences, and final opinions on the data presented. Believing in teamwork, Suzuki took the opportunity to ask the other board members to clarify some of the points discussed, before finally giving his opinion. Fischer then requested that Chen elaborate on the data presented, realizing that he had been waiting for an invitation. Like Suzuki, Chen responded without drawing any conclusions and left the decision to the chair, valuing the senior person's authority. He then turned to Salleh and requested more money for research. Salleh categorically refused, stating that he was solely in charge of finances and that the entire budget had already been allocated. Chen bowed to his authority.

Fischer now decided to wrap up the debate and come to a conclusion on the disputed issue. Miller immediately recommended a democratic vote: "Let's do it and fix it later if any problems arise," while Schmidt insisted on delaying any vote before all the data was in.

Suzuki smiled nervously and pointed out that the debate had to be continued until a decision was made and all were in agreement. He suggested that more time be taken in order to help everyone settle down, perhaps during lunch and even a round of golf. For his part, Salleh supported Miller's suggestion for a vote, stating that God would help them.

In order to show her respect for each person's views, Fischer asked each director individually to give his final views in an effort to satisfy Schmidt's need for hard data, Miller's action-orientation, Chen's sincere respect for authority, Suzuki's desire for group harmony and consensus, and Salleh's belief in seniority and religion. Thus, Fischer succeeded in helping all the board members to contribute positively to the final decision; they believed in it and carried the responsibility to proceed with the action items and strategy developed as a multicultural team.

In order to succeed with these cultures, keep in mind the following:

When working with the Germans, you need to do your homework before making a presentation. Openly challenge their views. Punctuality is highly valued, along with appreciation of others' titles and degrees. Germans value their privacy and have even larger personal space than Americans. If you meet these conditions, you will earn German respect.

To succeed with the Japanese, you must make an extra effort to be properly introduced and establish long-term relationships. Try to maintain group harmony, even if you personally disagree with a decision. Always focus on achieving group consensus that will eventually lead to group achievement. If you fit within the team, you will receive a deeper bow.

Arabs will be interested in your contacts, education, and position in society. They value authority and personal relationships. They may not be as elaborate in their information seeking as the Japanese and will base their decisions on intuition and their religious beliefs. They appreciate flattery and acknowledgment: provide these and you will get a bigger hug.

The Chinese value seniority and authority. This is usually achieved after hard work and recognition from their peers and families. Their decisions are usually not questioned by subordinates. In the meantime, however, they take care of the people under them, in both business and family matters. They will even link you into their expanded network.

On the other side, when dealing with Americans, be aware of their values of equality, independence, freedom, action orientation, and openness. Americans appreciate having all the cards on the table and discussing each one based on its own merits. Within the first few minutes of meeting Americans, you will be asked what you do. They will even go to war to save the underdog.

In conclusion, today's managers must be aware that every member of the team will come to the workplace carrying their own cultural baggage, which has been developed over time, based on cultural orientation and reward system. In order to create cultural synergy between diverse people, managers must be able to recognize their own basic cultural bias and how it differs from that of the people they are dealing with, as well as show respect and admiration for those other cultures. Only when this happens can cultural synergy exist; in other words, one plus one will be greater than two.

Managing Multicultural Teams

Martin McDonald, an American president of an Indonesian telecommunications joint venture, recently accepted a large bonus of stock options given to him by the board of directors. McDonald confidently accepted his job two years ago believing he could capably manage the five core groups of the company: an American team with technical expertise in the industry; a Japanese partner with practical construction skills; a Malaysian partner with extensive operational experience; Korean suppliers of advanced equipment; and Indonesians with in-depth knowledge of local markets.

Why did the board offer him the job, as opposed to the numerous other qualified candidates, and why did he confidently accept the challenge? Because McDonald had several years experience working in Southeast Asia. While there, he had not only acquired the cultural insight necessary to manage a joint venture of magnitude in the area, but he had also discovered the benefits of cultural diversity.

He knew that cultural barriers could be overcome if he made the effort to train his staff properly and balance the competing needs and desires of diverse cultures. The combined business strength of our partners, as well as the potential power of our diversity, would keep them one step ahead of their competitors, McDonald thought.

The situation in which McDonald found himself is not uncommon. As free trade opens local markets up to foreign competition, organizations are embarking on extensive global operations. Such efforts often require joint ventures between multinational organizations. In general, these partners offer strategic benefits like new technologies, stable international finance, local market expertise, and an availability of human resources.

While managers and executives commonly focus on business needs such as raising capital, procuring equipment, establishing operational plans, and providing technical training, the cultural issues that influence the joint venture's day-to-day operations are often overlooked. Yet these are the issues that can make or break an expensive joint venture operation. McDonald understood this sometimes-invisible reality.

Now let's see how McDonald addressed some of the multicultural mishaps that he encountered as he navigated his company toward profitability and a position as a telecommunications leader.

When McDonald first arrived in Indonesia, his main order of business was to set his employees on the right track. To do so, he called for several meetings of his top staff members. He expected his team members to be at the Friday morning meeting at 9:00 a.m. But, at 9:20 a.m., the final three of the six Indonesians members arrived, each accompanied by three uninvited members of their staff. A half an hour late already, McDonald had to change the meeting seating to accommodate nine extra participants.

While the meeting coordinator brought in nine extra chairs, McDonald noticed that the four members of the Japanese team had reorganized their seats so they could sit together. Everybody was still waiting for Budi, the senior Indonesian member, to arrive and deliver the formal opening remarks. When he began, he exceeded the five minute allotment by ten minutes. The 9:00 a.m. meeting was finally underway at 9:45 a.m.

Fortunately, McDonald had been prepared for these changes of plans. While he would prefer to start meetings on time, he, like many American business people, liked to follow strict time guidelines. He had studied the cultures he works with, however, and had accepted their differences. And so after presenting the meeting agenda and objectives he did not solicit any questions from the participants, as he might for a group of Americans. Instead, he recognized that Budi, the senior member, must first be invited for comment. After Budi was addressed, the rest of the Indonesian team joined in.

McDonald managed the discussion well. As a rule, he liked meetings to maintain their focus on final results and objectives. However, he did not criticize side conversations by the Indonesian members. These conversations comprised an important element of Indonesian decision making, whereas Americans would most likely wait until a set time after the meeting to discuss details.

McDonald, of course, didn't manage the meeting perfectly. About halfway through the discussion, he and Robert, the American technical director had a disagreement. The heated disagreement surprised the Indonesian and Japanese teams, and McDonald quickly noticed this. So instead of continuing the disagreement, he suggested a break. He had ordered coffee and snacks, which in addition to filling up the stomachs of the American, Japanese, and Indonesian teams, also helped relieve the tension of the argument. Before the meeting reconvened, McDonald and Robert settled their disagreement in private, deciding to simply announce their decision to the group in the second half.

When the meeting began again, McDonald wanted to conclude with a decision. He also sensed that the expatriate American team members were prepared for a democratic vote on an item they had been discussing. But he also understood that Yamaguchi, the Japanese team's leader, would want a week to consult with his headquarters in Tokyo. The Indonesian team he knew wanted more time.

So McDonald didn't press the issue. Although the issue might be seen as pressing, he knew that with a little schedule changing, possibly assigning some team members different immediate responsibilities, the current project deadline could easily be met. A second meeting was scheduled for the next week, at which time the project decision was made.

The case above exemplifies the possibilities for clashes between the American values of individualism, directness, and time consciousness; the Japanese interests in face-to-face discussion and consensus building; and the Indonesian values of hierarchy and seniority. At the core of the clashes are the differing values of task-oriented versus process-oriented cultures. Americans come to business meetings well informed, focused, and expecting an open dialogue. They expect to take action and assign responsibilities. Their Japanese partners place more emphasis on group harmony, consensus, and the need to discuss proposals and actions—they rarely make an immediate decision.

The Japanese traditionally sit as a group and come to meetings with ten questions and leave with twenty more. Decisions come later after achieving consensus. As in our example, they may even have to wait until headquarters in Tokyo decides the issue.

Furthermore, the Indonesian team expects a senior person to open and close important meetings. They also expect frequent breaks with coffee and snacks, and perhaps time to conduct their daily prayers. Indonesians may invite other members of their department to meetings, perhaps experts in the subject matter, and do not mind side conversations if they clarify an important point. And, of course, they expect seating according to seniority, as well as invitations to participate or speak up. They are the ones that are familiar with the local market and have the data.

With three sets of competing values, cultural clashes can intensify. Once cultural problems cause interpersonal clashes, teamwork can be seriously damaged. McDonald handled the situation appropriately because he believed that the company's ultimate goals of leadership and profitability would only be met if the needs of each culturally diverse team were met.

Overcoming Culture Clashes in Global Joint Ventures

As Budi Ibrahim, a Stanford Ph.D. in Telecommunications, accepted his boss' kind words of congratulations on becoming General Manager of IndoTelecom, a new global joint venture, he felt hesitant about what the new position would actually entail. Although Budi was obviously impressed with the technical expertise of his project's multicultural team, he worried about how he would lead his senior staff, who all had different cultural backgrounds: Kimura from Japan, Chen from Singapore, Schmidt from Germany, Marcel from France, and Sam from America.

Budi understood that as organizations expand their global activities, and as human resources are recruited from diverse technical and cultural backgrounds, most joint ventures nevertheless continue to focus on the strength that comes from expanding marketing territories, technology transfers, financial support, and even political policies.

Furthermore, Budi knew very well that local on-site management usually ignored the cultural diversity of its multicultural senior management teams, and thus usually suffered from numerous, sometimes disastrous, setbacks, even within a financially sound joint venture.

During his first week on the job, Budi arranged a dinner for the senior team managers at the International Club in Jakarta the night before their first day of formal business meetings. He felt this would be a good way to break the ice before the project began. At 7:00 p.m., the team members arrived and introduced themselves. When they were seated, Budi decided to maintain his edge by ordering orange juice in the event of any before-dinner business conversation. Surprisingly, his newly formed team did not follow suit. Sam, the American, ordered a martini, and Marcel then demanded a glass of cabernet sauvignon; Schmidt, a mug of cold beer; Chen, hot Chinese tea; and Kimura, some warm sake.

While each member enjoyed his drink, Budi opened the discussion by asking Marcel what he enjoyed most about Indonesia. Marcel elaborated for five minutes, saying that he enjoyed the cultural diversity of Indonesia, but was particularly impressed with the Dutch influence that he noticed, especially in downtown Jakarta. Schmidt, who had also commented on the Dutch influence, suddenly interrupted Marcel and complained about the constant traffic jam in the downtown area and the trains which, according to him, were always late, as were most Indonesians on their way to meetings. Sam chimed in, complaining about the early morning mosque prayer call over the microphone that woke him up every day at 5:30 a.m. He also complained that his privacy during this trip had been limited. In the meantime, both Kimura and Chen simply laughed and smiled.

The waitress came back and asked if everyone was ready to order. Chen, taking the lead since he was the eldest and most senior member, suggested that the team order several plates so that they could share their meal the Chinese way. He received agreement from both Budi and Kimura. Sam, however, said that he was on a diet and preferred only a soup and salad; Marcel ordered a very rare filet mignon along with another glass of cabernet. Schmidt gave explicit instructions to the waitress on how many sausages he wanted, what their optimum temperature should be, and insisted that they be complemented by a specified portion of sauerkraut, slightly warmed. He then ordered another mug of cold beer, saying that it was refreshing and appropriate since it was October—and time for Oktoberfest, a beer-drinking celebration. Finally, Kimura ordered Japanese sushi, but the restaurant was out of sushi. Very disappointed, he decided to have what Budi was having, *Nassi gori*, which was fried rice mixed with chicken and beef and topped with an egg.

During the dinner conversation, the Indonesian, Chinese, and Japanese were interested in establishing a sharing environment and everybody else seemed content carrying on (what appeared to be) their own monologues. While Schmidt demanded and commented on the virtue of quality and punctuality, and Marcel intellectualized and debated at length about Indonesian history, Budi quietly hoped that by tomorrow's meetings everyone would come together as a team.

Budi recognized the undeniable hints of culture difference and clash that his new team was experiencing. However, despite his desire to talk business before dinner, he was aware of the custom in most western European countries like France and Germany, as well as in the U.S. and Japan, to order wine, beer, or some other alcoholic drink beforehand.

Also, Marcel's expectation of others to have some knowledge of European (i.e., French) politics, history, culture, and language is typical. Chen's wish to order several plates for the group reveals the Chinese inclination toward establishing a sharing relationship, which contrasts with Sam and Marcel's respective orders, which demonstrate American and French individuality. Finally, Schmidt's insistence on detail, noted by his precise instructions to the waitress, was another reminder of how culture's effects can be seen even at the dinner table.

The meeting, which was scheduled for 9:00 a.m., did not start as Budi had planned. Sam came in on time and took it upon himself to start the meeting informally when he saw that Budi had not shown up by 9:15. When Budi did show up, followed by two assistants, he was embarrassed to see that the meeting had started. In front of the other managers, Sam explained that since they had another meeting at 10:15, he thought it would be better to get going. Budi smiled in spite of his feelings and restored control of the meeting. He gave his usual lengthy opening and soon thereafter asked Marcel to give the first presentation.

For most of the members, Marcel's presentation was difficult to follow, regardless of all the colorful overheads and detailed charts. For instance, Marcel talked comprehensively about the history of his company's success in the telecommunications field, how it benefited the French people, and how this project could benefit Indonesia. When Marcel finished, having talked for 10 minutes longer than he was allotted, Budi followed with some additional remarks. But before Budi had a chance to solicit questions from the participants, Sam suddenly began asking his own questions, urgently trying to clarify the objectives of the meeting and the project. This led to an open debate between Marcel and Sam. Schmidt joined in asking technical questions and in questioning whether everybody had done their homework; he wanted some numbers and facts, and he wanted them quickly. Marcel began to expand on Schmidt's concerns; this led to another open debate. Kimura, too, finally began asking questions, and Sam complained that Kimura posed too many questions and offered too few ideas. Finally, when Marcel asked if Chen agreed with the point of the presentation, Chen politely responded, with a smile, that he first would have to discuss the matter with his boss in Singapore. Obviously, matters were getting out of control.

What suggested a hint of cultural diversity at dinner last night could now be seen as full culture clash. Although Budi had spent time in the U.S. and had been trained in multicultural management, he realized that his present team, too, needed some multicultural skills in order for this global joint venture to succeed. Yet, his team still needed to come to an immediate decision after the break.

After the coffee break, which included afternoon prayer for the Indonesians, the meeting reconvened to vote on a new start date for the project. Budi, who at this point could almost anticipate the culture clash behavior of his team, remained virtually silent, except for his opening remarks. Not surprisingly, the team found it impossible to reach a decision. Sam, who was ready to vote on a new start date, could not understand why the meeting was being held up if Chen, Kimura, and Marcel all had to discuss any decision with their bosses before anything was finalized. Only Schmidt was ready to vote, since he had the numbers worked out and his boss had already directed him to make the final decision.

A serious situation was developing. Sam demanded that the Chinese, Japanese, and French immediately call their bosses (at that moment) in order to get a decision. In fact, Sam threatened to pull out of the project altogether if they did not make their calls. Naturally, Marcel debated the validity of this threat, citing the legal aspect of their respective contracts. Budi interrupted and insisted that everybody "cool off." He politely dismissed the team and ordered them to return that afternoon for an unscheduled meeting.

As Budi prepared his team for its first properly structured multicultural meeting, he recalled Sam's insistence on starting the morning session before his arrival. This, of course, showed the American style of acting independently. If Sam had known more about Indonesian meetings, he would have known that Indonesian meetings very often start late, and usually include opening remarks delivered by top management. Similarly, confusion about Marcel's presentation, even with colorful overheads and charts, showed the French tendency toward a comprehensive explanation frequently peppered with what the team members interpreted as vague allusions. In fact, Budi began to sense the depth of the cultural clash when Sam virtually cut him off with questions before Budi had a chance to solicit questions from the team members. This, of course, revealed the American value of full participation without necessarily complying with the formality of other cultures.

In any case, Indonesian protocol was overlooked by Sam, and this oversight led to a further disintegration of the meeting: an open debate (a normal event in French- or American-style meetings) on technical issues between Sam and Marcel isolated the Indonesian, Japanese, and Chinese members. Even more surprising was Schmidt's inquiry about "how the homework and numbers turned out for the rest of the team members." This seemingly innocent request by Schmidt once again showed the German characteristic of demanding details. And, when Sam reprimanded Kimura for asking questions but not offering any answers (a Japanese protocol during meetings), Budi was finally convinced that his team members were completely unaware of one another's culture and were definitely unprepared to manage a joint venture.

The team members' individual lack of awareness for their colleagues' respective cultures created an atmosphere of confusion and frustration. Even Budi did not expect the situation to get so hostile during the second half of the morning's meeting where, again, he saw how Sam used his decision-making ability to try and force his counterparts to come to a decision concerning the start date. Sam lost his temper because he was unaware of the extent of centralization of Chinese, Japanese, and French business systems. This disruption, as Budi recalled, forced an afternoon meeting to bring to light the multicultural issues that were threatening to unravel the whole project.

When Budi's team arrived at 4:00 p.m., they found open seating which was in contrast to the arranged seating of the morning sessions. Nevertheless, Budi arrived precisely on time, and improvised Indonesian custom by significantly reducing his opening remarks. He spoke to his team and re-addressed the problem of the new start date. After 10 minutes, and before Sam had a chance, he asked Kimura if he had any questions. After Kimura had a chance to express his concerns, Budi asked Marcel if he had any comment on what had been said so far. Marcel elaborated on a couple of items, but Budi diplomatically asked him to abbreviate his point so that the rest of the team members could have their say in the allotted time.

Budi quickly moved on to Schmidt and asked him if his work had led to any new technical concerns relating to the new start date. He went over a few new numbers, but nevertheless agreed to vote for a new start date. When Sam interrupted, Budi allowed the disruption, as most of the team had already spoken. Sam was comfortable taking over the meeting and he fervently argued his position.

Finally, Budi allowed Chen to set the agenda for the remainder of the meeting. Later, Budi suggested a coffee break so that Chen, Kimura, and Marcel could call their counterparts back home to get approval. The vote was taken after the break, with little or no hesitation, and the team reached a 4-to-1 agreement (only Sam objected). In the end, however, Sam went along with the vote since the majority had clearly won. Budi then asked Marcel to write the memo. The issue had been effectively settled.

In this case, Budi was able to manage and minimize the culture clash his senior management team had been experiencing before it had become too costly a problem. Based on his knowledge of multicultural management and negotiation, he allowed the individual members of his team, including himself, to express their concerns and expertise on their terms. His desire for group harmony was preserved while still allowing Sam, the American, to express his self-reliant and proactive style; Schmidt, the German, to express his concern for details and homework; Kimura, the Japanese, to focus on the process; Chen, the Singaporean, to be respected for his seniority; and, finally, Marcel, the Frenchman, to be allowed to elaborate and deliberate the issue thoroughly.

Conducting Training Across Culture

Deitel-Boors, a German engineer in the Indonesian telecommunications joint venture, had been assigned to train a group of Arabs and Japanese on maintenance of specific telecommunications equipment. A week before the training class, Deitel-Boors handed out a maintenance manual to each of the four Arabs and four Japanese.

Monday morning, at the beginning of the training session, the trainees were shocked with a two-page pop quiz. Both teams thought the session would start with a brief lecture by Deitel-Boors. Recognizing that most of the participants had not done their homework, Deitel-Boors decided to allow the teams a hands-on session with the equipment. In order to give them some time, Deitel-Boors returned to the office for a cup of coffee and to take care of some paperwork.

Ten minutes later, Mr. Ali, the technician from the Arab team, came into Deitel-Boors' office with specific questions. Ali was disappointed when Deitel-Boors asked him to go back and review page 15 of the maintenance manual. After 30 minutes, Deitel-Boors returned to the floor to check on the teams and was surprised to find the Japanese team still discussing how to open the front panel of the equipment. Meanwhile, the Arab team had split into two groups. Two of the Arabs were going through the manual while the other two were taking off the front panel. Deitel-Boors immediately recognized that he needed to come closer to the Arab team and establish a coaching style. He needed to provide continuous support. On the other hand, the Japanese members worked closely with each other, building consensus before moving to the next step.

By the end of the day's training, Deitel-Boors decided to recognize the effort of the teams, so he graded every member on their individual contribution. To his surprise, the Japanese team left the training session unhappy, despite the fact that Suzuki was recognized as the best performer of the session.

In this light, we begin to see how technology transfers across cultures can threaten the success of a joint venture if training, motivation, and work performance reviews are conducted without appropriate consideration of each trainee's culture. Deitel-Boors, with his values of self-reliance, risk taking, and individual achievement, had hastily applied these values in the training process. Although the Japanese and Arab teams are part of the joint venture business climate, training needs to adapt to individual cultures.

In training Arabs, one must consider their expectations of being coached and mentored by the trainer. Also, seniority level should be considered when setting up Arab teams, otherwise senior members will delegate most of the work to junior members.

For the Japanese, a visual and hands-on style is more effective than reading through a complex manual. The Japanese, however, welcome training where group participation and hands-on work is expected. Every member then contributes, forming a group and building consensus before moving on to the next step, and group recognition achievement outweighs any individual achievement.

Summary

This chapter has been your introduction to the fast-paced world of multicultural business negotiation and management. Now that we have seen some examples of the ways in which friction can be turned into multicultural synergy and strength, let's move on to an in-depth look and find out how to deal successfully with global cultures.

Working One-on-One with Americans

What would you talk about during your first encounter with Americans?
What should you emphasize in your first sales presentation?
What can you expect after four hours of tennis with your Texan colleague?

Since the end of World War II, America has played an important and influential role in the development of the global economic system. Not only has it worked with the United Nations and other organizations to promote the worldwide spread of capitalism, when necessary, it has also used its military clout to further the causes America supports.

Consequently, American cultural values are prevalent throughout the globe, and countries and cultures that have wanted to either do business with or compete against American companies, have sometimes found it necessary to adopt American business culture values and norms. Whether it is the corporate culture of a Silicon Valley start-up or huge conglomerates like IBM or General Motors, American businesses have a lot to offer in the way of successful business techniques and models.

Doing business with Americans, however, or adopting American methods of conducting business, is not always easy. For example, whereas some cultures, such as Japanese business culture, place emphasis on nurturing and maintaining close business relationships with suppliers and partners, Americans will often consult partners and friends for their services and needs, disregarding better offers in favor of experienced partnerships.

As the follow-up examples will show, there is no set method of doing business with Americans—each situation must be assessed on its own strengths and merits. Having a good foundation of knowledge pertaining to American business culture, however, will help you gauge "which way the wind blows" when doing business with Americans, and may make the difference between winning or losing that big, lucrative contract that can help you and your company.

When foreign companies and their representatives do business with Americans, they must be aware of the American styles of establishing relationships and communication, conducting meetings and presentations, as well as negotiation, and socialization. This chapter covers these topics in-depth, with specific examples, as well as exercises for increasing cultural skills, for both the novice and experienced reader.

Test Your Skills Dealing with Americans

In the following true-or-false statements, test your general knowledge of American business culture and values.

_____ 1. Americans usually tend to value material possessions more than spiritual enlightenment.

_____ 2. Most Americans like formality and rituals in daily interactions.

_____ 3. Americans usually rely on themselves for help rather than asking others.

_____ 4. Americans value time-control and are future-oriented.

_____ 5. Many Americans are open to sharing their personal space.

_____ 6. The majority of Americans use indirect messages to refuse an offer.

_____ 7. Americans tend to see themselves as group-oriented.

_____ 8. Americans are inclined to believe in equality and free competition.

_____ 9. Americans usually believe that being late for an appointment shows disrespect.

_____ 10. Shaking hands is important when you meet your American partner every time.

Most Appropriate Answers:

1. T; 2. F; 3. T; 4. T; 5. F; 6. F; 7. F; 8. T; 9. T; 10. F

Dr. Gonzalez goes to America

Establishing relationships with Americans can be a very difficult ordeal for people from other cultures. The following story demonstrates this in extensive detail.

Dr. Gonzalez, a waste management professional from Brazil, was attending an international conference in Texas on hazardous materials storage. During a break between speakers, he was approached by an American scientist, David Krouse. David casually said, "Hi, how are you?" Gonzalez replied, "Well, unfortunately, I missed the first speaker because my taxi was stuck in Houston traffic. And yesterday my flight was delayed leaving San Paulo, so I wasn't able to get a good night's sleep. I'm tired."

Krouse was turned off by Gonzalez's comments. Once he had finished speaking, Krouse smiled at him and said, "I hope you will have a good rest today," and wandered toward another group of businesspeople. Gonzalez felt slighted and embarrassed. "What did I do wrong?" he wondered. "Krouse asked me how I was doing, and I told him."

Krouse's greeting, however, did not necessitate a long, in-depth reply. Krouse was simply trying to break the ice with his question, "Hi, how are you?" He expected to hear, as most Americans do, a simple reply like "Fine, thank you."

Determined to make contact with more American businesspeople, Gonzalez introduced himself to an American standing in line at the refreshment table. "Hi, I'm Dr. Raul Gonzalez." The American shook his hand and said, "Good to meet you, I'm Mark Peterson. What do you do Raul?" Gonzalez replied, "I am the president of Waste Management of Brazil."

Pleased that Peterson addressed him by his first name, Gonzalez moved closer and lightly slapped him on the back, in a Brazilian way. He became animated, thrusting his hands and arms about as he laughed. Peterson backed away from Gonzalez, and returned to his seat immediately. Peterson's haste was not lost on Gonzalez. "How did I botch this meeting?" he wondered.

What Gonzalez failed to consider was Peterson's need for personal space. Peterson addressed Gonzalez informally, but his informality did not overlap with the arena of spatial relationships. Typically, Americans feel uncomfortable when their personal space is violated.

Leaving the refreshment table, Gonzalez heard a woman's voice calling to him. He turned and saw Sally Walters, a former business partner. "Raul, I didn't know you were attending the conference! It's so good to see you here!" She was full of smiles, and they talked for a few minutes about an upcoming speaker they were both eager to hear.

"I'm staying at the Hilton Hotel," Gonzalez told Sally. "Oh! That's just down the street from my hotel. Can you give me your room number?" Sally asked. As he wrote the room number of his hotel on the back of his business card, Sally complimented his gold Parker pen. "Do you like it?" Gonzalez asked. "Here, take it! I have plenty more back in Brazil."

Happy to finally be successful in contacting an American businessperson, and pleased with Sally's friendliness, Gonzalez asked, "Sally, would you like to join me for a drink and dinner tonight?" At this, Sally looked very uncomfortable. She said, "I already planned to have dinner with my boyfriend, John." She left, muttering an unenthusiastic, "It was good seeing you." Returning to his seat, Gonzalez wondered if he would ever have a strong business relationship with an American.

The situation above demonstrates the difficulties that can be encountered when communicating across cultures, with Americans or others. The rapid expansion of the global market in the latter half of the twentieth century has forced businesses to work with foreign cultures. Businesses that address issues of cultural diversity will improve their chances to succeed in today's global market. Let us examine the root causes of some of the cultural clashes with Americans.

American Cultural Values

During a management training program attended by American and Indonesian managers, we asked them to list their perception of what Americans value. The following table presents some of the respective answers received by participants.

American values as perceived by:

Americans	Indonesians
Control	Success
Money	Money
Position/Power	Control

Americans	Indonesians
Hard work	Individuality
Success	Pride
Recognition	Profit
Material Possessions	Logic
Family	Nation
Health	Hard work
Time	Family
Security	Business
Friendship	Friendship

Further, we asked participants to prioritize 20 values common among many cultures. These values were group harmony, competition, seniority, cooperation, privacy, openness, equality, formality, risk taking, reputation, freedom, family security, relationship, self-reliance, time, group consensus, authority, material possessions, spiritual enlightenment, and group achievement. We also presented the same questions to groups of Arab managers. The following table presents what these three groups indicated were their top five values from the given list of 20.

Indonesians	Americans	Arabs
Seniority	Equality	Seniority
Reputation	Freedom	Spirituality
Group Harmony	Openness	Reputation
Family	Self-Reliance	Family
Relationship	Cooperation	Authority

The differences in the lists above reveal quite a bit about American culture. For example, it is obvious from the list that Americans value their individual freedoms immensely. Equality, for one, is assumed by most Americans, and those who do not believe in it are generally perceived negatively. The American Dream is that of becoming rich through hard work, skill, and some luck. Americans assume that everyone has the opportunity to reach their full economic and intellectual potential.

American cultural lore is full of examples of achieving the American Dream: Ben Franklin ran away to Philadelphia as a young boy and grew up to discover electricity and to address the courts of kings; Abraham Lincoln was born in a log cabin and became president of the

United States. Numerous immigrants from Europe, Asia, and every corner of the world have left lives of poverty to find their fortunes in America.

Freedom is also highly valued by Americans. As an ideal, the right to say what one believes and vote in uncorrupted elections, is prevalent throughout American culture. Self-reliance and cooperation may seem, at first glance, to contradict one another. Self-reliance indicates that one does not need another's help, while cooperation is the key to successful team building. How can both of these values rank so highly when they are so opposite?

The key to understanding this contradiction may be to examine the American sport of baseball. In baseball, individual achievements are always emphasized: How many home runs did a player hit? How many games did a pitcher win? How many errors did a shortstop commit? On the other hand, only teamwork can win a game or the World Series. Everyone must work together to achieve the common good. Consequently, in baseball as in everyday American life, individual performance, teamwork, and cooperation are all applauded. These qualities are not opposed to one another but are actually complementary parts of a complete entity.

So don't let the emphasis on individual rights fool you. For example, whereas Americans may not list family as a top value in the context of business, the importance of family in American life cannot be overstated. Whether it is political candidates, the news media, or television commercials, one of the keys to selling an idea or a product in America is to relate it to the central family unit: the minivan, one of the highest selling classes of cars, is targeted at families; and family-oriented television shows dominate the primetime lineup.

The key, then, is to realize that while the five values listed above are an accurate representation of what Americans value most, the fabric of American society is complex and sometimes contradictory. Don't wonder how Americans can, in the same breath, espouse individual rights and cooperative teamwork—simply accept the reality that they will do so.

Now imagine what will happen if an American site manager, with typical cultural baggage, manages or negotiates with an Arab or Indonesian counterpart with *their* value of seniority, authority, relationship, group harmony, and spirituality.

After reading this section, test your American cultural skills by answering the following quiz:

1. In general, Americans most value:
   a. Social recognition.
   b. Happiness.
   c. Equality.
   d. Money.
2. Many Americans see themselves as:
   a. Modest and shy.
   b. Family members.
   c. Formal and ritualistic.
   d. Created equal to others.

The correct answers are 1. c. Equality, and 2. d. Created equal to others. Most Americans strongly believe in equality for everyone, regardless of race, gender, religion, nationality, or beliefs. They take this equality for granted and are likely to be offended by anyone who does not believe this. At the same time, however, they expect and respond to competitive situations. They will stand equal to each other but will then expect to compete and respect the winner.

American cultural values can be seen across the globe on television and in movies, and are reflected in the country's legal and political institutions. These values include freedom of choice, directness, openness, and self-reliance. Carrying these values over into American business communication, they have the potential to clash with Eastern cultural norms, as the following example of the first meeting between individuals from three different cultures demonstrates. Let us now find how these discussed values influence daily communication with Americans.

Meeting the Americans

So, what do you do, sir?

At a business conference in Cairo, Egypt, an American attendee approaches two men: a Japanese and an Arab.

American:	Good morning, gentlemen. I'm John Smith. *He extends his hand to the Arab and then to the Japanese.* Do you mind if I join you?
Arab:	*Shaking the American's hand with both of his.* Welcome, welcome, to Cairo. Please join us.

Japanese:	*Steps backward, bows slightly, then shakes Smith's hand. He says nothing and prepares to exchange business cards.*
Arab:	Are you enjoying yourself, John?
American:	Oh, sure, it's very nice here. What do you do, sir?
Arab:	I'm Salleh, from Egypt, and I'm the president of my trading firm. I'm here to meet our friends and look at some of the new products available.
American:	*Turning to the Japanese.* And your name, sir?
Japanese:	Silently hands Smith his business card.
American:	Glances at it quickly and puts it in his pocket. Oh, you're Mr. Suzuki.
Japanese:	Yes, with NEC Corporation.
American:	Oh, NEC! And what do you do at NEC?
Japanese:	*Smiles.*
Arab:	Well, should we all go to have some coffee and enjoy our new friendship together?
American:	I'm sorry guys, but I have to go and talk with someone from the French group. Maybe we can get together later. It was nice to meet you. Goodbye. *Walks away and introduces himself to the French group.*

In this exchange, the Arab was put off because the American cut the conversation short and declined an invitation to have coffee. Arabs place a high value on building personal relationships and want to get to know someone before discussing business matters.

The Japanese businessman was also uneasy because the American did not exchange business cards immediately, and he barely looked at the Japanese businessman's card before putting it in his pocket. In Japan, the custom is to study someone's business card to determine their company and rank, then to be silent briefly in respect for others. The American, with his "time is money" networking attitude, wanted to make as many contacts as possible—not just stand around idly and chat with one or two people.

This could be a problem for the American if he was trying to cut a deal with either the Arab or Japanese businessman. But what if the American had the upper hand? What if he represented a large retail distributor and the Arab wanted the American to carry his goods? In this case, although he has been slighted, the Arab may have to internalize his feelings and actually take the American up on the offer to discuss business at a later time.

Remember that Americans are individualistic, and this may show itself even more so if the American has the upper hand. While you may think your American partner is being rude or arrogant, understand that Americans probably won't see the situation the same as you do.

The following questions evaluate your skills for meeting Americans:

1. Your American acquaintance asks, "How are you doing?" She expects you to respond with:
   a. "I'm having a bad day."
   b. "Fine, thank you."
   c. "Sorry, but I'm in a rush."
   d. "I've been sick all day."
2. After exchanging business cards with an American, he will likely:
   a. Ask you to explain the meaning of your name.
   b. Admire the quality of your business card.
   c. Look at your title to see if you are an important person in your company.
   d. Ask what you do.
3. When talking with Americans, you should:
   a. Keep a half foot away from them.
   b. Keep two arm lengths away.
   c. Keep one arm length away.
   d. Avoid making eye contact.
4. When meeting with an American executive for the first time, you should:
   a. Hand your business card to her immediately.
   b. Wait for her to hand her business card to you.
   c. Shake her hand and exchange cards after a few minutes of discussion.
   d. Wait until the end of the meeting to give her your business card.
5. In a business introduction to an American, he may ask you to call him by his first name because:
   a. He is not interested in business.
   b. He likes harmony in discussion.
   c. His last name may be hard to pronounce.
   d. He wants to be comfortable during the discussion.

Most Appropriate Answers:

1. b; 2. d; 3. c; 4. c; 5. d

Tips for Meeting Americans

Mention your name clearly.	Don't talk about religion.
Be on time and prepared.	Don't offer a limp handshake.
Do not be afraid to discuss issues.	Don't offer an extended handshake.
Have a firm handshake.	Don't say "yes" if the answer is "no."
Smile and look in the eye.	
Say, "How are you? Nice to meet you."	Don't be dishonest.
	Don't complain.
Offer a pleasant greeting.	Don't stand too close.
Greet the senior person first.	Don't ask about salary.
Offer your business card for networking.	Don't ask, "How much money do you make?"

On the Phone with Americans

Telephone communication with Americans can be difficult to master, especially for businesspeople from cultures that emphasize compliments and established rapport. To succeed with Americans, however, directness and simplicity are key factors.

A common source of misunderstanding erupts when Americans answer the phone, for example, with, "Hello Bob, What can I do for you?" This opening demonstrates how much they value directness and immediately getting down to business, but it can be irritating to other cultures that emphasize formalities and long introductions. Asians, South Americans, and Arabs, who all value hospitality and accommodation, expect preliminary conversation about the other's well being, the weather, and other social topics, before discussing business. When Americans fail to do so, they are seen as pushy and abrupt.

The old American adage that "time is money" still holds true. Americans have a much shorter concept of time than their counterparts to the East. Nowhere is this better reflected than in business negotiations. Consider the following example.

An American distributor received a call from an Asian manager requesting more information about a product the Asian's company was considering purchasing. From the start, the Asian sensed that the American was anxious to close the sale and get off the phone. An Asian or Arab would typically begin such a call by asking about the other person's well being. When the Asian manager did this, however, the American gave a very brief response and quickly got down to business, saying, "How can I now help you?"

Americans highly value their time and put little emphasis on first building personal relationships in business. The American way of thinking is: "Let's do business, and then maybe we'll be friends." An Arab or Asian is just the opposite: "Let's be friends, and then we'll do business forever." To those unfamiliar with the American style of doing business, the American distributor may appear to be rude or uninterested. Americans, however, do not intend to be rude and may, in fact, be very interested. Their brief phone manners are simply a result of the task-oriented style of American business culture. The distributor's main objective is to close the deal quickly, preferring to avoid extraneous conversations as much as possible.

With this knowledge in mind, let's see how well you answer the following quiz:

1. If you receive a call from your American business partner, you should first:
   a. Ask him when he will issue a letter of credit.
   b. Ask him how his family is doing.
   c. Ask him what you can do for him.
   d. Say, "It's good to hear from you!"
2. You telephone an American supplier, but get his answering machine. You should:
   a. Hang up.
   b. Leave a brief message asking him to return your call.
   c. Leave a message.
   d. Call back later.
3. If you call your American supplier to find out why your urgent order hasn't been processed, she will probably:
   a. Apologize for the delay and promise to call when she's fixed the problem.
   b. Put your call on hold until she discovers the source of the problem.

    c. Promise to get back to you by fax.

    d. Ask you to call back later.

4. When negotiating with an American client over the phone, you should promise:

    a. Punctual delivery.

    b. Free samples of your product.

    c. An all-expense-paid trip to Egypt.

    d. All of the above.

Most Appropriate Answers:

1. c; 2. c; 3. b; 4. a

Tips On Phone Etiquette with Americans

Briefly introduce yourself.
Mention the purpose of
your call.
Offer a brief greeting.
Ask if the time is right to talk.
Speak directly and clearly.
Respond directly to inquiries.
Leave a message, if the
person is not available.

Don't ramble or offer small talk.
Don't interrupt.
Don't shout or swear.
Don't make jokes.
Don't get too personal.
Don't put someone on hold for
long.
Don't hang up suddenly.
Don't eat while on the phone.

Writing to Americans

How skilled are you at communicating with Americans through letters, e-mails, and faxes? The following questions will test your skills:

1. Dr. John Smith, the managing director of your American client would prefer to be addressed as:

    a. Dear Dr. Smith,

    b. Dear Mr. Smith,

    c. Dear John,

    d. Dear Sir,

2. When trying to persuade an American supplier, you should mention:

    a. The deadline for submitting the quote.

    b. The commission you will lose on the deal.

    c. The problems that you will occur if they don't make an immediate decision.

    d. That he will lose an opportunity and you as a client if he doesn't act immediately.

3.   In your proposal to the marketing manager of an American organization, you should focus on:

    a. The mutual benefits this deal would bring.

    b. The possibility that the benefits of this deal may promote her to VP of marketing.

    c. The fact that she is invited to visit your company in Cairo.

    d. The fact that you are willing to sponsor her son's trip to Cairo.

4.   To speed up the delivery of a late shipment from an American supplier, you should:

    a. Ask the manager for a personal favor.

    b. Thank him for his continued cooperation.

    c. Give him a two-week ultimatum.

    d. Promise to secure another order with him.

5.   When writing to an American firm for the first time, it is very important to:

    a. Begin your letter with a flattering introduction.

    b. Have your letter signed by your company's president.

    c. Make reference to your contact source.

    d. Be specific as to the purpose of the letter in the first paragraph.

Most Appropriate Answers:

1.c; 2. d; 3. a; 4. c; 5. d

Even the formality of a business letter varies across cultures. For example, consider what happened to my colleague, Dave Perkins, an American engineer. Not long ago, he took a trip to Japan and Malaysia to meet with Dr. Noburu Saito in Osaka and Dr. Omar Faiz in Kuala Lumpur. Afterward, he wrote them both letters to follow up on the proposal he had made. When he showed me the two letters, which began "Dear Noburu" and "Dear Omar," I told him he was unintentionally offending both of his hosts. Using the first name in the salutation of a letter, while common in American culture, is too informal in others.

A proper salutation for his letter to Japan would have been "Dear Saito-*san*." Opening a letter with -*san* eliminates titles and does not overly distinguish the receiver, thus keeping with the Japanese desire to maintain established harmony within the group.

In a letter to a Malaysian or an Arab, though, just the opposite is true. Titles are very important in both of these cultures. Their letters may use three or four titles before the name. Thus, by opening his letter with "Dear Omar," my colleague was ignoring the man's title. Even if he had known the Malaysian well enough to be on a first-name basis with him, he should still have referred to him as "Dr. Faiz," or at least "Dr. Omar," in the salutation of the letter. Recently, I received a letter from a German, signed Prof. Dr.-Ing. Hans Bullinger. What might his reaction be if an American wrote back with "Dear Hans"?

Let's scrutinize another case, that of Budi Ibrahim, president of a tapestry company in Indonesia. Budi recognized that a large percentage of his sales were to American tourists. He believed that the sale of his product in America would skyrocket if he could find a good distributor. Through a friend in the American Embassy, Ibrahim received the address of Clark O'Donnell, an importer in New York who specialized in Asian products. Ibrahim wrote a two-page letter to O'Donnell, explaining his role as company president, his education, and the size of his company. He also mentioned that he was a good friend of the American ambassador to Indonesia. Ibrahim concluded the letter by wishing happiness and well being to the American, and inviting him to visit Jakarta. A month passed, but Ibrahim did not receive a reply. He sent another letter, but O'Donnell still did not reply. Ibrahim assumed that O'Donnell didn't have time for his business.

O'Donnell, however, did not reject Ibrahim's business because of his products. He rejected it because of Ibrahim's indirect writing style. Ibrahim did not adopt the American style of writing business letters, which tends to be clear and succinct. The letter didn't need to mention a relationship with the ambassador, nor did Ibrahim need to engulf O'Donnell with flattery. Ibrahim should have written a half-page letter in which he emphasized his company's accomplishments and reputation, as well as the reasons why his products would sell well in America. This is what Americans expect to see in their business correspondence: "What's in it for me?" Don't unnecessarily dwell on who you are.

Another detail to remember when writing letters to Americans is that they do not especially value hospitality and building personal relationships. An American friend remembered how he once received a letter from an Egyptian exporter with whom he wanted to do business. The American was annoyed that the letter went on for two full pages, full of personal greetings and reflections on the company's past activities, before ever getting to the point of responding to the American's proposition.

In response, my American friend sent a brief note again pushing for a "yes" or "no" answer to his proposal, with a 48-hour deadline. He never got a reply. Later, when he met his Egyptian contact again, he wondered why he was received coolly. I explained that the Egyptian had put all that effort into his letter in an attempt to establish a relationship, and so was probably angry that my friend had not taken the time to respond in kind and, moreover, had given him an ultimatum. In this case, the American's desire for immediate feedback clashed with the Arab's desire to create a hospitable long-term relationship before doing business.

Tips for Writing to Americans

Put your subject up front.
Arrange your information in a logical sequence.
Respond to their specific concern.
Use complete names.
Be short and to the point (not flowery).
Include a polite close with regards.
Be direct and concise.
Use correct words and short sentences.
Use "Dear" and "Sincerely."
Summarize at the end with action items.

Avoid reckless grammar and spelling.
Never use all caps.
Don't be overly polite.
Don't be timid in asking for help.
Don't use slang language.
Don't use long words.
Avoid hand-written corrections.
Don't skip a tier of management.
Avoid unclear, vague and long letters.
Don't get personal.

Presenting to Americans

Mr. Kawamata, an electronics salesman from Japan, and his two assistants traveled to San Francisco for a week to give a presentation to an American distributing firm. A deal with the American distributor would secure their company's share of business in the American market. It also would offer Kawamata and his assistants an opportunity to demonstrate their value to their company.

The presentation began with a description of the Japanese company's product line. Kawamata then outlined a strategy for marketing his products. Several of the American executives interrupted him immediately, voicing their concerns about the marketability of the products by requiring his response to several urgent questions. Their discussion was not inflammatory, but candid and to the point. Unfamiliar with the direct style of the meeting, Kawamata refrained from expressing his opinions to the American executives. To maintain harmony, he simply nodded at their comments and told one of his assistants to take notes.

Kawamata intended to address the concerns of the Americans to his superiors when he returned to Tokyo, but the Americans did not receive any indication from him that he would do this. The Americans wanted to receive direct feedback to their inquiries. At the end of the presentation, the Americans felt that Kawamata had failed to provide this immediate feedback, and they decided to search for another supplier. The Americans believed that Kawamata's silence meant that he wasn't taking their concerns seriously.

Of course, Kawamata gave utmost respect to the Americans' concerns. He simply failed to express his response adequately. His failure to adapt to American corporate culture resulted in a major setback for his company. He also hurt his future chances of working with the American company.

Test Your Skills for Conducting Meetings with and Presenting to Americans

Now that you have read the example of Mr. Kawamata, answer the following quiz to test your skills for conducting meetings and presentations to Americans:

1.   As a project manager, you are conducting a presentation to American executives. They will be most interested in:

    a. The name of your graduate school.

    b. Your title and the number of people who work underneath you.

    c. Your salary.

    d. Your accomplishments in the last two years.

2. You are conducting a presentation to an American firm. Do you start by:

    a. Apologizing for not speaking clear English.

    b. Asking everyone to introduce themselves.

    c. Thanking them for their time.

    d. Informing them that they must make a firm commitment by the end of the meeting.

3. When meeting with joint partners from America, you should:

    a. Prepare the agenda prior to the meeting.

    b. Present the agenda and topics of discussion at the beginning of the meeting.

    c. Expect full participation.

    d. All of the above.

4. To close the sale by the end of your presentation to American managers, you should:

    a. Invite the negotiating team to dinner at the Hilton Hotel.

    b. Ask the senior manager to sign the order immediately.

    c. Ask the technical director to give you his personal bank account number.

    d. Offer a special discount if they make their decision before the deadline.

5. In American business meetings, you are expected to:

    a. Wait until the end and state your position firmly.

    b. Talk about how difficult it was to get to the meeting.

    c. Maintain group harmony and not ask embarrassing questions.

    d. Express your ideas openly and rationalize them aggressively.

6. At the end of an American business meeting, the participants may:

    a. All go to the cafeteria to have a drink.

    b. Write a conclusion and/or action plan with specific responsibilities and dates.

    c. Conduct behind-the-scenes discussions to change the conclusion.

    d. Apologize to each other for any confrontations they had during the meeting.

Most Appropriate Answers:

1. d; 2. b; 3. d; 4. d; 5. d; 6. b

Tips for Presenting to Americans

- Prepare an agreed-upon agenda.
- Be prompt in starting time.
- Prepare and pass on minutes of meeting.
- Remember that the chairperson presents first.
- Focus on issues one at a time.
- Solicit input from all attendees.
- Expect open debate.
- Share problem-solving ideas.
- Reach decisions before the meeting is closed, if decisions are required.
- Assign individual action items.

The American Decision-Making Process

In reaching decisions, most American managers will:

- Define a list of problems.
- Allot time to discuss.
- Be direct and to the point.
- Be involved and assertive.
- Focus on the bottom line and on straight answers.
- Ignore personal relationships.
- Be action oriented.
- Conduct quick discussions.
- Produce tentative solutions.
- Assign action items and responsibility.

Negotiating with Americans

On sale for $9.99!

Negotiating prices with Americans can prove to be difficult if one is not aware of the pressure tactics that American salespeople use. Take Mr. Sukarno, an immigrant from Indonesia who needed to purchase a second automobile for his wife so she could shop and pick up the children from school and soccer practice. He decided to purchase a Ford minivan because it would suit his family's needs.

After trying out a few models, Sukarno and his wife decided to purchase a mid-model that they both liked. The car salesman said, "I'll give this van to you for only $27,995. That's a steal as far as I'm concerned." Sukarno told the salesman that he couldn't spend more that $25,000. The salesman replied, "I can give you the base model for $25,500, but only if you agree to purchase leather seats, air-conditioning and a CD player, radial tires, and an alarm system."

"These extras will add up to a lot more money, won't they?" Sukarno asked. "Yes, but these extras are necessary nowadays," answered the car dealer. "The alarm will prevent your car from being stolen, and if you plan to do any driving this summer, believe me, AC will be your best friend."

Convinced that the minivan was the best deal he would be able to find, Sukarno gave in to the dealer's pressure tactics and purchased the van. With the extras, the van cost $30,095. What happened? Sukarno was a victim of unfamiliar sales tactics. If he had had more experience dealing with American salespeople, he would have purchased the minivan for a much lower price.

It's now or never!

When making purchases from Americans, make sure that you check out competitors' prices. Don't fall into the same trap as the subject of our next example. Mr. Wu from Singapore had traveled to the Silicon Valley to visit family, and decided to purchase a hundred computers and several servers for his accounting firm while in the area. He knew that he would find the most competitive prices in the Silicon Valley.

His first stop was to the Global Computer Store, where he found a model compatible with the needs of his company. Wu asked the computer salesman what the unit price was for 100 computers. The salesman said, "Including the software and software licensing contracts, I can sell a hundred computers for a unit price of $1,650 each." Wu replied that this was too much money for his limited budget. "How about $1,500?" asked the salesman. "That's as low as I can go."

"This price is attractive," Wu told the salesman, "but first I must discuss the matter with my superiors." The computer salesman said,

"You must decide quickly; my boss is only allowing me to sell the computers for $1,500 for the next 24 hours." The salesman offered to let Wu use the store's telephone to call his superiors in Singapore.

Fearing that he wouldn't be able to find a better price, Wu telephoned his superiors and described the salesman's offer. They were hesitant to allow the purchase, as they were unaccustomed to making expensive deals in such little time. But they were also afraid to lose the deal. They approved the purchase, fearing this was an opportunity they couldn't afford to miss.

The company, of course, did not get the best possible deal. Wu succumbed to the pressure tactics of the American salesman. American salesmen often state that a deal must be made immediately. If he had been more familiar with American sales tactics, Wu would have shopped around and probably found the same computer for a lower price. He could have then returned to the Global Computer Store and renegotiated the price of the computers for as low as $1,200 per unit.

Encountering the American Negotiators

Following is a general guideline on what Americans are most likely to do, and how to counter those tactics the next time you meet them.

	Americans	You
Group Composition	Middle managers with marketing orientation negotiate at the first meeting.	Include your technical staff to challenge them.
Establishing Rapport	Short time for establishing rapport, followed by attention to tasks.	Prolong period of initial contact to get control.
Information Exchange	May/May not follow up on any requested information.	Repeat your own requests to get to the bottom line.
Persuasion Tools	Buyers are pressured to make immediate decisions in "use or lose" offers.	Focus on self-interest of individual negotiators and how they will gain from the deal.

	Americans	You
Decision Process Decision Makers	Ensure that facts back up decision makers. Middle managers are usually empowered to make decisions.	Compare their offer with their competitors. Focus on personal gain of immediate negotiator.

Working with Americans

What will a dozen red roses do?

Be careful not to sexually harass American coworkers. Detrimental side effects can result to those who violate the rights of others in the American workplace. Take, for example, Jacques LeCroir, a young French engineer who had recently begun working for an American hi-tech firm in San Francisco. The American firm chose Jacques over several American, German, and Swedish candidates. The salary and benefits offered to him were more attractive than the packages offered by other companies to his fellow classmates. Jacques believed his six years of exemplary work at the Sorbonne had finally paid off.

After working with the company for one month, Jacques recognized that the secretary of his department, Jennifer, was very friendly and helpful to him. She was also very attractive, and he knew that she was single. Jacques complimented Jennifer on her appearance and playfully tickled her from time to time. When she did nothing to resist his flirting, Jacques concluded that Jennifer wanted to go out on a dinner date with him. He brought to Jennifer a dozen red roses on a Friday morning and asked her out on a date.

Not only did Jennifer decline Jacques' offer, she also informed his boss of his frequent passes at her. She interpreted Jacques' offer as the final straw in a series of sexual harassment incidents. Jennifer said that she could not be comfortable working around Jacques, and asked her boss to transfer him to another department.

Fearing the worst, the boss decided to transfer Jacques to a site 50 miles away in the farm city of Modesto. But Jacques' family and friends had already made plans to visit him in San Francisco during the

Christmas holidays. "How will I explain this to them?" he contemplated. "A dozen long-stemmed roses transferred me to the city of Modesto!" He should feel lucky that his antics didn't result in worse consequences, however.

Can you do my job?

Don't be surprised when an American boss asks questions pertaining to your interests in the company. Employers will often allow you the opportunity to sell yourself to them. Be careful, though, not to commit mistakes similar to those in our next example.

Fong Chang, a Chinese immigrant with a degree in computer science from Stanford University, had worked for Surge Semiconductor in the Silicon Valley for just over a year. Mr. Russell, his boss, had decided to review his past year's performance.

"Well," the boss said, "I must say that we've been quite happy with your work. Your input on the Phase Two project really opened some doors for us. We have no complaints about your work." Fong thanked Russell and said that the year he worked for Surge had been very rewarding. Russell then said, "Well, tell me, then, where do you want to be one year from now? Let me know what your ambitions are while working for Surge."

Embarrassed, Fong blushed and smiled sheepishly. He did not give Russell any idea of how he would like to move up within the ranks of Surge Semiconductor. Within a week, he decided to leave his job at Surge and look for another job.

Fong quit his enjoyable and promising job because he misunderstood his boss' inquiries. Russell offered Fong an opportunity to sell himself. He liked his work and wanted to learn about his long-term goals with Surge Semiconductor. Fong, however, interpreted Russell's inquiries as a sign of abandonment. Because of his Chinese cultural background, he expected his boss to be more of a patriarch who expressed concern about his workers and directed them appropriately.

Ignorance of the American value of direct and open communication cost Fong a great job. He may lose more jobs if he doesn't learn about the differences of American and Chinese cultures.

Can you help?

As discussed previously, another extremely important American value is independence. This frequently shows up in the workplace, as this next example shows.

Nho Dahn had recently been hired by an American laser manufacturing company. He had lived in America for three months, and this was the first job he had had that paid well. He wanted to save enough money to send his wife and daughter in Vietnam to America. After five days on the job, however, Nho encountered difficulties with the equipment he was using. He asked his supervisor how to fix the problem. The supervisor gave the technical manual to Nho and told him to read through the manual and fix the problem himself.

Two hours later, Nho finished repairing the machine. A few days later, however, another problem occurred with the machine. Again, he went to his supervisor, who told him to read the manual and to fix the problem himself. The supervisor became angry when this happened a third time. He noted in his personnel file that Nho had very little initiative. He also expressed his anger to Nho directly. "This is not the way we do things in America. You can't come to me with every little problem you have. You must learn to depend on yourself and try first to solve your problems alone."

This concerned Nho. He realized that he must try to work independently and go to his supervisor only when all other options had been exhausted. He also worried that these incidents may jeopardize his employment when his performance was reviewed at the end of the year. Keeping his job was Nho's main concern. He feared he may never be able to send his wife and daughter to America if he was forced to find a lower paying job.

Test Your Skills for Working with Americans

With the above situations fresh in your mind, review the following quiz to test your skills for working with Americans:

1. Working under an American supervisor, you should:
   a. Be polite and not interrupt his instructions.
   b. Not let him know that you did not understand.

      c. Hide your mistakes until he discovers them.

      d. Maintain ongoing honest communication about work problems and progress.

2. You are working hard to finish your project. Your American coworker is sitting down reading the newspaper. She might:

      a. Come very close and look at what you are doing.

      b. Bring you a cup of coffee to keep you awake.

      c. Try to help you only if you ask her to.

      d. Ask you to stop working and join her for a movie.

3. During his performance appraisal, an American employee might:

      a. Agree fully with his manager's evaluation.

      b. Defend his performance and justify his actions.

      c. Ask his managers to write down his future goals.

      d. Not ask questions about his promotion or salary increase.

4. You are on a training assignment with a U.S. company. You should:

      a. Introduce yourself to all department personnel.

      b. Get permission from your supervisor every time you leave the office.

      c. Learn to depend on yourself to solve your problems.

      d. Try to establish harmony within your group.

Most Appropriate Answers:

1. d; 2. c; 3. b; 4. c

Tips for Training Americans

Keep to a schedule.
Clarify benefits to participants.
Use handouts and slides.
Invite participation.
Be timely, organized, and
to the point.
Explain subject matter.
Keep a class size of 12 to 15.
Provide a break every
two hours.
Provide an agenda and the
necessary tools.

Don't be an unprepared
instructor.
Don't direct lectures.
Discuss opportunities.
Keep the class from being boring.
Don't leave people out of class
activities.
Avoid over-crowding.
Don't get unfocused or off the
subject.
Avoid bad training environments.

Use examples.
Establish goals and methods.
Provide positive feedback.
Provide role-play activities.
Don't interrupt people.

Don't publicly reprimand or get too personal.
Don't use improper or inaccurate information.

Tips for Motivating Americans

Set goals and give responsibility.
Assign challenging work.
Change work occasionally.
Promote and pay for performance.
Give personal thanks and praise.
Reward with good bonuses and salary raises.
Give out team awards and goals.
Explain opportunities.
Be open and friendly.
Establish feelings of worth.

Avoid repetitive tasks.
Avoid unfair blame or pay systems.
Don't assign work that's too complicated.
Don't give limited information.
Don't be harsh or critical.
Don't be discouraging, biased or prejudiced.
Don't set impossible goals.
Don't reprimand in public.
Don't ignore comments or stifle ingenuity.
Avoid a lack of rewards.

Tips for Performance Reviews of Americans

Start and end on a positive note.
Provide realistic feedback.
Establish expectations.
Give credit properly.
Discuss areas of concern.
Discuss solutions and set dates.
Give rewards linked to performance.
Give opportunities to discuss openly.
Be honest and objective.
Discuss strengths and weaknesses.

Don't lose previous reviews.
Avoid criticisms or discussions in public.
Avoid references to age, sex, religion.
Don't be subjective or prejudicial.
Avoid indecisiveness.
Avoid discussing reviews with others.
Don't treat reviews as a task.
Don't misuse reviews.
Avoid oversight.
Avoid inconsistency.
Avoid surprises.

Plan with goals and results.
Provide guidance for
improvement.
Permit feedback and
discussion.
Highlight achievements.

Avoid being too general in your
comments.
Avoid looking at your watch.
Don't ridicule employees.

Socializing with Americans

Friendship or friendliness

In another scenario, Raj Sehgal, a chemical engineer from India, was recently hired by an American firm in Texas. An American who worked at the firm, Bill Porter, knew that Raj was an outstanding tennis player, and invited him to his country club to play tennis on a Saturday afternoon. They began playing at one o'clock. Raj played better than anyone Bill had played against in a long time. Both men enjoyed the other's company. They didn't finish playing until 5 p.m.

After they showered, Raj asked Bill to join him for dinner. Bill declined. "I've made dinner plans with Mark and, later on, I'm taking my friend Sally to a movie." Raj said he understood, but he was actually quite upset. He had sweated all day long playing tennis in the hot sun and expected to spend part of his evening with Bill. He had to go back home with two McDonald's hamburgers for dinner as his wife had canceled her plan to cook and was away visiting her mother.

Bill's actions should not have upset Raj, however. He should consider that Americans often have different types of friendship. One friend may be a tennis partner, another a frequent dinner guest, and another a sailing companion. It often takes time for one friend to assume several different roles.

Also misleading to foreigners is the American habit of making casual invitations. An American participant at one of my seminars told me this story: He was in Cairo visiting a business acquaintance. "Let's have lunch sometime," he told his Egyptian friend. The Arab went home and told his wife to prepare a lavish meal. The next day, when the American visited his friend's home, he was shocked to find a six-course meal waiting for him, and what's more, the Arab now expected to be treated to a similarly elaborate meal at the Cairo Hilton!

When Americans say "Let's get together" or "Let's have lunch," it can cause confusion for people unfamiliar with American culture. Americans generally say things like these to show their desire to keep in touch or as a polite ending to a conversation, not necessarily because they want to plan an activity in the near future.

Be ready for a hot dog dinner

And don't be surprised to discover that Americans are very relaxed socially. Mafous Naguib and his wife, Nadia, were recent Egyptian immigrants to America. Mafous had worked for a tourism publication company for two months and had become good friends with David Cranston, his immediate supervisor. Mafous invited David and his wife to dinner at his apartment on Saturday. "Mrs. Naguib," he hinted, "will prepare some specialties from Egypt."

Nadia slaved all day in the kitchen. She prepared a six-course meal that included leg of lamb, rolled grape leaves, shish-kebab, and a special dessert. The Cranstons genuinely enjoyed the meal, and reciprocated the Naguibs' hospitality by inviting them to dinner in two weeks.

The Naguibs were stunned, however, upon arriving at the Cranstons' for dinner. The meal consisted of hot dogs, steak, baked potatoes, and vegetables! Nadia estimated Mrs. Cranston had spent no more than one hour preparing the dinner. The guests were cordial and enjoyed the meal, but Mafous began to feel uncomfortable working with his superior.

Mr. and Mrs. Naguib should not have been surprised when Mrs. Cranston did not overextend herself. Americans usually do not expect their hosts to spend all day preparing dinner. Mrs. Cranston probably had no idea how long Nadia spent in the kitchen.

Have another drink

While Americans are often relaxed on social occasions, however, they are not rude. Especially watch your alcoholic intake when dining or socializing with American business connections. Patrick Mallory, an Irish aerodynamic parts salesman, was in the U.S. to promote his company's new landing gear. A purchasing agent for an American airline manufacturer had agreed to meet him for an early afternoon lunch. Patrick recognized that a deal with this company could substantially increase his own company's share of the American market.

The American met Patrick at an upscale seafood restaurant. The two decided upon their dishes and Patrick ordered a carafe of wine.

The lunch was long, as the American did not hesitate to ask very specific technical questions regarding the landing gear. Time passed and Patrick ordered another carafe of wine. Then he ordered yet another.

After drinking so much, Patrick became somewhat boisterous. He was easily annoyed by the American's persistent questions about the landing gear. Upon finishing a fourth carafe, Patrick said rudely, "Look, we can only discuss the landing gear for so long. This lunch has been going on forever. Are you going to purchase or not?"

The American stood up to leave and said he would call Patrick tomorrow with a decision. He never called, though. He didn't want to do business with an inconsiderate drunkard. Patrick woke up the next morning with a severe headache. If he didn't refrain from drinking so much he would return to Ireland without any new clients. His superiors would then give him a real headache to worry about—the prospect of unemployment.

Test Your Skills in Socializing with Americans

Answer the following quiz to test your skills in socializing with Americans:

1. Your American friend is interested in buying a King Tut picture for his son while he is in Egypt. He expects you to:
   a. Surprise him with the picture as a gift.
   b. Take him to the market and help him select the gift.
   c. Advise him as to where he can get the best buy.
   d. Ask your wife to take him out shopping.
2. Mr. Ahmed from Cairo has just left the office of an American partner who said, "We should get together sometime." Ahmed should:
   a. Invite his American friend to dinner at his house.
   b. Consider it to only be a friendly comment and do nothing about it.
   c. Expect his American partner to invite him for dinner at the Hilton.
   d. Invite the American for dinner at the Hilton but have him pay.
3. Your American coworker has invited you to play tennis with her for the second time in a month. This could mean that:
   a. You are now her close friend.
   b. You can talk to her about your problems with your family.

c. She expects you to solve the technical problem she has at work.

d. She just enjoys playing tennis with you.

4. This is your first week of training in an American company. Your department secretary seems very friendly and helpful. She may be:

a. Expecting you to invite her to your country.

b. Doing her job.

c. Interested in going out to dinner with you.

d. Expecting you to bring her some flowers.

Most Appropriate Answers:

1. c; 2. b; 3. d; 4. b

Summary

Americans don't have to be difficult to work with. If you understand American culture, your business relationships with them can be extremely rewarding. Consider the following tips when interacting and negotiating with Americans:

- Remember that Americans communicate directly and openly. They like to lay everything on the table from the start.
- Be concise and direct with your written correspondence and telephone calls.
- Be aware that Americans increase their profits by selling their products in package deals.
- Focus on the benefits your company can provide to your American clients.
- Be punctual in your appointments with Americans. Punctuality is considered courteous and respectful.
- Know that Americans are often independent problem solvers. Expect them to rely on themselves before they go to a coworker or supervisor for help.
- Be aware that Americans are short-term oriented and focus on immediate gains.
- Remember that Americans stand behind their commitments firmly.
- Deal with everyone on the negotiating team equally. Avoid looking down on women or on young businesspeople.

- Be persistent but not overbearing.
- Know that Americans evaluate business propositions on their technical merits and immediate benefits.
- While discussing business with Americans, create an environment that allows the participants to express their views openly.
- Make the most of your opportunities. Don't turn down an opportunity because it lacks immediate monetary gains. The rewards will come later.
- Be aware that the internal politics of most organizations may influence their relationships with you.
- If an American company gives you the opportunity to do work for them, make sure you do an exceptional job. American companies evaluate performance rigorously but fairly.

If you keep these suggestions in mind, you can deal successfully with Americans.

Facing the Japanese Salaryman

*How would you start your sales presentation to Japanese clients?
How many counter offers should you make when negotiating
with the Japanese?
Where will you entertain your Japanese supplier?*

Boasting one of the strongest economies in the world despite recent short-term setbacks, Japan is one of the big players in the global economy. Not only must the Japanese be dealt with as intense competitors anxious to capture markets that have thus far eluded their grasp, but they must also be addressed as a large consumer market ready for increasing consumption. Yet, finding a niche in the Japanese market has historically been a difficult task, especially for Western economic powers. Trade wars were common headline news with political leaders complaining of unfair trade practices on the part of Japan, and business leaders imploring Americans to purchase domestically produced goods.

The escalation of this trade war has cooled off in recent years. The reasons for this vary. Japanese automobile companies, for example, have set up manufacturing plants in the United States. Japanese and American companies have also worked together on various joint venture projects. Still, competing with the Japanese is no easy task. Whether looking to enter the Japanese market or to make a sale to visiting Japanese representatives, their cultural background must be taken into account.

In this chapter, we will focus on the Japanese salaryman, the key person that most foreigners interact, negotiate, and have to compete with. The chapter will identify the inherent cultural values of most Japanese and characteristics of the Japanese salaryman. We will provide detailed information on effective communication, meetings, negotiation, and marketing to Japanese organizations. Specific examples will be presented on certain encounters with the Japanese salaryman and how to enhance your relationship and gain a competitive edge in the Japanese market.

Test Your Skills Dealing with the Japanese

Answer the following true-false statements to test your skills dealing with the Japanese:

___ 1. If a Japanese person smiles and nods his head, he definitely likes what you are saying or offering.

___ 2. When a Japanese person sucks air through his teeth, it is a non-verbal sign that he has a problem.

___ 3. Japanese supervisors will usually give minimal instruction to their foreign subordinates to encourage them to work in groups.

___ 4. In a group situation, the Japanese sometimes use silent periods to sense others' feelings and thoughts.

___ 5. Japanese culture rewards individual more than group achievements.

___ 6. In Japanese culture, group harmony and consensus are important and highly respected.

___ 7. Most Japanese managers have a private office with a family picture on the wall.

___ 8. The Japanese are often direct and not concerned with losing face.

___ 9. Most Japanese decisions are made on the negotiating table with foreigners.

___ 10. When a Japanese person says "yes, yes," he is confirming his agreement.

Most Appropriate Answers:

1. F; 2. T; 3. T; 4. T; 5. F; 6. T; 7. F; 8. F; 9. F; 10. F

A Personal Tale: My Encounter with the Japanese Salaryman

When I first decided to enter the Japanese market with my multicultural training seminars, I wanted to make a presentation to the management at Toshiba, one of the largest and most successful Japanese electronics conglomerates. I asked a professor friend at Tokyo University for a reference to someone at Toshiba, and he kindly gave me the name of a manager in the training department, a Mr. Suzuki.

I immediately drafted a proposal and sent it to Mr. Suzuki, along with a copy of my new book, proposing to meet with him during a visit to Japan the following month. Two weeks passed without any response, so I decided to take the initiative and called him directly. He immediately thanked me for the information, but apologized for not being able to meet with me. I then called my professor friend and found out that they had just met. Apparently, Mr. Suzuki did not have a strong enough relationship with my friend to entertain my request, and so I was not properly introduced.

Not giving up on Mr. Suzuki, however, I invited him to lunch the next time I was in Japan doing business with Hitachi. He accepted and later invited me to make a presentation at his office and to find out about my program at Hitachi. When I arrived at the office, I was surprised to find 10 people in the conference room. On the presentation table was an American flag, a Japanese flag—and, in recognition of the country of my birth, an Egyptian flag. I felt confident that my proposal was well received, but I never received an offer. I later found out that Mr. Suzuki was not the proper sponsor to defend my proposal against other managers in the company that I needed.

I put this knowledge to use when I approached the next Japanese company. At Sony Corporation, I sought the highest introduction possible. Earlier, I had attended a conference in Tokyo where the late chairman of Sony, Mr. Akio Morita, was giving a speech. After his speech, I asked him for the opportunity to visit his company. He looked to his assistant with a smile and the assistant asked me to call him on my next trip to Japan. Two months later, the assistant set up a meeting with Mr. Yamamoto, the manager of Sony's training department.

At 11:00 a.m. sharp, I arrived at the reception desk at Sony, where I was met by a young lady named Yoko. She apologized that Mr. Yamamoto had been called to a meeting, and inquired whether I had

brought any information for him to review. Disappointed, I nevertheless handed her my material and a copy of my book, wondering why
my meeting had been overlooked. Later, I realized that most Japanese
managers will not meet with you until they have a good amount of
information about your organization and have a consensus from their
team to meet with suppliers like me.

One month later, I received a fax from Yamamoto indicating that he
was now ready to meet with me. He was very interested in our programs, and I felt that he would make a good sponsor. After three
months, however, I learned that Yamamoto had been moved to a different position. He did refer me to his successor, Mr. Hara, but I was
nevertheless forced to start the whole process over again!

Unfortunately, Hara informed me that he had already developed a
relationship with one of my competitors. I immediately began to point
out the benefits of my programs over those of my competitors. Hara
simply smiled and asked me to be patient, reminding me that Japanese
do not terminate easily a good relationship. Six months later, I was
awarded my first contract with Sony.

Learning from my experiences, I now sailed into the Fujitsu
Corporation with ease, but this time I had to negotiate prices. As I
expected, Fujitsu countered my first price with an offer to pay 50 percent of my proposal, claiming budgetary restraints. I countered with a
discount of 10 percent, and, after a delay of two weeks, my sponsor
came back with a final offer at a 20-percent discount.

Recognizing the lengthy process that the Japanese undertake to
make decisions, I decided to accept their final price. It was for less
money than I would usually accept, but it did give me the opportunity
to be offered a second program after three months. To my surprise,
they offered me 20 percent less for the follow-up program. Although I
explained that my price was already discounted, they maintained their
offer, claiming that my high price might destroy the harmony among
them and other Japanese suppliers. I declined.

Six months later, after recognizing that the experience I would gain
by doing business with Fujitsu would be worth the discounted price, I
decided to accept their offer. Now that I had established a relationship
with Fujitsu, they were willing to offer me a third program. Later, and
to my astonishment, they asked for another 20-percent discount when
they offered me a fourth program to guarantee more programs. I considered this too low for my expertise, and I decided to drop them as a
client.

That was how I discovered the essence of the Japanese keiretsu system, in which a company guarantees business to a supplier on one key condition: that the supplier always adheres to the company's budget.

These experiences illustrate some of the ways in which the Japanese conduct business, and they are also a reflection of Japanese culture as a whole. From personal introductions and negotiation tactics to decision-making processes and other expectations, such as the keiretsu system, it is important for managers from other cultures to understand Japanese business practices.

Japanese Cultural Values

Every society accumulates a set of unique cultural values. These values are reflected in the business culture of each society. Due to its geographic isolation, Japan's political and cultural doors were closed and locked for centuries. As a result, the Japanese developed a set of values which enabled them to survive and peacefully coexist within sharply defined boundaries. To this day, these values include group harmony, consensus, and achievement. In recent years, Japan has officially opened many of its barriers to politics and trade, but its deeply rooted cultural values are slow to change with the times.

From childhood, the Japanese are molded by the values that Japan holds dear. Parents and grandparents teach Japanese children the importance of group harmony, achievement, and group consensus. These values are reinforced as the child interacts with peers and encounters Japanese social institutions, such as schools and government bureaucracies. When Japanese children finish their education, most begin work with a Japanese company. The values instilled in them at an early age are reinforced in the Japanese work environment.

The primary source of business-related cultural conflicts is the approach taken by companies seeking to do business with other companies. When American companies make a proposal to Japanese companies, the executives involved approach the deal with the values they have inherited. Americans apply their values of freedom, equality, independence, risk taking, and competition, often unaware that Japanese values lay on the opposite end of their cultural spectrum. Independence and competition are important qualities for American managers to incorporate into their work, whereas successful Japanese managers must learn to work well within their groups and accept the consensus of their teams. Clashing values often result in failed business relationships.

During our management training seminars, we asked Japanese participants to prioritize 20 values common among many cultures. These values were group harmony, competition, seniority, cooperation, privacy, openness, equality, formality, risk taking, reputation, freedom, family security, relationship, self-reliance, time, group consensus, authority, material possessions, spiritual enlightenment, and group achievement. We also asked the same questions to groups of American and Arab managers. The following table presents what these three groups indicate are their top five values from this list.

Japanese	Americans	Arabs
Relationship	Equality	Seniority
Group Harmony	Freedom	Spirituality
Family	Openness	Reputation
Freedom	Self-Reliance	Family
Cooperation	Cooperation	Authority

Obviously, this table illustrates the vast differences between the values of these three cultures. You can see how friction arises when any two of these three cultures interact. The differences in the lists above reveal quite a bit about the Japanese who stress building relationships before any business will start. This is followed naturally by group harmony and cooperation in all aspects of decision making and management. Caring for elders and family members is still an important part of Japanese life.

Americans value their individual freedoms immensely. Equality, for one, is assumed by most Americans, and those who do not believe in it are generally perceived negatively. The American Dream is that of becoming rich through hard work, skill, and a little luck. Americans assume that everyone has the opportunity to reach their full economic and intellectual potential. On the other hand, Arabs look for and value seniority and authorities who are guided by spiritual feeling for decisions. They will try to keep their word or reputation with their family and close members.

The Japanese Salaryman

Most foreigners interact with the Japanese salaryman. Salarymen are employed by most Japanese offices, and are the epitome of the young Japanese corporate worker. Let's discover what values the salaryman holds, and take a look at his daily activities so we can learn how to work with him successfully.

Most Japanese high school students dream about being salarymen. They believe this will give them the security they need to be employed for the duration of their lives. They study hard and try to do well in their interviews with potential companies such as Sony, Fujitsu, and Toyota. After passing rigorous interviews, they are selected not only for their technical qualifications, but also for their possession of traits that will enable them to work well in groups. Once they are accepted, their first few months on the job are generally dedicated to introducing them to the company's policies, culture, and business practices. They are assigned to a department and a group within the department. Their first task is to simply work effectively within their assigned groups, rather than to accomplish any complex activities on their own. Their bosses evaluate their communication and interaction with group members.

The salaryman's day usually starts at 6 a.m., when he takes an approximately one-hour train ride to work. Most new hires are given space within a company dormitory. This is done primarily so they can spend time with their groups. The new salaryman is expected to be punctual in everything he does, which includes participating in the company's morning exercise routine and watching the company's morning television broadcast. He is expected to dress formally in a white shirt, slacks, a tie, and a company badge. Most companies also provide their employees with a company suit jacket.

The salaryman works in a large room with 10 to 12 desks. Each desk is shared by usually two employees. The boss's desk is usually facing everyone to monitor their work. The salaryman's mentor will give him an assignment and help him complete it with his team.

Lunch is an extremely important social activity for the salaryman. From 11:30 a.m. to 1 p.m., he joins three or four of his team members for lunch. They relieve the tension they may feel by smoking, discussing their work, and talking about the boss. It's rare to find the salaryman spending his lunch alone.

Communicating with foreign visitors is a unique experience for the new salaryman. He is often asked by his boss to join a meeting with foreign visitors. He joins the meeting to watch and listen to how his boss communicates with foreigners. This is the salaryman's first experience interacting with foreigners in business. After he has gained experience working with foreigners, the boss will give the salaryman more responsibility in handling foreign visitors. It is rare for a foreign visitor to meet with only one salaryman—the foreigner will usually encounter two or three Japanese employees. Normally, two of them will be veteran employees, and the other a newer salaryman.

At 5 p.m., the business is officially closed, but nobody leaves until after the boss leaves, which is typically an hour later. Two or three times per week, the employees will get together after work to eat, drink, smoke, and talk. Between 9 and 10 p.m., the salaryman rides the subway train home. The married salaryman expects his wife to be waiting for him with a hot bath and a bowl of steaming rice. He will already have had dinner with his friends. He then falls asleep, dead tired, setting his alarm for 6 a.m. the next morning. During the weekend, he catches up with extra sleep.

The salaryman's performance is evaluated based on how he works within his group, his group's contributions to the department, and how his department contributes to his company's profits. He looks forward to the company's bi-annual bonuses in the summer and winter and normally uses this money for vacations with his family or to purchase investments. Typically, his salary is managed by his wife, who gives him a daily allowance. Salarymen love entertaining foreigners, as long as they or the company picks up the tab.

After three to four years of successful work with the company, the salaryman is offered a transfer or a promotion to a higher position in another department or another city. He doesn't dare refuse. These frequent changes pose a challenge to foreigners who establish relationships with them. Foreign businessmen usually have to start from the beginning again, establishing a relationship with the replacement salaryman. To succeed with the salaryman, you must identify his level of seniority, the length of time he has worked in his position, and when he will be transferred.

The phenomenon of the Japanese salaryman is indicative of many of the cultural norms of Japan. The values of harmony, group togetherness and cohesion, and adherence to rules of etiquette all show themselves in the study of the salaryman. The process of becoming a salaryman also explains the resilience of Japanese values, and how these values can remain so strong in a drastically changing world.

Mr. Bell's First Trip to Japan

Mr. Bell was a marketing manager for Telestar Telecommunications, an American firm. During an exhibition of his company's products in San Francisco, he was approached by two members of Tokyo Telecom. Mr. Yamamoto, Tokyo Telecom's representative, reviewed Telestar's brochure, inspected their products and, after an extensive discussion, told Bell that he was very interested.

A month later, Bell received a letter from Yamamoto stating that Tokyo Telecom wished to discuss a joint venture with Telestar. Bell was excited at the possibility of entering the Japanese market. He immediately told the good news to his boss and informed Yamamoto that he would visit Japan immediately.

Bell spent two weeks preparing a presentation to highlight Telestar's technological and cost advantages. After confirming the date for his arrival in Japan, he booked a flight to Tokyo. Upon arriving at the airport, he took a cab from Narita airport to his hotel in Tokyo. To his surprise, the cab fare was $200 for the almost one-hour trip. He checked into the Hilton where he discovered that he had to pay $250 for a room.

Bell's meeting with Tokyo Telecom was scheduled for 9 a.m. He wasn't aware of Tokyo's morning traffic jams, and left the hotel at 8:30. To Bell's dismay, he didn't arrive at the office until 9:30 a.m. when Yamamoto and his team were waiting for him. Yamamoto recommended that Bell try the underground subway.

Bell proceeded to shake each hand, while each employee attempted to hand him their business cards. Bell recognized that the Japanese businessmen were pulling their cards from their business card holder while he was fishing around for his own business card in his wallet. He saw that this did not please them, but he couldn't fathom why. Each member of the Japanese team inspected his card closely, while Bell simply dropped their cards into his shirt pocket. He looked as if he was in a rush to get into business.

Yamamoto then invited Bell into the guest room, where he was offered coffee. After accepting, Bell asked, "How's business?" Yamamoto paused, and politely responded that it was fine. Bell then asked Kenichi what he did in the company. Kenichi replied humbly, "I just joined the company, and I'm Mr. Yamamoto's assistant."

After sipping the coffee, Bell opened his briefcase and removed the documents for his presentation, including the company catalog he'd prepared for the presentation. Yamamoto informed Bell politely that they were waiting for the boss to arrive, after which they would move to the conference room to conduct the presentation. Bell realized that he needed to slow down.

The boss arrived, and the group moved to the conference room to begin the presentation. Bell began with a multimedia presentation of his company's technological wizardry and line of products. He talked for nearly an hour before asking the group if they had questions. Nobody responded. Bell assumed his presentation had been made clearly and was understood by the group.

Bell, however, had been conducting a one-way presentation, which did not sit well with his prospective clients. Japanese businessmen usually run their meetings interactively, and Bell should have directly asked Yamamoto if he had questions, not the group. Yamamoto would have replied immediately, and other members would have then become involved in the discussion. Because Bell's long one-way presentation and approach concerned Yamamoto, he offered his staff a break from the presentation. During the break, the group members finally began asking Bell questions, and then the presentation resumed.

At 11:30 a.m., Yamamoto indicated that it was time for lunch. Bell had been given money by Telestar to take Yamamoto and his staff to lunch and made the appropriate invitation. Yamamoto accepted immediately and invited his boss and junior assistant along. Lunch was a great opportunity to have an informal exchange of information. Bell felt at ease with the group during lunch, but not when he saw the $400 lunch bill—much more than he expected.

After lunch, Bell was bombarded with technical questions by the group, many of which he was unable to answer. He wrote down the questions he couldn't answer, and told Yamamoto that he would fax the answers to Japan once he arrived in America.

After returning to San Francisco, Bell looked at the $5,000 company bill he had accumulated during his visit and wondered how the deal would go. After a long two months of silence from Tokyo Telecom, he received a fax thanking him for his visit. At this time, however, it was difficult for them to engage in business with Bell's company. Bell didn't know what to do. Did they mean never? How should he proceed? Bell had no idea of his standing with his prospective clients due to his lack of understanding of Japanese culture. He needed more preparation and awareness of the norms of the close-knit culture of Japanese corporations. He may have not recognized that, perhaps, the Japanese company was in the process of information gathering and was not necessarily ready to sign in! Now he had to be more patient and keep the line of communication open.

Working for the Salaryman

In their overseas joint ventures, the Japanese tend not to include local managers in the decision-making process. They usually create two separate lines of management: the Japanese and the local managers.

Although they appear to share work, the Japanese usually control the decision-making process; the local staff only provides information and marketing. Most decisions are made in consultation with Tokyo or with the base office. This process usually frustrates the local staff, which expects to be part of the organizational decision-making process. In time, the local staff begins to feel that their opinions and expertise are not valued. Eventually, they withdraw completely from decision-making responsibility, giving full control to the Japanese team. When the Japanese team leaves the factory to go back home, problems arise and quality drops.

In overseas operations, many Japanese experience anxiety in their interpersonal relations with local workers and soon become isolated. Adding to this sense of isolation is the fact that many Japanese managers see themselves as personally representing their company in an overseas operation. In strong contrast, most foreign workers view themselves and their Japanese colleagues as mere employees.

Some Japanese tend to avoid dealing immediately with personal problems or lack of performance. They prefer to let problems slide rather than deal with them head on in the American style. As deadlines approach, these Japanese managers become frustrated and push their local workers to meet deadlines. The workers, who have not had much feedback on their performance, see the Japanese managers as rude and authoritarian.

Most Japanese managers enjoy drinking and socializing after work. This is also the time for informally exchanging business. The following morning, many foreign managers feel left out and surprised at not having been included in the discussion. In contrast with the Japanese, most Arab workers and managers do not drink alcoholic beverages because of their religious beliefs. Moreover, workers and managers in the Arab world generally do not mix socially, thus minimizing the opportunity for informal discussions. Further, when a local employee makes a mistake, the employee discovers that the entire Japanese management staff knows about it, from last night's drinking session, by the next day. The worker becomes acutely embarrassed about the incident and may begin to mistrust the Japanese supervisor for advertising the mistake.

In one case, a large Japanese company hired a new graduate from Stanford university with a Ph.D. in computer science and relocated him with his family to Tokyo. The American employee was very sharp and worked hard and came up with a new design within 6 months that the company was looking for. He was sure that this would help his six-month contract to be extended to full-time employment with the company. To his shock, at the end of his contract, his Japanese boss indicated that the company would not renew his contract. The Japanese manager complained that he did not fit very well with his team. Although he was creative and meeting deadlines, he rarely joined the group for lunch, dinner, or karaoke fundrinking time. Further, at 5 p.m. sharp, he usually left the office to join his family, while other members of his team stayed late.

Japanese supervisors also tend to be quite conservative about giving praise or other forms of positive feedback. This is usually because they are afraid that they will make an inappropriate or insulting remark in a foreign language. Most overseas workers, however, expect coaching and encouragement from their supervisors. They are motivated by positive feedback and encouraged to be innovative. When a foreign worker presents the Japanese supervisor with an idea to improve a process and the supervisor responds with only polite interest, the worker's motivation is severely reduced.

Foreign workers will be more productive if managed by supervisors who not only have the required technical qualifications, but who also possess the specific cultural skills necessary to gain the respect of local workers. This is particularly true in the Arabic-speaking countries of the Middle East, where flattery is common and highly valued. To an Arab, words of flattery and personal encouragement from a superior will have a much more positive impact than will any promises of promotion.

In the Japanese language, voice pitch is low and tone is constant, so as not to convey undue or inappropriate emotion. People from other cultures, however, are less hesitant to express their emotions more openly, and this is reflected in the changes in volume and tone of their speech as most South Americans or Italians will do who have to watch their voice tone.

In general, Japanese culture places a greater value on nonverbal communication than do other cultures. Indeed, even silence is considered a virtue in Japan; conversations often contain periods of silence during which each participant senses the thoughts and feelings of the other. In other cultures, periods of silence during social interaction are considered awkward and uncomfortable. In Arab cultures, for example, silence is usually reserved only for sad occasions such as mourning, and Americans tend to interrupt silence with self-disclosure or arguments intended to elicit a response. The Japanese tendency toward silence and reluctance to acknowledge something with a definite "yes" or "no" frustrates most foreign workers, who label the Japanese as vague or ambiguous.

Dress is another area that can have culturally specific meanings. In most Japanese factories, workers and managers wear the same uniform. In other cultures, dress and appearance display social status, so high-level managers wearing ordinary working clothes will not be given due respect. Before transplanting your factory uniform to another country, make sure you know what is culturally appropriate dress in that country.

Similarly, the design of office space is also a reflection of culture. The open-space floor plan of most Japanese workplaces reflects the value placed on inner harmony and group discussion. The Japanese do not use space to gain privacy or to show power, status, or authority. Foreign executives, however, expect their own private office as a sign of their power and authority. So, if in their overseas operations the Japanese try to lay out their offices as if they were in Japan, local managers and supervisors may feel as if their power and status have been taken away from them. Even the workers feel a little uncomfortable when the lines of authority are blurred.

In addition, business discussions are conducted openly in Japanese companies, and typically include everyone involved. Even important business meetings and those that involve personal matters are discussed as a group. This sort of arrangement is not acceptable to some other cultures and local management.

Motivational tools vary widely among cultures. For example, status and title are important motivational tools in Arab cultures and in many developing countries. The Japanese values of group harmony and equality do not motivate foreign managers of Japanese-owned plants to excel by title or status. If Japanese managers eliminate the expected competition and reward system for status and title, they will take away some very important incentives.

When making performance evaluations in overseas operations, the Japanese practice is to allow all Japanese managers in the department to review and comment on the performance of each foreign worker, even if the worker reports only to one manager in the department. Many foreign workers feel that this does not lead to a fair evaluation, and the bad feelings that result can serve to de-motivate employees and reduce productivity. Some foreign workers in Japanese companies feel discriminated against in terms of medical care, personal development, salary, and promotional opportunity, when compared with their Japanese counterparts.

In some joint-venture projects, Japanese medical doctors are sent from Japan for the Japanese staff, and local employees feel that the company has more concern for the Japanese staff than for them. Isolation and hard feelings result. In some cases, Japanese companies even provide overseas Japanese staff with food shipped directly from home. In poor, developing countries, when local workers are never invited to share in or to taste some of these imported foods, resentment develops and morale falls.

Enhancing Relationships with Japanese

Even if your company's products and technology are the best in the industry, the door is not automatically open for you to conduct business with Japanese companies. With the Japanese, one must first go through the lengthy process of nurturing a relationship. The relationships the Japanese have amongst themselves start early in their educational lives. These relationships are nurtured through their alumni gatherings and are based on mutual obligations.

In order to succeed with a Japanese business contact, you must first find a contact through a person with whom the contact has a mutually obligatory relationship. It is then your responsibility to make your relationship flourish through continuous communication and visits. If you don't have a good contact to begin with, your prospective relationship will not go far. Part of your relationship will be the seasonal greeting. If you receive a greeting card from a Japanese prospect, it is a good sign that the prospect is interested in your services. You should reciprocate this communication in order to show that you are interested as well. If you stop it, it may mean that you are not interested any more in doing business.

Relationships should be nurtured not only with seasonal communication, but also with interpersonal activities such as lunch, dinner, drinking sessions, and meetings on golf courses. The Japanese take more time to build relationships than in other cultures. The extra time they take is used to watch you and find out whether you can work harmoniously with their company. They want to ensure that their relationship with you will be productive and that the chances of failure are minimal. To them, there is no divorce after marriage in business. Both personal and business investments will be lost.

Information is exchanged by the parties via careful written and personal visitation. This gives team members involved in the decision-making process the opportunity to evaluate products, services, and quality. It is rare that the relationship will result in a business deal unless every member of a Japanese group trusts the prospective client.

Invitation to a karaoke bar, for instance, where they talked about matters of interest other than business and laughing together result in becoming true acquaintances and may be the last step toward signing the contract.

Tips for Marketing to the Japanese

Take note of the following tips:

- Your proposal will be highly considered if you have been introduced to the company by a respected Japanese contact.
- Formal meetings with foreigners are conducted mainly to receive information or ask questions, not to make any decisions.
- A strong manager within the Japanese organization must sponsor your proposal and defend it to the other parties involved.
- Top management will question the sponsoring managers until all involved parties have agreed. Consensus is key.
- The Japanese will look for potential market shares, adaptability of your products, and your harmonious and cooperative attitude.
- Decisions are made behind the scenes during a series of informal meetings and only after all parties agree.

Let us now look at the following scenario for tips in communicating with the Japanese.

On the Phone with the Japanese

Who is calling, please?

International telephone calls can also be a source of friction between people from different cultures, as demonstrated in this sample call by an American computer manufacturer to his Japanese hard-disk supplier about a missing shipment.

Japanese:	Hello, this is XYZ Distributors, Takahashi speaking.
American:	Hello, Takahashi, this is Michael Ellis from Future Computers in the United States.
Japanese:	Oh yes, Mr. Ellis. Did you receive the disk drives?
American:	No, I haven't. That's why I'm calling. Our production line is stalled because they were waiting for them.

Japanese:	Oh, I'm very sorry, Mr. Ellis.
American:	Well, when did you ship them?
Japanese:	I need to check with my department staff to find out.
American:	Fine, I'll hold while you check.
Japanese:	I'm sorry, we must first have a meeting to discuss the problem.
American:	Another meeting? Can't you just check with the shipping department, *now?*

This telephone conversation reveals how the American values of directness, self-reliance, and action orientation can clash with Japanese values of group harmony and consensus. The American wanted to find a quick resolution to the problem, while the Japanese wanted to discuss the issue at a meeting with his colleagues and usually cannot make the decision by himself. To the Japanese, the American came across as pushy and abrupt—while to the American, the Japanese seemed indecisive and overly apologetic. In fact, both were simply adhering to their own cultural values and norms.

A similar misunderstanding once occurred when I was making an intercontinental call to a business contact in Tokyo. As my contact spoke, he kept asking, "Are you still there, Farid?" There was nothing wrong with the connection, and I was listening to him intently, but because I wasn't saying "*hai, hai*" ("yes, yes") as he talked, he was not sure if I was following what he had to say. When I started to do that, my Japanese contact seemed more comfortable and the conversation went much more smoothly.

I have also found that it's important to listen carefully when a Japanese person prefaces a comment with "by the way." An American might use that phrase to switch to a less important topic, but, for the Japanese, it is a signal to start talking about serious business matters. He is giving you a hint!

The emphasis the Japanese place on etiquette can become a thorn in one's side when dealing with them over the phone. Keep the following points in mind when engaging in telephone conversations with the Japanese:

- Speak slowly and clearly—do not be ambiguous.
- Send a fax or letter on a particular subject before calling.
- Identify your country first, then your company, department, and name.
- Inquire about the person who you are calling and state their department.

- State the main purpose of your call.
- Listen as much as you talk, and don't worry about occasional silences.
- Do not interrupt the other side.
- Do not expect a direct answer on the phone.
- You may follow up with a written summary of the main point.

As with most cultures, be sure to reiterate important points and confirm your partner's understanding of them. Also, confirm prices, dates, and follow-up actions. This will not only give you a good idea of the position you hold in relation to the Japanese company, but will also serve as a means for you to make your expectations known. Always conclude your conversation with an expression of thanks and appreciation. Following up your call with a fax or letter often proves a vital tool in nurturing the relationship you develop with your partners.

Writing to the Japanese

In this section, we will compare a Japanese business letter with an American business letter.

Letter to a Japanese Businessman

Dear Mr. Ohshima,

I was happy to receive your call today and am sorry it took us so long to get connected. I am thankful for Mr. Shinichi's introduction and hope you enjoyed your Golden Week holidays.

Our company is one of the leaders in the field of multicultural management and negotiation. Our programs develop the cultural competency of today's managers who deal with diverse employees, suppliers, and clients. Our training has been of great value to major Japanese organizations.

As JapanCorp expands its global communications, I believe that our programs will be of great value. I hope we will have the chance to meet within the next few months to discuss our mutual interests.

Thank you again for your call; I am looking forward to continuing our communication. By the way, I will be traveling to Tokyo in July. If you are available for a meeting at that time, please let me know so that we can make arrangements.

Sincerely,
David Weller
Sales Representative

Letter to an American Businessman

Dear Mr. Perkins:

Our company is the leader in the area of multicultural management and corporate training. We provide intensive training and consulting services that help develop the cultural competency of managers and executives who deal with culturally diverse employees, suppliers, and employees. Our programs have been adopted by corporations such as Sony, NEC, Samsung, HP, Apple Computers, and others.

As AnyCorp expands its international activities, our programs and expertise will be of great value in dealing with the global cultural diversity it will encounter. If AnyCorp has an interest in our programs, please contact me so that we can plan to introduce our programs. You may be interested in our newest program—developing flexible corporate cultures.

Thank you very much for your time, and I look forward to hearing from you.

Sincerely,
David Weller
Sales Representative

In the letter to Japanese clients, the writer only suggests that they meet to discuss their common interests. The writer recognizes that the Japanese client's goal at this point will only be to develop a relationship, not to award a contract. The second letter, though, is much more straightforward. The writer actually suggests a series of programs for the prospective client.

Japanese Nonverbal Messages

Be especially careful when presenting to a group of Japanese businesspeople and take note of what appears to be growing confidence in your ideas. More than any other form of interaction and communication, nonverbal signals and norms have a manner of fooling even the most seasoned veteran.

The Japanese treat visitors according to the level of interest in their proposal.

During my frequent visits to Japanese companies proposing my training programs, I noticed the following nonverbal messages reflecting their interest in my training services. If my host invited me to present my proposal in the big hall where everyone works and sits on the smoking couch, he is not interested but is just entertaining my visit.

If he invited me to a private room without a door, however, it shows a higher level of interest but not enough. If he takes me to a closed room with nice pictures on the wall, it is a good sign. If he offers me green Chinese tea, it is no good. Japanese or Brazilian coffee would be a better sign, especially if he offers me orange juice after the discussion. If he then invites his boss to meet with me afterward, it is a very good sign. Now, if he thanks me for coming, shakes my hand, and lets me go, it is okay. But if he takes me back to the elevator door and bows twice when I am leaving, we will be very close to a contract. Finally, if he takes me down to the street and calls a taxi for me, I can rest assured that the contract has been won!

Some nonverbal messages require special attention. Waving the hand from right to left means "No." Tilting the head expresses disagreement or strange feelings. If you encounter either of these two signals, do your best to switch negotiation or discussion tactics. They may be warnings of impending difficulties.

Here are more specific pointers to remember when dealing with the Japanese:

- A Japanese person's smile does not necessarily indicate agreement. It may even reflect sorrow or embarrassment for you.
- Sighing means relief in Japanese culture.
- If a foreigner requests a yes or no answer, the Japanese will usually just smile.
- Remaining silent means that they are thinking or simply have nothing to discuss. Do not give your discount now.
- Slouching or relaxing in a chair implies boredom.
- Removing glasses or stretching ears indicates confusion.
- When Japanese people pat their head, they are disappointed or don't understand.
- Crossed arms means possible refusal, disagreement, or wonder.
- Eye contact with a twisting of the neck is an indication of a hostile attitude. Direct eye contact is impolite.
- Crossing the legs is a sign of relaxation.
- The Japanese point to their nose with their finger when talking about themselves.
- The Japanese stay behind senior members when walking with them.
- "Yes, yes" means, "I understand what you said, but I haven't agreed yet."

- "Okay, next!" indicates a desire to change the topic of discussion, not "Yes."
- "By the way," means to listen carefully; the person is giving you an important clue.
- Pauses may occur quite frequently. Don't always feel that you must fill the empty space with extraneous words.

As always, use your knowledge of the Japanese culture to avoid situations that are unacceptable to the Japanese. What may seem to you to be a spirited discussion may be perceived by them as a breakdown in various cultural barriers, including the relationship of subordinates to superiors and the disrespect of hierarchical status.

Conducting Meetings and Presentations

Let us now test your skills for meeting with and presenting to Japanese with the following quiz:

1. After your initial meeting with a Japanese negotiating team for a joint venture, they will be most concerned about:
    a. Production costs.
    b. Current profit margin.
    c. How much they can trust you and their potential market share.
    d. Management style.

The most appropriate answer here is (c), how much they can trust you and their potential market share. Remember, the Japanese are similar to Westerners in that they worry about market shares, prices, and potential growth. They also, however, clearly desire good relationships with business partners.

2. The Japanese seek meetings with foreign business people in order to:
    a. Seek further information.
    b. Check on the foreign company's credibility.
    c. Present the Japanese market strategy.
    d. Identify if there is a lawyer in the group.

The Japanese want to know as much as they possibly can about potential partners and allies, thus (a), seek further information. The reason they seek this information is, not surprisingly, because they need it in order to make a decision about whether or not they can trust the potential partner. They will probably come to the first meeting with 10 questions and then generate 10 more for the next meeting.

3. When negotiating with the Japanese, it is important to:
    a. Speak softly.
    b. Speak humorously.
    c. Speak in a strong, tough tone of voice.
    d. Use flattery.

The answer to this question is related to the Japanese value of harmony in relationships. When negotiating with the Japanese, it is important to (a) speak softly, which indicates that you respect your counterparts. Do not use much flattery, otherwise, they will not believe you.

4. While trying to sell a product to the Japanese, the most important strategic factors to consider for winning them over are:
    a. Lower prices.
    b. After-sale service and continuous supply availability.
    c. Brand-name products.
    d. Beautiful designs and multiple color selections.

When trying to sell a product to Japanese clients, your priorities should be c, b, d, then a. Also, take note of a product's appeal to the younger Japanese generations, with their inclination toward brand names and Western market goods.

Presenting to Gusaki International

Lynn Pottie, a recently appointed VP of marketing for RPI Automation from California's Silicon Valley had just arrived in Tokyo for a meeting with her Japanese VP, Mr. Tanaka, whom she had not met before. The Japanese team had just arrived to the reception hall with one person in the front and three following Mr. Tanaka. Lynn immediately prepared her business card and handed it to the person in the front followed by a warm handshake. She suddenly noticed the three people behind him were in shock. Apparently, in her American culture, she expected that the lead person is the VP and so she gave him her first attention. In Japan, you have to be introduced. The person in the front is the assistant, and he is supposed to introduce the VP. Lynn would have to recover from her first culture clash.

Tanaka accepted the apology and now Lynn was ready for the get-acquainted meeting with the VP. Unfortunately, Mr. Tanaka's English was not as fluent as Lynn expected, and so he has invited his assistant to help in the translation. Now Lynn concentrated on speaking to the junior Japanese assistant and neglected to give enough personal attention to Tanaka, which made him again uncomfortable. Lynn eventually became aware of the problem and began to show pictures and samples of her product line to Tanaka, which finally put him at ease.

The Japanese follow strict rules in personal introduction and even in seating arrangements. The boss must be introduced and, in meeting rooms, seated far away from the door with perhaps an impressive picture on the wall behind them. The Japanese learn well with visual presentations and interaction. It is necessary for foreign businesspeople to utilize plenty of visual aids, samples, and pictures. Doing so helps to open a dialogue, and communication among the presenter and the Japanese will improve despite problems in language.

Written documents should be sent either before the meeting or left for a post-meeting reading. An effective presentation to a Japanese audience must focus on full participation from all employees. Questions must be directed to specific persons within the group. Comments must be solicited by other members. When dealing with the Japanese, one must recognize that decisions will not be reached within the meeting room, but rather by the members of the decision-making team after the meeting is adjourned.

To obtain feedback on their presentation, foreign businesspeople must use the drinking and dining time after meetings to seek information about the outcome of their proposals. At this time, hosts may give indirect clues about the potential for a deal's success. It is important, then, that a strong relationship be developed with at least one member of the Japanese team being dealt with—someone who can explain how to succeed with the company. As mentioned before, these relationships take time, dedication, and mutual obligation.

After conducting business meetings and presentations, it is essential to communicate with whoever is in charge of the Japanese team. Let them know what your expectations of the meeting are. It is also helpful to maintain a relationship over the telephone so that you can keep abreast of their ongoing discussions. Remember that your success with the Japanese depends on your ability to maintain mutually beneficial relationships through continuous communication with them. Here are specific tips and taboos that you should remember:

Cultural Tips for Conducting Meetings and Presentations

- Japanese meet with foreigners to collect information, not to make decisions.
- Utilize visual images as much as possible in order to minimize language barriers.
- Make your presentation as participatory as possible.
- Direct your questions to specific persons. Don't ask general questions.
- Don't insist on a yes or no answer.
- Don't be taken in by smiling or nodding.
- Use break time to seek inside information from your Japanese connection.
- Respond to questions by the Japanese with questions directed toward them.
- Watch their nonverbal messages: smiling, nodding, hand gestures, scratching heads, taking off glasses, taking notes, and sleeping.
- Maintain a harmonious environment and avoid conflict whenever possible.

Cultural Taboos in Conducting Meetings and Presentations

- Not exchanging business cards immediately.
- Not giving full attention to business cards.
- Keeping business cards in your pant back pocket or wallet or shirt pocket.
- Speaking with a loud or emotional voice.
- Arriving late due to unforeseen traffic or unfamiliarity with surroundings.
- Not clearly identifying the boss.
- Not giving senior persons full attention, especially when talking through an interpreter.
- Placing business as the top priority rather than relationship.
- Refusing signs of hospitality: a cup of coffee, lunch, karaoke, etc.
- Speaking quickly.
- Insisting on a yes or no answer.

The Japanese Decision-Making Process

While many foreign organizations believe their technological and price advantages will open the doors of Japan to them, they are unaware of the decision-making process they must undertake to be accepted in Japan. With this in mind, let's look at the case of Victor Brown.

Victor Brown of Telemarketing International was concerned about the status of his proposal and meeting with the Japanese firm Toto. He was formally introduced to Mr. Kawasaki, a member of Toto's marketing team, two years ago and had visited Kawasaki's office three times in the past year. Victor had made two presentations to Toto's marketing team so far and was disappointed because he had expected to close the deal much sooner.

The Japanese, however, tend to take a long time making decisions. The first step of the decision-making process is for a Japanese manager to sponsor the foreign company's proposal. This Japanese manager must be persuasive and have widespread contacts within the organization. Many foreign business people contact Japanese representatives who are not appropriate for their needs. They therefore receive no response from the Japanese—not because their products or prices are unappealing, but because there is nobody on the Japanese side who will write a proposal. Finding the person within a Japanese organization who is able to write and promote a proposal is very difficult.

When a contact within the Japanese company is ready to write a proposal, they must begin the lengthy process of seeking the approval of everybody involved in the proposal. Several one-on-one meetings are held between the managers involved in the decision before the formal meeting is held to make a final decision. During this informal meeting process, many questions are generated and communicated to the foreign firm for response.

Once a sponsor feels they have secured an agreement from all concerned parties, the formal meeting is held by the departments involved in the decision-making process, the proposal is discussed, and a general consensus is secured. The agreement is then submitted to the top manager for approval. The top manager must be assured that all parties involved in the implementation have been agreed on and that they are all ready to work on it. If the top manager feels otherwise, the proposal is generally rejected, and the original Japanese sponsor must lobby the proposal from the beginning again.

Upon reaching a final agreement, the foreign organization is informed that business will commence. If the Japanese offer is not acceptable to the foreign party, the Japanese may consider a second, and possibly a third, offer. Japanese businesses will not go beyond three rounds of negotiation. This is due to the length of the consensus-building process among the Japanese members and department, not necessarily because of the terms of the agreement.

One of the challenges that foreign organizations face is the turnover of Japanese managers. It often takes as long as a year to establish the relationships that are needed to succeed. Unfortunately, these sponsors are shifted to other positions within the company every three or four years. If you find that your sponsor has moved to another job, it's important that you use their name as a reference with the person who takes your sponsor's new position. Remember that the new person may not be as powerful a sponsor. Many foreign organizations encounter junior managers who are unable to write and promote their proposals.

Encountering the Japanese Negotiators

The table below lists characteristics of Japanese negotiators, complemented with the best practices for foreign representatives.

	Japanese	You
Group Composition	Usually comes in 3–4 junior and middle managers.	Bring 1–2 higher-level managers to seek high-level manager.
Establishing Rapport	Try to establish harmonious cooperative relationships.	Reciprocate but focus on step-by-step results.
Information Exchange	Keep seeking information without giving in too much.	Do not give in all at once. Give some but insist on receiving as well.
Persuasion Tools	Spend a lot of time to build relationships through evening dinner-and-drinking sessions. Claim budget and market conditions during compromises.	Share time with them but focus on your sponsor relationship. Show your compromising attitudes and long-range interests.

	Japanese	You
Decision Process	Middle managers seek support from those involved. Senior managers question and approve final decision.	Be patient but in continuous contact with your sponsor. Do not prolong negotiation process more than two rounds to avoid their withdrawing.
Decision Makers	Senior manager makes decision.	Identify and focus on middle manager who makes the recommendation.

Social Etiquette

Following are some social etiquette tips that you will need for establishing strong relationships with Japanese partners:

- Utilize lunch, dinner, and drinking time to build strong relationships with the Japanese.
- You may offer gifts after initial relationships are established.
- Take care in wrapping gifts, and present them in nice shopping bags. Don't expect that the gift will be opened in front of you.
- Utilize seasonal holidays and special occasions to exchange greetings.
- Maintain communication through telephone calls, faxes, letters, and visits.
- The Japanese welcome foreigners to visit their homes, and look forward to visiting the homes of foreigners.
- Don't be shy if you are invited to a karaoke lunch—it is a time to make mistakes, laugh, and be at ease with your Japanese hosts.

Summary

Once again, compare the Japanese culture to other cultures. You might even try returning to these questions after reading some of the following chapters. When dealing with an array of diverse cultures, comparing and contrasting serves as a learning exercise surpassed only by hands-on experience. Whether you are a small business owner, an expatriate assigned overseas, or a middle- to upper-level management executive, the information and lessons presented in this chapter will help you in dealing with the Japanese. The practical skills you have gained apply to the many business and social situations in which you will inevitably find yourself.

Remember that when interacting with the Japanese, your first instinct should be to make sure that you are following these proper rules of etiquette. While you will need to be able to interpret Japanese messages and understand the implications of their various interpersonal clues, etiquette should always remain your top priority. With time, you will pick up the clues that the Japanese are giving you regarding your marketing style, your presentation, or your company's product.

Finally, keep in mind the homogeneity of Japan. Whether you are from a Western country, such as the United States or France, or if you are from a different Asian country, such as Indonesia, chances are that you have dealt with much more diversity than your Japanese counterparts. Therefore, use your experience to your advantage and be flexible and understanding about the needs of Japan. The rewards will definitely be worth the effort.

Competing on the Battleground with Koreans

4

What are the "Isms" of Korean culture?
How do you negotiate price concessions with Koreans?
What is the main difference when dealing with Koreans vs Japanese?

The complexities of dealing with Koreans lie in their similarity to other Asian cultures and their assimilation of American business practices into their corporate cultures. Over the last several years, I have communicated and negotiated with, and trained managers from major Korean organizations. Based on these experiences, I have learned some valuable lessons about doing business with them. By examining the values that Koreans adhere to, I have learned how their cultural values influence their daily business communication. When Koreans work on projects intra-culturally or inter-culturally, their cultural values have a direct bearing on the way they conduct business.

Any executive working with a Korean organization can see the influence of cultural values on business, particularly when looking at everyday business encounters such as personal introductions, telephone calls, meetings, presentations, and negotiations. And Korean culture certainly isn't uniform across the entire nation. Cultural values and their manifestations vary from region to region and from organization to organization. These values play a very important role in Korean corporations, locally and globally: the values behind the actions will be the driving force for the Koreans, influencing the success or the failure of their global joint ventures.

In this chapter, you will test your skills for dealing with Koreans. It will provide you with insight into the Isms of Korean cultural values, including meeting the Koreans, communicating with them on the phone and in writing, conducting effective meetings and presentations, enhancing your relationships with them, avoiding pitfalls, and understanding their decision-making process. This chapter will also provide tips for training, motivating, and reviewing their work—along with important social etiquette to enhance your negotiation with them on the battleground!

Test Your Skills for Dealing with Koreans

Answer the following true-false statements to test your skills for dealing with Koreans:

____ 1. Most Koreans are taught to challenge the boss's orders.

____ 2. Dedication, loyalty, and team spirit take precedence over job skill.

____ 3. In Korea, most final decisions are made by the consensus of middle managers.

____ 4. Most Koreans utilize their intuition and spirituality when making their final decisions.

____ 5. You may expect that signed contracts between partners may be considered null if situations change.

____ 6. Koreans usually exhibit a suspicious attitude toward foreigners.

____ 7. Korean workers show more loyalty to the company than towards their boss.

____ 8. In Korea, bonuses are often given during birthdays and the Chinese New Year.

____ 9. To impress a Korean, point out your degrees and the size of your house.

____ 10. Many Koreans will use emotional appeals rather than factual information in order to persuade you.

Most Appropriate Answers:

1. F; 2. T; 3. F; 4. T; 5. T; 6. T; 7. F; 8. T; 9. T; 10. T

Personal Tale: Be Ready, Fire!

In my early attempts to introduce my multicultural management and global negotiation training seminars in Korea, I communicated with a Korean management organization to market my programs. After my first meeting with the director, I was referred to a junior manager, with whom I negotiated terms and prices for two months.

At the end of the negotiations, I talked with the junior manager on the phone from California and received his confirmation. Based on this, I asked my staff to begin developing promotional materials. To my astonishment, however, two days later the junior manager faxed me and claimed that the director had not consented to our agreement. A done deal was not a done deal!

After a few more rounds of negotiation, a contract was agreed upon, but only after I had learned the valuable lesson that in Korea only the boss makes the final decision. Like the junior manager, Korean workers simply try to satisfy their immediate superiors by executing their boss' orders in an unquestioning manner. The junior manager was really still negotiating with me.

While initiating my relationship with another Korean conglomerate, I found that, from the outset, they expected me—as a consulting expert—to function as a commander and recommend what should be done, often with no payment. They looked for my generosity at the beginning. After an elaborate dinner, for example, this new client expected me to draft detailed recommendations for them free of charge. Had I not given the client this information, though, I would have been denied a contract. Koreans expect your initial expertise free, especially if you are American, European, or Japanese. Once you have shown yourself to be an expert in your field, however, they will look to you as their commander in charge, and will entrust you further with their business.

Facing cultural differences in ethics can be confusing when working with Koreans. I experienced this several years ago when I was given the chance to deliver my training programs to a leading Korean electronics firm. At the time, one of my new books had been on the market for two months. Although this company did not want to place an order of my book for the company's participants, my agent asked me to deliver several copies of the book one week ahead of the program. I assumed the books were for the participants to read in preparation for the program.

During the first day of my seminar, however, I nearly suffered a heart attack when I discovered that my client had reproduced my hard cover book in a paperback version, which the program manager was reading through. The manager's excuse for producing my book without permission, and violating my copyrights, was that the book was not available yet in Korea!

Later that night, to placate me, the manager brought three copies of the book to my hotel and shredded them in front of me. Although I suspected that another hundred copies had already been produced behind my back, I did not press the issue, recognizing that the client was valuable, and that the whole episode was just a clash of ethics. Maybe because I was the "professor," I had to give away my knowledge for free.

Getting paid by Koreans is sometimes another exercise in frustration. As my book gained respect in the market, a local Korean firm approached my American publisher to translate and sell the book in Korea. My publisher accepted the offer and prepared a contract that specified the advance payment of $2,000 in royalties. My publisher, however, had yet to receive any payment six months later when my book was translated and put on the Korean market, where I found it on sale at a book store.

The Korean company's excuse for thus violating my copyrights was that they forgot to pay. My publisher had to threaten them with a lawsuit in order to convince them to finally pay the contracted fees. To the Korean publisher, it was acceptable for them to translate, sell and then later pay. From my publisher's point of view, the Korean publisher had to pay first and then translate, sell, and make profits!

Many non-Koreans complain that, when communicating with Koreans, they sometimes seem blunt and aggressive. This can be explained by looking at the Korean value system and the priorities of those values. When a Korean first meets someone new, the Korean has no previous relationship with this person upon which to build a trust. The Korean thus considers this person excluded from the so-called "family/network group." Therefore, the manners of the Korean may seem insensitive. Also, during interactions with others, if Koreans feel that the other person is lower in status or authority they expect that person to automatically concur with their point of view. It is obvious, then, that many would initially find Koreans blunt and aggressive, especially Americans, who value equality and are known for challenging another's opinion.

In my experience, I have found that most Korean organizations are run like military compounds—dwelling on hierarchy and levels of authority. I now realize that I would have been more successful initially with Koreans if I had graduated, not from engineering and business schools, but rather from a military academy.

These examples do place foreigners dealing with Koreans in frustrating positions. As soon as you are accepted and have a trustworthy partner, however, you will find that Koreans are social, humble, responsible, and ready to help you in your business ventures.

Korean Cultural Values

In working with Korean managers, we asked participants in our frequent management training workshops to prioritize 20 values that are common among many cultures, which have been described in previous chapters. We also asked the same questions of groups of Japanese and American managers. The following table presents what these three groups indicate are their top five (out of 20) values.

Korean	American	Japanese
Family Security	Equality	Relationship
Cooperation	Freedom	Group Harmony
Relationship	Openness	Family Security
Group Harmony	Self-Reliance	Freedom
Spiritual Enlightenment	Cooperation	Cooperation

Looking at the differences in cultural values gives us our first clue as to why cultural clashes exist between Americans, Koreans, and Japanese. Koreans place great value on building strong cooperative relationships first between family members. Close family comes first. This explains why many Korean companies have been established, run, and maintained by family members or their close contacts. Entire companies and networks have been built based on family ties.

Conducting business with group harmony within their culture is another tendency that is based on Korean values. Group harmony is the reason that they prefer to work only with groups that are connected through family ties: they want to minimize any conflicts they may have with outsiders, especially with people from different cultures. You may also notice that Japanese and Koreans have more in common than with Americans. One can now see why American business people may have cultural friction with both Japanese and Koreans. Clashes in business usually come from clashes in cultural norms.

Koreans are also guided by spiritual beliefs that are based, in general, on the teachings of Confucianism. The tenets of Confucianism require that followers exercise complete loyalty to hierarchical structures, whether that structure occurs in one's family, company, or the government. The boss is in charge. Furthermore, you may note that the Koreans differ from the Japanese in the value that Koreans place on spirituality. This is because the Koreans follow more of the teachings of Confucius, and even Christianity, more than the Japanese, who in general give spirituality a lower priority.

Another subtle difference between the Japanese and the Koreans is the context in which group harmony plays a role. To the Japanese, it is important to preserve the harmony in any group, be it the department, the company, the community, or prospective client or supplier. For the Koreans, however, the most important group is the family. The Koreans are more apt to focus on the family than any other group. Until you are trusted, you are a stranger.

These cultures developed by their respective sets of values through the process of Korean culturalization. Of course, Koreans have developed their own system of cultural development. The Korean father, mother, grandfather, and grandmother, for example, teach the Korean child to value the support of the family. They also teach the child the importance of close contact and cooperation with other family members, and how to cultivate relationships within the family.

Through the family, Korean children will also learn to adhere to the principles of Confucianism. As the children grow older, each institution that they participate in teaches a new set of cultural norms and reinforces the values they have already learned. School, business, and government all play a role in reinforcing proper values of Korean culture.

The following Isms of Korea are important clues to keep in mind when addressing the various business and social issues you will encounter as you expand your presence in the Korean market, and when you start to deal with Korean coworkers and employees.

The Isms of Korea

- Collectivism/Family
- Authoritarianism/Superior vs. Subordinate
- Connectionism/Personal Relationships

- Conservatism/Tradition
- Exclusivism/Grouping
- Fatalism/Acceptance
- Secularism/Worldly Accomplishments

The Korean Code of Conduct is mainly based on Confucianism, which implies:

- Total loyalty to a hierarchical structure of authority
- Duty to the parent
- Minutely defined form of conduct between children and adults
- Distinction between the roles of husband and wife
- Trust between friends

Keeping these cultural values in mind will help you open and expand your business opportunities when dealing with Koreans.

The Company as an Extension of the Family

To understand Korean organizations, you must keep in mind that the family is the central unit of the Korean company. It follows that all connections, contacts, and business networks are based on relationships within the family. Making connections in the Korean business world can only start with an introduction from someone within the family member network.

The Korean company-family is entirely self-sufficient. Clients, suppliers, and employees are all related to or close friends of a family member. The family unit as an executive governing group is exemplified in top Korean companies, such as Daewoo, Samsung, and Hyundai. These companies all achieved success because they had strong family ties. Recently, the Korean government has been trying to break down these family ties, with limited success.

The sense of obligation within the family is strong; in the principles of Confucianism, Koreans will always adhere to the authority of the father, the boss, or the head of the company. Members are expected to support the company through direct loyalty to the boss. Thus, family connections or personal ties are a must for any foreign firm to enter into and succeed in the Korean market. Since it is unlikely that foreigners will have such connections, it is imperative that foreign companies seek the help of a well-connected agent.

The honor of the company is also important to a Korean. When working for a Korean company, loyalty, commitment, and sacrifice are demanded of all employees, even more so than quality of work performance. Dedication and team spirit take precedence over job skill. Group harmony is valued more than group achievement or consensus. Most managers emphasize personal ties and cohesiveness among employees. The result is often greater productivity which may come at the expense of lower creativity.

Korean companies will also find success by having connections in the government and, once again, this success is linked to the family: the more family members/connections you have, the more likely it will be that some of them will hold top government positions. My own experience in the Korean market exemplifies this situation. When we tried to negotiate a contract with a large Korean organization, the company sent a training manager to attend one of our free marketing presentation. He politely indicated his interest, but gave no response when we tried to elicit further feedback about our proposal. Later, we realized that we had to go through our agent to meet his superiors in the company. Luckily our agent had an old, well-cultivated, family-related friendship with a superior manager who was able to provide us with a stronger reference.

Meeting the Koreans

The following tips are important to consider if you want to impress your new Korean partner and start a win-win relationship on solid ground:

- Bow slightly when greeting another person for the first time in a day. If one person is of a much lower status, only that person bows, while the other may respond verbally.
- You may place your hand over your heart after shaking hands to show respect to seniors.
- Make a good first impression. Koreans will form their overall impression from how you act and speak.
- Dress is a sign of position and respect, so do not dress informally. Shorts, backless dresses, and similar attire are not appropriate in public.
- In conversation, you may refer to a technical degree, school attended, place of birth, and residence. Show, however, your sincerity, politeness, and humility.

- Indicate your personal references (connections) and interest in maintaining the relationship.
- Elderly people should be shown kindness and respect at all times. Always offer priority to them—give them your seat on a bus, help them cross the street, and carry things for them.
- Social harmony should be preserved at all costs, even if this means telling small lies and behaving indirectly.
- When passing objects to someone of equal or higher status, use your right hand, both hands, or your right hand supported by your left. When passing objects to someone of lower status, you may use either hand, but not both.
- You may discuss personal hobbies and personal tastes. Personal questions are seen as a way of getting to know another person. If you don't wish to answer, change the subject.
- Status is very important. It is determined primarily by profession, family, and age. Acknowledging other people's status will improve social relationships. Also, be sure to act according to your own status.
- When addressing Koreans, always use their titles to show respect: Director Lim, General Manger Park, Dr. Lee. If possible, learn titles in Korean, as this will establish closer relationships.
- Koreans may initially sound aggressive and tough. They have a friendly gesture and cooperative attitude, however, once they trust and decide to work with you.
- They have high respect for authority and seniority, so use your rank, title, authority level to your advantage.
- Koreans will put themselves down in front of superiors. If you feel that you are a boss, you should then help them.
- Be a reasonable, trustworthy, hardworking person, open-minded and sensitive to Korean culture.
- Affection among people of the same sex is a way of showing friendship.
- Show appreciation for Korean culture and enjoyment of Kimchi!

Avoid These Taboos

There are, of course, some don'ts you must adhere to when dealing with Koreans. Once again, keep in mind that the following social mistakes can seriously jeopardize your relationship with Koreans.

- Do not dwell much on your connection to authority.
- Mentioning the name of your connection to your counterpart's boss is considered a challenge or threat.
- Criticism should be avoided whenever possible. When it is absolutely necessary, be tactful, gentle, and private.
- Showing public anger is impolite and can permanently damage relationships. Keep your temper at all times.
- Don't be offended by initially aggressive attitudes or misled by enthusiasm. Keep your feet on the ground.
- Don't stare at the elder or look down upon others.
- Don't go directly to the subject.
- Don't point your finger at your counterpart.
- Don't ask your counterpart's age.
- Don't show affection between the sexes in public.

On the Phone with Koreans

During my engagement with one Korean company, I received a call from a staff member who wanted to discuss some business matters. After a few greetings and discussion, I wished him well and told him that I was looking forward to seeing him soon, indicating the end of the conversation. I noticed, however, that my caller did not hang up the phone. I thought that he perhaps had something more to say, so I kept talking to him about different subjects, including the weather in Korea and California, and pausing in between in order to give him the opportunity to say goodbye and hang up, which he never did. After 20 minutes, I finally had to hang up, with nothing to talk further about. I later realized that since I was at a higher level than him, he could not hang up first. In Korean culture, the senior person has to hang up first. If I had known that at the time, I could have saved him some phone charges.

Here are a few tips that I have since learned in communicating with Koreans on the phone:

- Give a brief greeting.
- Don't get over-excited.
- Make the call brief and clear.
- Stick to the point.
- Don't be rude.

- Reaffirm agreements.
- Do not use the phone to discuss matters with or report to a Korean superior.
- Do not hang up on a superior!

Writing to the Koreans

You are negotiating a deal with your Korean counterpart. Which of the following answers is correct? In writing to him, you should start by:

a. Asking about his family.
b. Asking how his business is doing.
c. Acknowledging his point of view.
d. Giving him an ultimatum.

If you were negotiating with an Arab, you would begin by asking about their family and the condition of their business and end by wishing them happiness and prosperity. If you wish to maintain harmony while negotiating with a Korean, however, you should always (c) acknowledge their point of view first, in a polite and flattering manner. Most Koreans will temper their authoritative attitude by using courteous words such as "frankly speaking" or "appreciate," and you should follow suit.

This negotiation style is in direct contrast with the American style. Most Americans like to deal with problems directly and sequentially in a step-by-step manner. The Japanese, on the other hand, come to the negotiating table with an attitude of humility. They often start by either thanking their counterparts or apologizing for some invisible slight. When confronted by a disagreeable option, in order to preserve harmony the Japanese will often politely ignore the offending point of view, usually in silence or with a smile.

Again, which of the following answers is correct? When negotiating through written correspondence, you should use these key phrases:

a. "This is my last offer."
b. "I appreciate your situation, but I'm giving you my best offer."
c. "It is very difficult for us to reduce the price."
d. "If you double the order, I'll give you a discount."

Most American managers would probably apply their values of competition, directness and risk taking to try to influence the Korean. In order, however, to negotiate successfully with Koreans, you must adhere to their negotiation methods: you must use (b) kind expressions of your friendship to achieve your desired goal. Saying, "we appreciate your offer" or "we acknowledge your point of view" are effective ways of complying with the Korean negotiation system. Although you and the Koreans may not have the same point of view, it is important that both parties kindly acknowledge each other's position in order to fit in with the Korean cultural patterns.

Korean Letters

Following are examples of typical business letters sent by middle managers in Korean corporations.

Letter #1

May 11, 1999

Dear Sir,

I received your fax from Mr. Lee, my manager. I am Park S.H. in the education and training department.

We are very sorry to offer a later answer concerning your fax.

We read the materials that you sent us. We are very sorry to inform you that we cannot invite you at this time, because we have other commitments. A future meeting will be a good chance to get information and talk about our matter of concern.

I hope we will meet some other time. Thank you again for your fax.

Sincerely,
Park S.H.

Letter #2

Dear Sir,

I am very sorry to say that the terms you presented are beyond our ability to host the program in terms of revenue.

I know that you deserve our proposal, but we expect you to understand our market situation. Maybe we will have another chance to cooperate for mutual benefit.

Thanks for talking and hope your business will be successful.

Sincerely,
S.S.H.

Letter #3

Dear Sir,

I have received your message regarding your contractual agreement. We feel our relationship with Global Success is a comprehensive and long-term one in terms of us being integral parts of a whole. In this spirit, I am forwarding herewith a draft of our agreement, which you can add to and revise as you deem appropriate.

I would like to conclude our agreement prior to undertaking any project with you. I am looking forward to receiving your comments and opinions on the context of our working relationship.

Sincerely,
Lee K.M.

As these letters show, most Koreans will get directly to the point, with few greetings or introductions. In order to show their humility and politeness, they will almost always apologize for something. They may then acknowledge prior communication, point of views, and other subjects, and end with their expectations for a long-term relationship with a brief wish for success.

Tips for Written Communication with Koreans

- Acknowledge others' views.
- Comment on personal situations.
- Ask questions related to people.
- Use respectful and formal language: refer to happiness, success, prosperity and health.
- Give your best regards to related people and close with a greeting.
- Use language like *frankly speaking* or *I appreciate it very much*.
- Be aware that bluntness is common in Korean written communication.
- Use words and phrases like *in consideration, with deep understanding, in appreciation, final offer, we appreciate, in discussion with management, according to, finally, as discussed,* and *please consider*.

Conducting Meetings and Presentations

1. When conducting a meeting with your Korean delegation, you should:

a. Arrange seating according to age.
b. Talk about yourself at great length.
c. Ask everybody to introduce him- or herself.
d. Ask for the vote on the final decision.

When meeting with Koreans, follow Korean culture in its respect for seniority. The boss must be seated at the center of the table, far away from doors. Behind the boss may be a fine art work or picture. If you share the meeting, make sure to give the floor for the boss to open up the meeting and motivate others. Do not dwell much about yourself or your position. You can ask participants for a brief introduction when each will show modesty and humility. Final decisions will usually take place after the meeting in consultation with top management based on the recommendation of middle managers.

2. No one has asked any questions during your presentation. You should:
    a. Ask the senior executive for his opinion.
    b. Ask the oldest person if he has a question.
    c. Ask if anybody has a question.
    d. Keep talking.

In meeting with Koreans, you may find them hesitant to interrupt the speaker in a show of respect for the speaker's seniority and knowledge. The speaker is supposed to be the professor. Junior participants may be reluctant to ask questions until a senior person does so. You should first ask the senior for their opinion and feedback, followed by an older person for their wisdom and opinions. Others may follow and start asking questions. If it is close to the end of the meeting, you should ask the junior persons for their opinion before the senior, otherwise the junior one will reiterate the senior's position. Keeping your meeting with Koreans engaged is a skillful art.

Tips for Conducting Meetings with Koreans

- Notify the participants of the topics before the meeting.
- Arrange seating according to seniority.
- Avoid long introductions and false statements.
- Don't discuss subjects not on the agenda.
- Participants should each present their own ideas.
- Koreans' decisions are often drawn out in the meeting.
- Accept the majority and respect the minority opinions.

- Keep to the schedule.
- Be polite and avoid interrupting others.

Also, avoid calling for an urgent meeting. This will put Koreans on the defensive and may cause them to question your competence and reliability. Do so only when unavoidable. Additionally, it is a good idea to conceal any anger you may feel about your Korean partners' opinions. Remember that quite often your partner's opposition may be simple posturing.

Enhancing Relationships with Koreans

1. To succeed in your relationships with Koreans, you should show:
   a. Credibility.
   b. Stubbornness.
   c. Flexibility.
   d. Politeness.

All of these are important traits that you must exhibit in order to establish a profitable relationship with Korean. Be polite, demonstrate your credibility, be flexible, and yet still be stubborn enough to finally get the job done.

2. Most Korean organizations conduct business in which manner?
   a. Democratic
   b. Militaristic
   c. Socialistic
   d. Family-like

In order to enhance your success in working with Koreans, you're best prepared if you're a graduate of a military school! The Korean lifestyles for family, company, government, and nation follow militaristic patterns. The father, boss, or president charts the strategy, and family members, company personnel, or the army nation executes it.

3. In order to enter into a business relationship with a Korean company, you must work your way from:
   a. The bottom level up.
   b. The middle management level up.

    c. The top-level management down.

    d. The top management down to the middle-management level.

Because the Koreans value and respect authority, one must (c) try to reach the highest level possible and move down the chain of command. Otherwise, at each level you will encounter a special authority that you must "bow to." The chain of command is so well defined that if you begin at the bottom, getting a proposal or a plan approved will be a long and arduous process.

Each level up, the manager in that department will look at your proposal and then stamp it with an approval. Korean managers enjoy displaying their authority, and each level of the company will hold up your document for a certain amount of time just to prove that it can. It may be a long time before your proposal ever gets to someone in a decision-making position.

4.   In Korea, a successful businessperson must:

    a. Conform to the hierarchical structure of authority.

    b. Be loyal to his company.

    c. Fulfill his duty to his parents.

    d. Expand his network through family connections.

It is important to adhere to all of these values in order to succeed in doing business with Koreans. All of these elements stem from Confucianism and are an integral part of Korean culture.

5.   In order to succeed in entering the Korean market and selling products to Korean companies, you should:

    a. Participate in a well-publicized exhibition in Seoul.

    b. Ask for a recommendation from the local Korean consulate.

    c. Visit the potential client in Korea.

    d. Recruit a well-connected local agent.

Unless you are an executive from IBM or Sony, or have a new invention, you will be better off entering the market through a well-connected agent. Your first agent may not be the proper one. They may not have the connections you look for. The agent you need must have connections to high-ranking officials in Korean organizations. In most situations, the effective agent is involved in some kind of reciprocal relationship with the higher-ups: they stand to gain by referring others to that company.

6. When dealing with Koreans, it is important to keep in mind that, in a Korean company, decisions are usually made by:
   a. The program manager.
   b. Top managers.
   c. Middle- or upper-level managers.
   d. Group consensus.

In Korea, most of the decisions are made (c) based on a consultation between middle- and upper-level managers. The team that negotiated the deal will be informed of the decision only once the plan is ready to be implemented. This style of decision-making again stems from the military chain of command that most Korean organizations follow. To use the military analogy again, the captain and the commander will jointly decide on a course of action, approve and stamp it, and the soldiers or employees will carry out the orders.

Persuading Koreans

Your first offer to a Korean company of $100 will most likely be:
a. Ignored.
b. Reduced by 50%.
c. Reduced by 20%.
d. Reduced by 10%.

Price negotiation with Koreans is a tough and lengthy process. Your offer will usually first be cut by 50% (b). In a round of bargaining and exhibiting your credibility, politeness, and stubbornness, they will settle at 10–20% below your original offer. Next time you offer a price, make sure to mark it up at enough room or you will lose.

Characteristics of the Korean Negotiator

Here are some traits of Korean negotiators to keep in mind:

- They evaluate the facts according to a set of personal values.
- They use loaded words and offer bargains that propose rewards.
- They appeal to feelings and emotions in order to reach a "fair" deal.
- They use their power, status, and authority to their own advantage.
- They look for compromise, and try to make effective statements.
- They focus on people and their reactions.

In order to counter the above traits, you must:

- Establish a sound relationship at the outset of the negotiation.
- Show your interest in what the other person is saying.
- Identify values and adjust to them accordingly.
- Be ready to compromise.
- Appeal to your partner's feelings or interests.

Many foreign executives find negotiating business deals with Koreans frustrating. Non-Korean companies often have difficulty reaching agreements with the Koreans, exchanging products with them, and even receiving payment on time from Korean companies. Unless you understand Korean cultural values and how they influence business, you will certainly encounter problems and misunderstandings. The Korean negotiation style can be summarized by two main points: negotiating is an emotional experience for the Koreans, and expectations that their authority will be respected at all times by the other side.

In negotiating, a Korean's primary concern is to touch the business contact's personal feelings. A Korean's arguments will not stem from technical concerns about your proposal, but from emotional concerns about you as an individual. They want to come across as feeling comfortable with their business counterparts; they want to like them personally. They consider the two of you as a "group" and they want to maintain harmony within that group. Based on these mutual feelings of friendship, they want you to give them a special or reduced price. Koreans feel that their partners in negotiation should make concessions because of their level of authority and good will.

Keep the following in mind:

- **The Korean military style of negotiation must be addressed.** If you are not accustomed to this style of negotiation, as with most Westerners and many other negotiators from other Asian countries, you will have to learn the ropes.
- **Koreans are tough price negotiators who will play on your emotions.** Use this to your advantage! If they want to play hardball, play with them and be just as uncompromising. They will respect you for this, and eventually an agreement will be reached.
- **Subordinates will strictly adhere to their boss' requests.** This goes back to the military nature of the Korean management style.

Remember, militarism is a part of Korean culture, so it is pervasive in all areas of Korean life.

- **You must specifically state what is and is not covered in the contract.** Stating what is not covered in the contract is more important than what is in it. This will save you a lot of hassle down the road. If you fail to do so, you may be in for some surprises when your Korean partner asks for certain items or benefits that were not mentioned in the original agreement.

During my training at one of the Korean companies, I found that they had been taping my presentation without my consent or previous agreement in the contract. They assumed that it was okay to tape me. They claimed that they needed the tape to enhance their study of the subject. What would you do? I just asked for a personal copy for me, too.

Following are a few important tips to help in persuading your Korean partners:

- You must try to pump the Korean person's Kibun. Kibun is a combination of a Korean person's self-esteem, mood, feeling, and inner spirit. Koreans will ask about the boss's Kibun before they go to see the boss.
- If there is bad news, avoid telling it directly. You may delay it to the late afternoon rather than in the morning. Do not disturb one's Kibun early in the day.
- Relationships are the keys to success. It takes time, dedication, mutual obligation, and continuous communication.
- Try to communicate with the highest position possible; otherwise, you will encounter many gatekeepers.
- It is wise to compromise at certain times to allow a Korean partner to save face or maintain a respectable image.
- Be sincere and make others comfortable. Remember that Koreans start with a suspicion of foreigner's intentions.
- Patience is highly valued. You must be patient when services are not performed on time, when someone is late, or when things are not done efficiently. Do not blame anyone or show anger.
- It is important to be introduced by a Korean. Note, however, that they may negotiate against you, including your agent.
- Keep your lines of communication open by informing Koreans of your new products and experience until they feel comfortable with you.

- Take initiative with them on price offers, terms, conditions, and even the format of a contract. They may see you as their consultant with more knowledge in the field.
- Use ceremonies, holidays, and promotional events to wish them well and get closer to the person or group in charge.
- Time in negotiation is very important, and participants tend to make compromises because of time loss. Read time limitations very carefully, and use them to your advantage.
- Don't make impulsive decisions. Discuss matters, then hold off on actions for at least 24 hours. I noticed that most faxes sent to me from Korea are often signed the day before they are sent. Koreans may make decisions and then think about them for a while before acting. Be patient.

Contracting with Koreans

When contracting with Koreans, the following points are important to keep in mind in order to complete and sustain a successful business relationship.

- Take the lead in proposing terms or contracts so that you have the advantage. Otherwise, you may have to deal with a prolonged process of concessions. Read the other side's terms carefully.
- Contracts should be flexible but spell out all terms, as well as what is not included. Don't ever assume anything.
- Give them more than one option to choose from. Do not just disagree.
- Establish a friendly relationship with one person on the team. This person will tell you the whole story and help to mediate if problems are encountered.
- Koreans start negotiating from an extreme or absurd position and attempt to conduct their deals by appealing to your emotions.
- Stand firm at the beginning and repeat your offer.
- Give in on small items but hold back on major things; expect concessions each time. Three to four rounds of offers, each with small concessions from both sides will do.
- Be ready to compromise when negotiating with Koreans, and try to sell your second contract before your first closes. It is the honeymoon time!
- In getting paid you must be on top; otherwise, they may take forever, blaming it on the accounting office. They may delay payment unless you put on gentle but persistent pressure.

"Passing the buck" and avoiding responsibility are also common practices among Korean business people. All of these culturally-based business customs may frustrate the foreigner new to the Korean market. I once had to take on the Korean tax office to prove my eligibility for a tax waiver. Even my agent took the side of the tax office. Korean loyalties lie with their family members and close personal contacts. As an outsider, it is often very difficult to initially fit in.

In general, contracts with Korean companies must be clear, yet flexible enough to allow for change. Contractual obligations may change along with changes in the business relationship. For instance, if there is a sudden increase or decrease in sales volume, the Koreans will see this as a reason to change the payment conditions stated in the contract. For them, the contract is just a relationship, not a binding agreement as in the American legal sense.

The Korean Decision-Making Process

Because Koreans value and respect authority, one must try to reach the highest level possible and move down the chain of command. Otherwise, at each level you will encounter a special authority to whom you must "bow." The chain of command is so well defined that if you begin at the bottom, getting a proposal or a plan approved will be a long and arduous process.

At each level, the manager in that department will look at your proposal and stamp an approval. Korean managers enjoy displaying their authority, and each level of the company will hold up your document for a certain amount of time just to prove that it can. It may be a long time before your proposal ever gets to someone in a decision-making position.

The Korean style of decision making is a result of the military-style chain of command that most Korean organizations follow. To use a military analogy, the captain and commander of a company jointly decide upon a course of action, and their soldiers carry out their orders.

Koreans want to come across as feeling comfortable with their business counterpart; they want to like them personally. Koreans consider both parties in a negotiation as one "group" and they want to maintain harmony within that group. Based on mutual feelings of friendship, Koreans want you to give them a special or reduced price. They feel that their partners in negotiation should make concessions because of their level of authority and goodwill. And, very often, the Korean style of negotiation is commonly referred to as normative behavior.

Koreans evaluate facts according to a set of personal values. They either approve or disapprove of your offer; they agree or disagree. They use loaded words and offer bargains that propose rewards. They appeal to feelings and emotions in order to reach a "fair deal." They use their power, status, and authority to their advantage. They look for compromise and try to make effective statements. They focus on people and their reactions.

Keep the following in mind:

- Koreans defer decisions to management. The top manager makes the final decision and questions the subordinates extensively.
- Koreans utilize their intuition and spiritual feelings for final decision. They will take a spiritual break of 2–4 days to make a decision depending on the magnitude of the decision.
- Once a decision is made, however, they move like an army to implement it.
- In a big organization, your contact is not the decision maker even after you come to an agreement with them—the boss still has to agree. Your contact may come back with the bad news that the boss did not agree.
- They need to see the whole picture and then focus on one item at a time.
- Major companies can't move until they have a program in place. The boss has to decide on and approve it. Then they will march like an army.
- Koreans really need time to think about issues spiritually. In any given team, each person will think alone for some time. A leader will emerge and then they will discuss the issue as a group.
- Give Koreans time to think about the issue. At the beginning, they are suspicious about foreigners.
- They are not as creative as some other cultures. They look for orders from the boss and then follow them in a military fashion. They will reach the target, however, without retreating.

Encountering the Korean Negotiators

The following table presents how Koreans will conduct their negotiations and how you can counter them in the categories below:

	Koreans	You
Group Composition	Consists of 2–3 middle and junior managers.	Bring 1–2 higher level managers for more respected position.
Establishing Rapport	They will set a tone for skillfully alternating the spiritual with exchanges of facts.	Accept their style, including their spiritual tone. Stress on facts.
Information Exchange	They will ask many questions, but reveal little; they may sound blunt or aggressive.	Reveal limited information until contracting has advanced.
Persuasion Tools	They will integrate you into their process over time through ceremonies such as dining, drinking, and visits to shrines.	Display your know-how and credentials to gain their respect. Add to your original offer.
Decision Process	They will engage in tough bargaining process until a compromise is reached.	Be willing to compromise. Be patient, credible; stress their benefits from the deal.
Decision Makers	The top manager makes final decision based on recommendation of middle level.	Reach the top level through a middle manager to help show credibility.

Enhancing Your Negotiation Success with Koreans

Following are several suggestions for enhancing your negotiation success with Koreans:

- Establish a sound relationship at the outset of the negotiations. Maintain a reputation of high quality and uniqueness.
- First establish the level of your authority as a consultant, expert, provider of new technology, etc. Then extend your hand to help them with the necessary information.
- You may have to make a proposal first, as they look to you as the boss, professor, or consultant for the first input. They will then think about and discuss the proposal, receiving the boss's approval before making any commitments.

- Be ready to compromise. Compromise as often as possible. This will show your sincerity in negotiating cooperatively. They may compromise on one element but ask for another.
- Give Koreans some time to think about issues, collect more information, and build a spiritual feeling, trust and confidence in you. Then they will talk seriously.
- From time to time, review your conversations with Koreans in order to get a sense of their real feelings.
- Remember that it is a two-way relationship from which both parties must benefit.

Working with Koreans

The following cases test your skills for working with Koreans:

1. When working with Koreans, it is important to establish group:
   a. Harmony.
   b. Consensus.
   c. Achievement.
   d. Loyalty.

It is important for Korean managers to establish (d) group loyalty from the outset of their project. This is in contrast with Japanese managers, whose first job is to establish and maintain group harmony, consensus, and achievement.

2. In Korean companies, employees believe they work for:
   a. The company.
   b. The boss.
   c. The group.
   d. Themselves.

Most Korean workers dedicate themselves to serving the boss' interests and goals, which again leads to serving the company through the chain of commands. In turn, they expect that the boss will take care of their needs. In the U.S., workers generally work to achieve their own self-interest. If they do a good job, they will be acknowledged by the system. In contrast, most Japanese will dedicate themselves to serving the group so the company will take care of them.

Training Koreans

What would be the appropriate way to begin a training session for Korean managers and staff? The example that follows displays some of the do's and don'ts of training Koreans.

Michael Penrose was a British technical consultant and trainer. He earned his degree in computer engineering from a renowned British school and traveled overseas to America to receive an MBA. He had worked with several American and British companies, successfully training their workers on how to implement computer information systems into the structure of their organizations.

As the owner of his own consulting business, Michael hoped to dramatically increase his returns by expanding his business to Southeast Asia. Since he had some good friends from Korea, he used his references to obtain a contract with a growing electronics firm. When the time came to train Koreans, however, Penrose knew that his Korean cultural background was lacking. Therefore, he prepared for his new job by researching the cultural norms of Koreans and devising his own plan for successfully completing his contract.

Since he was training managers of different levels, he first devised two different training groups. His long-time assistant worked with the lower-level managers, and he himself took the upper-management group. He did this because Koreans expect strict separation of management levels—remember their military culture. Also, while he usually had a laid-back teaching style when working with the Americans and the British, he took a more authoritarian stance when dealing with and training the Koreans. They expected him to act as a knowledgeable authority, and he did so according to their expectations. He also gave tough, intense assignments, expecting the best out of his students and pushing them to their limits.

For his own sake, he set up several group discussions, which relieved the pressure of speaking in front of a class for hours at a time, and gave him time to rest. When all was said and done, Penrose achieved his goal and, due to a successful first series of seminars, was awarded a year-long contract. His business expanded, and he was fortunate enough to return to beautiful Korea several times—all the rewards of preparing for the expectations of Korean culture!

Tips for Training Koreans

As you might expect from our discussion of Korean culture as a whole, successful training programs depend on a variety of factors.

Check out the following list. Keep in mind the cultural factors mentioned previously to explain the reason for the following:

- Don't mix the levels of managers.
- Trainers are the authority.
- Strict rules and intense activities are expected.
- There is no need for preparation for training. They learn as they go.
- Group discussions are encouraged to relieve the instructor.
- Fifteen to twenty participants make up an appropriate class size.

Not surprisingly, I noticed that one of the keys to successful training of employees is the allotment of appropriate amounts of time for recess. Korean employees and trainees will expect breaks every hour to hour and a half. This is a time for cigarettes, coffee, and refreshments for participants. As an instructor, break time will also be important for you to try to gather feedback from participants. Also, provide a well-documented training manual. Koreans will expect this, and the success of your program may very well depend on your written documentation. They are encouraged to spend time after class reviewing notes and reading materials.

Motivating Koreans

Group achievement is valued higher than group harmony or consensus. Consequently, effectively motivating Koreans is dependent upon the skills of the manager, and in finding a balance between the needs of the individual and those of the group, or in the larger sense, the corporation.

Because Koreans identify themselves with their company and job, however, this task is not as hard as it may seem. Keep the following tips in mind when developing a motivational strategy for your Korean employees:

- Personal loyalty may take precedence over fairness.
- Workers are often motivated by the carrot-and-stick, or shin sang pilbol, approach.
- Koreans are mostly managed by paternalism.
- Reward and punishment are applied on a group basis.
- Personal ties and cohesiveness among Korean employees result in greater productivity.
- All employees receive a present on their birthday.
- Koreans are extraordinarily sensitive to slights and setbacks which damage their "kibun."

If you are having trouble motivating your Korean workers, take into account that they often resort to ritualistic, face-saving facades. This also occurs when motivating Korean negotiators to follow your plans or to assimilate your ideas of how to proceed. When this happens, don't hesitate to emphasize your rank and social class. A good idea is to display "gentle stubbornness," "firm flexibility," and "polite obstinacy". This will give your partner the message that, while you may understand their point of view, you are not willing to completely compromise your position.

Promotions within Korean Organizations

Most Korean organizations base their promotions on the following criteria:

- Personal record: age, military service, education, time served with company.
- Performance evaluation.
- Evaluation of abilities: foreign language skills, in-company education, ability to teach within the company.
- Professional licenses.

Social Etiquette When Dealing with Koreans

In dealing with Koreans in a social environment, keep the following in mind:

- Drinking is an important part of social and business relationships for men in Korea, and may well be much more than Westerners are accustomed to.
- Eating is done with chopsticks and a large spoon. The person with the highest status should begin the meal.
- Excessive talking during the meal is considered impolite. Slurping is seen as a sign of enjoyment.
- Generosity toward friends and acquaintances is important, including the giving of expensive gifts and preparing more food than a Westerner might think necessary. Being at all stingy is impolite.
- Gifts are very important. When visiting someone's home, bring fruit, flowers, cakes, or alcohol. When giving money as a gift, put it in an envelope.

- Invitations are usually informal and verbal. They are often not given by the person hosting the event and may be given only a few hours before it.
- The person who extends an invitation is the one who pays. It is considered an honor and a matter of pride. There is no such thing as "Dutch treat" in Korea.
- Throwing away rice is considered wasteful and bad luck.
- Koreans usually sing at social gatherings. At parties, the most honored person is given the first chance to sing. Other people are then each given a turn. Be prepared to sing at any social gathering.
- Shoes should be removed before entering a home or temple.
- Tipping is not usually necessary. If the service in a restaurant, hair salon, or taxi has been especially good, a small tip would be appreciated.
- Touching children is a natural expression of interest and affection.

Summary

An understanding of the Koreans' cultural values can provide insight into the potential for the success or failure of your business ventures with them. In order to succeed with Koreans, you must adhere to local cultural values, at both the individual as well as the organizational level. Remember, the spiritual values of the Koreans and the strong family connections between employees of Korean companies are the two most important elements of Korean culture, and these elements will always influence how Koreans conduct business. Enjoy your next negotiation with Koreans and do not be concerned with their initial offense. During dinner and drinking sessions, you will find them just as warm and human as in other cultures.

Dealing with Indonesian Paks

*How do you impress your Indonesian counterpart
in your first meeting?
How do you plant your seeds for future business in Indonesia?
What will assure you that a negotiated deal is a done deal?*

In the late 1990's, Indonesia experienced both economic and political turmoil as the Ruphia, its currency, devaluated and its leadership went under the most dramatic change in close to 40 years. World leaders waited to see whether Indonesia would survive these immense changes. In this country with the fourth largest population in the world, however, business is now returning to a state of normalcy. This is due to basic Indonesian values: respect for elders and seniority, and maintaining harmony and relationships among Indonesia's diverse cultures. This is something that the prospective business partner, expatriate manager, or future employee of an Indonesian firm should keep in mind.

In this chapter, we will cover the many values of Indonesian business cultures and provide you with the knowledge you need to interact successfully with your Indonesian partners and potential clients. It will also cover the many essences of doing business with Indonesians, thereby helping you to improve your skills in negotiating with and managing Indonesians.

The chapter begins by testing your current skills in dealing with Indonesians. It will then present the inherent cultural values of

Indonesians and show how these compare to those other cultures in the book. Several of my firsthand experiences and those of other people dealing with Indonesian business communities will be presented. Specific examples with tips and taboos in your first encounter with Indonesians, conducting business meetings, and presenting to and enhancing your relationship with Indonesians will be discussed in detail to improve your skills. How to persuade, train and motivate Indonesians will also be presented. Finally, we will present brief tips on several social norms one must adhere to when sailing across the Indonesian business islands.

Test Your Skills Dealing with Indonesians: True or False?

Test your knowledge of basic Indonesian cultural values with the following true-or-false statements:

____ 1. Indonesians value group achievement more than group harmony.

____ 2. The use of "Pak" before someone's name shows more respect for your counterpart.

____ 3. Most Sumartan Indonesians value risk taking more than Indonesian Javanese.

____ 4. In order to succeed with Indonesians, you must exhibit your own individual technical ability in addition to a cooperative attitude.

____ 5. Upon meeting an Indonesian, the individual will be first interested in finding out where you are from.

____ 6. Upon completing a deal with Indonesians, your counterpart will appreciate a token gift.

____ 7. Your personal references are weighed more highly than your technical capabilities by the Indonesian.

____ 8. For an Indonesian, a 5% markup is usually sufficient.

____ 9. Most Indonesian taxi drivers will insist on a 10% tip rather than leaving the amount up to you.

____ 10. Most major decisions are made by team consensus rather than by the president of the organization.

Answers:

1. F,; 2. T; 3. T; 4. F; 5. T; 6. T; 7. T; 8. F; 9. F; 10. T

Personal Tale: Who Do You Know?

In my first attempt at introducing my multicultural management and training seminars to Indonesia, I wrote directly to the editor of *Warta Ekonomi,* a local business magazine that hosts international speakers on a monthly basis. When I received no response, I called one of my Indonesian friends in California, who immediately pointed out that I should try to contact the magazine's top person, the publisher.

My friend was kind enough to find out the publisher's phone number for me and I immediately made the call. Upon introducing myself, I presented myself and my past achievements and accomplishments. To my surprise, however, the publisher was more interested in who I knew in Indonesia and the schools I had attended 25 years earlier. I realized that Indonesians place a higher value on connections and status than on accomplishments.

Finally, the publisher offered me the opportunity to speak at one of his magazine's monthly dinner meetings. I accepted, hoping that this would open the door for my programs in Indonesia and build a connection. Because I was more familiar with American and Japanese businesspersons, I began my post-presentation conversations with either the typical American introduction, "What do you do, Mr. Ibrahim?" or the Japanese, "Which company are you with, Ms. Indrawati?"

I later realized that when most Indonesians introduce themselves they ask, "Where do you come from?" and then "Who do you know in Indonesia?" These questions are their ice-breakers. My inquiries were somewhat forward. Now I adopt the Indonesian style of introduction when meeting them and, not surprisingly, have found that my chances of success have greatly improved.

Indonesian Cultural Values

In order to succeed in Indonesia, one must make an effort to understand the diversity of Indonesian cultural values. Indonesia consists of many islands and many local sub-cultures. Although Indonesians, as a people, have basic values, you should do your best to be aware of the local culture of your Indonesian partner, such as Javanese (Java), Batak (North Sumatra), Sundanese (West Java), Padang (West Sumatra), Manado (North Sulawesi), or Ache (North Sumatra).

As a nation, Indonesians subscribe to three basic national cultural values: Pancasila (their basic beliefs), Gotong Royong (cooperative spirit), and Bhineka Tunggal Ika (unity in diversity). Using traditional cultural symbolism, the Pancasila refers to five basic beliefs of the nation as a whole: a belief in God, democracy under one nation, social justice, respect for human rights, and unity/consensus.

While working with a team of Americans and Indonesians, we asked both what they valued most. The following table illustrates how they answered.

Valued Most by Indonesians	Valued Most by Americans
Religion	Religion
Family	Relationship
Self-Improvement	Unity
Consensus	Prosperity
Relationship	Tradition
Loyalty	Family
Friendship	Nationality
Seniority	Simplicity

As this table shows, religion, family, relationship, consensus, seniority, and nationality are key values of an Indonesian's life. As with the previous chapters of the book, during our management training workshops with Indonesian managers, we asked Indonesian participants to prioritize 20 common values. We also asked the same questions to groups of Arab and American managers. The following table presents what these three groups indicated were their top five values from a list of 20.

Indonesians	Americans	Arabs
Relationship	Equality	Seniority
Group Harmony	Freedom	Spirituality
Seniority	Openness	Reputation
Family	Self-Reliance	Family
Cooperation	Cooperation	Authority

As our research points out, Indonesians highly value relationships, which leads to cooperative partnerships. They communicate and deal with others in harmony and avoid conflicts. They show respect to seniority in family, office, government, and nation.

They do not value risk taking, self-reliance and group achievements, however, as highly as other cultures such as Americans. Now imagine American managers working in Indonesia with their values of equality, freedom, openness, and self-reliance. They will probably have frequent culture clashes with their peers, boss, and coworkers. Although Arabs stress seniority like Indonesians, they are less keen on group harmony and place more emphasis on authority and one's reputation.

In order to succeed in negotiating with and managing Indonesians, you must be aware of this spectrum of values. In your business experience, you may have to deal with government officials or persons in private enterprise. Following are some of the values unique to the subcultures that you may deal with in Indonesia.

An Indonesian Civil Servant's Values

- Ceremonial rituals with visitors
- Relationships
- Seniority: respect for the boss
- Material possessions
- Formalities: rules, regulations, flag ceremony, morning exercises
- An emphasis on seating arrangements
- Individual acknowledgment of people

Private Businessperson's Values

- A less formal but more disciplined approach
- Simplified processes
- Business kept within family and friends
- Material gains
- A relaxed atmosphere
- Friendly negotiations
- Humorous conversation

As noted, when dealing with government officials, formality is expected during ceremonies, appreciative gestures, and when forging future business relationships. In contrast, when dealing with Indonesian private enterprises, one may be less formal, keep interactions simple, and focus on tangible returns such as money and repeat business. As more Indonesian entrepreneurial businesses emerge, a relaxed, friendly, and humorous culture appears to be developing.

As mentioned, Indonesians place more emphasis on maintaining harmony with their partners and on how a deal will benefit each participant. These facts were ingrained in me when I asked some participants in my training programs to draw a picture of Indonesian culture.

Some simply drew a group of old and young Indonesians sitting around in a circle, ready to eat from the same bowl. We have to share everything, the drawing said. One must respond by developing a negotiation stance that emphasizes group benefits and aims toward a win-win proposition for everyone involved.

Another interesting picture drawn by participants showed Indonesians as confused ducks wondering where to go. A farmer with a long stick tried to direct the ducks in a certain direction, indicating that everyone waits for directions and go/no go decisions from the boss. The picture also had a duck that had to take the first step forward toward the target. There were also a couple of ducks about to get tapped on the head as a way of motivating them to move forward. From this picture, we can see that clear direction by the boss, sticking together, and acting as one team are very important values in Indonesian culture. They would not move before the boss said, "Go!"

In negotiating with Indonesians, one must keep in mind the priority of their values: relationships, cooperation, group harmony, seniority, and family values. They are very status-oriented, as shown by their attention to good dress, posture, and how they fit into the group. Expect much group negotiation but not quick decisions. Foreign businesspeople should have a good reference within the organization who will introduce them. Then they must identify the influential person who will sponsor their project. Finally, the person who is the ultimate decision maker must be persuaded. In the end, everyone involved "must eat from the cake that has been baked by all."

Meeting Indonesians

Establishing good relationships with Indonesians can be a rewarding experience. You will have plenty of business if you understand the key factors that Indonesians look for when developing a business relationship. Let's look at the following personal story.

Going to the Top

After my first seminar in Indonesia, I noticed that several participants were eager to introduce me to their friends and colleagues. I had spent several days working with them, establishing credibility, friendship, and trust and building close relationships. Now, in return, they wanted to show me their appreciation by offering me their connections. This was a show of respect for the senior person (the professor) and a way for them to show who they knew. It was also a way to reciprocate for what I had done for them.

One of the participants introduced me to the managing director of a large automobile manufacturing company. During our meeting, the managing director asked me for two copies of my book, one for himself and one for the president. He said that if the president read the book and was interested in the program, its introduction was almost guaranteed.

After two months, I phoned the director. He said he had not yet given my book to the president and, as a result, was unable to give me the necessary personal introduction to the director of the training department. Believing that two months had been too long from my American perspective, I decided to try my luck directly with the company's training manager during my next visit.

After a three-hour presentation to the training manager and his staff, I received some complimentary words and promises to get back to me. But several months again passed without any progress. So I recalled my mentor's recommendation about being introduced to the highest possible person in an organization. I concluded that I had not been patient enough; I should have waited for the president's recommendation. Later on, I realized that nothing will move before the blessing and agreement of the big Pak.

This requirement that you be introduced to the highest person possible reflects the Indonesian value system. I have found that Indonesians' respect for seniority will cause them to look solely to the boss to make decisions. The boss is the father figure in the organization and the final decision maker. Communicating with and seeking the commitments of high-ranking officials help to reassure that your business will go through. Do not ignore, however, the lower ranks who will be in charge of the implementation process—you should also maintain a harmonious relationship with them as well. They do the paper work to speed up or slow down internal processes and get you paid on time. You have to get them involved and make sure they are happy at all times.

Let us now look at the following quiz and see how well you will do in meeting Indonesians:

1. When meeting an Indonesian businessperson for the first time, you:
    a. Shake hands.
    b. Present your business card.
    c. State your name and company and then shake hands.
    d. Open your arms to give him a hug.

Usually Indonesians will offer (a) a soft handshake. They will then engage in pleasantries to find out where you are from and the people you associate with. They will later present you with their business card as a record of the meeting. Find out the level of seniority of the person and show an appropriate level of respect. Giving an Indonesian a hug is not common as it is among Arabs, unless you are an old friend.

2. While introducing yourself, you should first mention your:
   a. References.
   b. Education from a famous university.
   c. Position in the company.
   d. Hobbies.

You will probably mention (a) your references and how close you are to them. This will enhance how well you will be trusted in their community and country. Your earned degree(s) from a famous local or overseas university will also put you a step higher. You may proceed in inquiring about their hobbies in order to discover interesting topics of discussion. Don't dwell on your position or authority within your company. One of my friends gave me a clue that the president of the company I was going to meet had a collection of butterflies. He was very happy when I presented him with a small collection of butterflies during my first meeting with him.

3. To thank your Indonesian partner, send him/her:
   a. A thank-you letter signed by your company president.
   b. A round-trip airline ticket to visit your country for a week.
   c. The bicycle that the partner talked about for his/her son.
   d. A money order.

If you are in a business relationship with an Indonesian, an appropriate gift from your country will be appreciated. A (b) round trip ticket is considered part of the promotion if you are engaged in a large project. A thank-you letter (a) highlighting her contributions to the project will be greatly appreciated.

4. To enhance your relationship with your Indonesian partner, you should:
   a. Invite him to visit your country at your expense.
   b. Introduce him to your best friend and family.
   c. Join him Friday night at a nightclub since he loves to dance.
   d. Send him greeting cards every holiday.

Introducing your partner to your best friend and member of your family (b) is a show of admiration and appreciation. Joining your partner at dinnertime followed by (c) a club will put you in a relaxed atmosphere, which will enhance your relationship. Cards for greeting and religious holidays (d) will also be greatly appreciated, but be sure to continue sending them throughout your business relationship and for some time afterwards.

5. You want to build a trusting relationship with your potential Indonesian customers. You should:
    a. Offer your personal accountability.
    b. Mention your last sales to another big organization.
    c. Let them drive your new Mercedes around the parking lot.
    d. Describe your product's 24-month warranty.

In order to encourage your Indonesian customers to proceed with the sale, your (a) personal accountability to finish the job will make a great impact. They can count on you if problems arise. A reference to a person in (b) another organization with whom you have dealt successfully will establish greater credibility. Make that contact feel you are part of the team and will support them if problems arise. Most Indonesians are team players.

6. You notice that when Indonesians talk to their bosses, they address them as Pak Bambang, Pak Farid, etc. This means:
    a. "I'm sorry."
    b. "Yes, sir."
    c. "Please."
    d. A show of respect.

Pak is a term of respect, the equivalent of the English term *Papa*. If you hear others calling you Pak, that indicates a great respect for you. It is usually followed by the name of a senior person rather than a subordinate. You usually do not use Pak for a person of a lower level than you unless you have a respect for that person's ability, too.

7. The first impression you make is the one that Indonesians remember most. Knowing this, you:
    a. State your powerful references clearly.
    b. Watch your tone and style of speaking.
    c. Wear a neat and proper cloth.
    d. Show up late in order to display your power.

The best answer to this question is (b). Indonesians value interpersonal harmony, relationships and politeness in social interactions. They are made uncomfortable by rudeness, confrontation, an overly intense or emotional manner, or pushiness, all of which they regard as arrogant and self-centered. It is important to maintain a polite and respectful manner. It is also important to (a) state your references clearly. Relationships, family, networking, and hence references are key assets in creating credibility in Indonesian society. Indonesians are status conscious, so dressing well is a good idea; however, you don't want to dress ostentatiously. To display your power by not showing up on time will be construed as rude and arrogant.

Tips for Enhancing Your Relationship with Indonesians

Greet people with a smile.
Shake hands gently and softly.
Show respect for seniors and elders.
Speak politely and listen to others.
Relax and enjoy the encounter.
Mention your name and give out
a business card.
Ask about hobbies.
Show kindness toward subordinates.
Make eye-to-eye contact.
Offer coffee and sweets.

Don't touch head or use left
hand.
Don't be too familiar.
Don't use foot gestures.
Never be frontal.
Don't talk in a rude manner.
Don't address someone by a
disliked nickname.
Don't use firm handshakes.
Don't stare at Indonesian girls.
No body touching.
Don't push for an immediate
decision.

Interacting with the Paks

Here are further tips on how most Indonesians will interact with their superiors:
- Subordinates stand with their hands held loosely in front.
- Subordinates stand until asked to sit down.
- Subordinates speak first, explaining the purpose of their visit.
- Boss listens quietly.
- Boss shakes head in acknowledgment as subordinate speaks.
- Subordinates ask the boss to solve the problem, if possible.
- Boss promises to look into the matter.
- Boss counsels subordinates to be patient.

On the Phone with Indonesians

Most Westerners who are anxious to close sales on the phone may have a difficult time doing so with Indonesians, even in today's world of interconnected global business. Keep in mind the following tips and taboos during your next phone contact with your Indonesian partner:

Speak slowly and clearly.
Socialize first.
Be prepared for long communication.
Say congratulations, thanks, salamat.
Answer with your name.
Give a nice greeting, and conclude politely.
Introduce yourself first.
Hang up softly.
Be patient and receptive.
Leave messages, if necessary.

Don't get angry, loud or vulgar.
Don't eat while on the phone.
Don't push for decision.
Don't be offensive to races or religions.
Don't put one calling on hold for a long time.
Don't call someone at home after 9 p.m.
Don't greet before asking, Who is this?
Don't speak too quickly or loudly.
Don't swear to God.
Don't interrupt caller.

Writing to Indonesians

Written communication is often the most common way of communicating across cultures—reports, letters, fax, and e-mails are all greatly important. Because this is so, written communication must be carefully worded to avoid costly mistakes that may cause embarrassment and lost deals. Note the following:

Before you write:
Check for correct spelling of names. Can you type the following names correctly the first time? Mr. Lesjanto Tjiptobiantoro or Mrs. Widie Tjahjanto
Use we, rather than I or me.

Introduction:
Begin with a greeting or good wishes.
Acknowledge past correspondence or business.

Body of the letter:
State your purpose clearly.
Avoid confrontations or threats.
Mention your reference and relationship.
Stress open, personal communication.

Conclusion:
Close politely.

Do you know what the following titles mean?

a. drs.
b. dra.
c. Ir.
d. DR.
e. dr.
f. Pak

A man with a Bachelor's degree is indicated by the title *drs.,* and a woman with a Bachelor's degree is indicated by the title *dra. Ir.* is an engineer's title, while *DR.* is a person with a Ph.D. dr. is a medical doctor. *Pak* is an address of respect for an older or senior person or being polite to someone you respect—Pak Budi, Pak Farid.

Before I recognized the above, however, I was communicating in writing with an Indonesian who signed the correspondence with dra. Egiest. I was not sure if this person was a man or woman. I took it as a man and so responded back by "Thank you Mr. Eigest, . . .". Upon arriving to Jakarta, I was embarrassed when I found that Mr. Eigest was really Miss Eigest!

Here is a sample of an appropriate letter to an Indonesian businessperson:

Mr. Bambang Barato
General Manager, Engineering Dept.
Indonesia Corp.
Jakarta, Indonesia

Dear Pak Bambang,

Thank you for your continuing cooperation and interest in our products. You and your staff have shown great progress in our recent seminars. We are sure that by working together we will achieve our goal of improving your company's international market shares.

As you know, I will be in Jakarta next month to conduct seminars to several other clients. At that time, we may be able to hold a program for other members of your staff, as well.

The price of the programs will be the same as it was in November. Also, we might be able to reduce the cost if you decide to opt for two programs, as we can then waive the travel expenses. As you know, program costs include program delivery, extensive workshop manuals, and air travel expenses for two instructors.

If the above proposal is of interest to you, please contact me. I look forward to communicating with and seeing you again in the near future. Thank you very much.

Sincerely,

David Smith
Sales Representative

As you may note, the letter starts and ends with a friendly introduction, and maintains a harmonious relationship and a show of helping attitudes. This is a basic and important Indonesian value. Next time you write a letter, memo, or even an e-mail, stop for a moment and re-read it with an Indonesian, or other, culture in mind. With minor changes in words, you will get the order! Following are further tips to use in your next message to your Indonesian partner.

Date, use proper heading, and title.	Never use red ink.
Do not state the purpose first.	Do not push for immediate
Write in black or blue.	decision.
Put a salutation and	Avoid the use of colored paper.
signature at end.	Avoid rude content.
Use good paper.	Avoid private letters faxed
Be brief and clear content.	without covers.
Use "Dear sir" or "Pak."	Avoid bad content arrangement.
Be polite, even for bad news.	Don't skip the salutation!
Open with greetings.	Don't beat around the bush.
Write letters that are long.	Avoid being arrogant.
	Avoid a threatening attitude.

Conducting Meetings and Presentations

More chairs and donuts, please

During Bobby Smith's first week in Indonesia working on a telecommunications project, he invited five managers from his division to discuss the status of the project at an 8:30 a.m. meeting. He arrived on time to discover that only two of the managers had arrived. Fifteen minutes later, the rest arrived, but each one was accompanied by three subordinates. Wondering why, Smith now needed to bring nine additional chairs into the already crowded room.

Smith tried to open the meeting and set the agenda but to his surprise, several members had not reviewed his letter of invitation and were unclear as to the meeting's objectives. Smith thus had to spend 15 minutes reviewing the agenda of the meeting. Ten minutes into his presentation, he was annoyed by several side discussions that took place while he was talking. He was not sure why or how to handle it. At about 9:30, he felt that they were looking at their watches and so, he called for a coffee break, and was surprised that the Indonesians complained that there were no snacks or donuts.

It is not unusual for Indonesians to arrive late to meetings. Bosses usually arrive after every one is in. So, everyone tries to be the boss, by coming in late, thus appearing more important. Most managers will invite 2–3 subordinates to accompany them in order to answer detailed questions and to carry supporting documentation. Side conversations are also common and may reflect either boredom, or an effort to clarify issues among themselves rather than interrupting the speaker, or it is time to build consensus among members. Finally, Indonesians expect snacks with every morning coffee or afternoon refreshment break. All of these expectations are normal for Indonesians, but they were new to Bobby. Hopefully, for the next meeting, he will be better prepared.

The following quiz will further help you to conduct effective meetings and presentations with Indonesians:

1. You are making a business presentation to your Indonesian clients. You begin by:
   a. Thanking everyone for the opportunity to present your product.
   b. Telling them your name, title, and achievements last year.
   c. Apologizing for not speaking Indonesian.
   d. Presenting each person with the gifts you brought.

Thank everyone (a) for the opportunity to present your product and your wish to conclude the meeting with a win-win agreement. If it is an important meeting, they will expect a senior person from your/their company to introduce the first topic. The seniority of the person indicates the importance of the meeting. Telling them (b) your past achievements in Indonesia will be highly considered. Saying a few Indonesian greetings will also be appreciated. After a long meeting, a token gift from your company is a nice momento. According to the importance of the issue, another lower-level boss may come to close the meeting, if it is a full-day event.

2. Halfway through your presentation, you realize that nobody has asked any questions. You should:
   a. Continue with your presentation.
   b. Ask if anyone has a question.
   c. Ask the senior person if he has a question.
   d. Ask the oldest person if he has a question.

A successful presentation in Indonesia must involve the audience. Indonesians will be hesitant to ask questions or participate in the beginning as a show of respect for the presenter's expertise and seniority. At some point in the meeting, you will want to (c) direct your attention to the senior person, after which you can ask other attendees to participate. They are waiting for the senior person to talk first. At the end, however, don't ask the senior person for an opinion first; otherwise, all junior persons will respond the same way that the senior person did. Give junior participants a chance to give their opinion at the end before the boss does.

3. At the end of your presentation, you want to close the sale. You should:
   a. Invite everyone for dinner at the Hilton hotel.
   b. Ask the senior person if he will sign for an order now.
   c. Thank them again for being patient and cooperative.
   d. Remind them of the deadline in order to get the special discount.

You should thank the audience (c) for being patient and cooperative. Don't pressure the senior person or the group for a yes or no answer in the meeting. They will probably need some time to digest and discuss the information as a team. The boss will probably ask for the team's opinion later on and then will make the final decision. It is appropriate to invite some of the senior participants to dinner at a nice restaurant. Take this chance to discuss hobbies, world affairs, the diversity and beauty of Indonesia, and other non-business subjects.

4. You have not heard from your Indonesian partner in several weeks, so you make a telephone call. To motivate him, you:
    a. Remind him of the deadline date.
    b. Ask him how can you help speed up the decision.
    c. Remind him how much you rely on him.
    d. Ask him for his boss's phone number to complain.

Again, it is important to maintain ongoing communication with Indonesians. Many non-Indonesians may feel that the other side is committed and wait for their response. Later, they may discover that the Indonesian was just entertaining their request without any real commitment. In this case, it is better to (c) remind your partner that you are relying on them and hope that the project goes through for mutual benefit. Offer to help resolve any issues that are still under consideration. Show a helping hand rather than a demanding attitude. If you blame or load the problem on them, your partner will disappear. Make your partner's problem yours and they will feel supported and will move on.

Tips for Conducting Successful Meetings and Presentations

Do:

- Select comfortable facilities and chairs.
- Be on time, but be aware that their boss may not be on time.
- Seat the senior member in the middle of the room far from the door.
- Give recognition and attention to the boss.
- Create an informal atmosphere; spend time greeting people.
- Thank participants for attending the meeting.
- Take attendance by signing people in for important meetings.
- Clearly state your objectives and the agenda.
- Mention the important points from the previous meeting.
- Deliver your presentation in a clear and polite way.
- Conduct an open discussion with an emphasis on interpersonal harmony.
- Give time for the audience to ask questions.
- If the meeting is long, provide many breaks with snacks.
- Have someone record the minutes of the meeting.
- Report the result to higher-level management and secure their commitment.

Don't:

- Deviate from the meeting's objectives.
- Make significant changes.
- Discuss many topics at one time.
- Take a dominating role in the group.
- Act superior to the audience.
- Point at someone in the audience with your finger (do it with your whole hand).
- Be emotional or confront others.
- Speak too long.
- Push too hard for answers.
- Exceed meeting time by more than an hour and half.

Persuading Indonesians

Who will make the decision?

Earlier in this chapter, I discussed my experiences in establishing relationships with Indonesians. Once I understood the Indonesian introduction and proposal process, I was easily able to reach Mr. Danang, the president of a medium-sized data transfer organization. My presentation to him went well, and I expected an immediate sale. Danang asked me, however, if I would have dinner with him to further discuss my proposal and the introduction of our programs.

I happily accepted his invitation, and during our dinner we discussed such topics as prices, our hobbies, our families, and world affairs. After a three-hour dinner, Danang then referred me to his assistant, who was to handle the final negotiations. To my disappointment, the negotiations with the assistant did not go well; the company could not afford the cost of my programs, which Danang could have told me directly. By referring me to the assistant, he was just passing the buck—and the $200 dinner bill. It is very seldom that Indonesians will directly refuse an offer or say no to you; it is considered impolite and rude and may harm future relationships. Thus, you have to listen to the unspoken words.

Armed with my newfound knowledge, I began to make progress with a large Indonesian telecommunications company. After the usual process of introduction to the president and negotiation with team members, the program manager in charge, Mr. Santoso, proposed dates and prices for my program. I took this as final confirmation.

After I faxed him the contract for his signature, Santoso surprised me by replying that he needed to hold off another week for approval from the corporate vice president of finance, who was returning from an overseas trip. I immediately realized that the deal was not yet done. Once again, the boss has the final say.

Eventually, the deal did go through, and I learned that I had to maintain continuous and patient communication with Indonesians in order to stay abreast of important developments. Be certain not to display disappointment or anger if your Indonesian partners temporarily delay your sale, for doing so may cause them to simply delay the sale indefinitely.

Planting a Seed for the Spring Harvest

Recognizing the importance of building relationships, I recruited an Indonesian agent, Mr. Komurddin, to market my programs in Indonesia. After three months of entertaining and visiting important clients, Komurddin suggested that I bring along several copies of my book to potential clients. The interpersonal marketing was rigorous. We spent almost half a day with the prospective client company, scheduling meetings with three of its important directors. Each meeting consisted of about 40 minutes of waiting and being introduced to the director's staff, but only five to 10 minutes presenting, merely to hand each director a signed copy of my book and business card.

I realized that Komurddin was just planting seeds with the directors. Free samples (i.e., copies of my book) were given in order to develop a relationship and the spirit of cooperation that could eventually lead to the introduction of my programs. Later, I found that this was part of a lengthy process that Indonesians follow to prepare the groundwork for submitting official proposals. They must first guarantee that key people involved in the project are aware of it, will be satisfied with its outcome, and are ready to sign on. Then a proposal will be submitted. My friend will probably be visiting them again seeking unofficial approval from the boss to submit the official proposal.

Now I've got it!

After several successful programs with one of Indonesia's leading telecommunication companies, the participants told me that one of the directors had realized the value of the program to his company. A potential expansion of my program in the company became possible.

I asked one of the participants to introduce me to the director, which he did. I secured a meeting with the director in which I elaborated on the value of the program for the top members of the organization. The director asked me to prepare a presentation to the Board of Directors, which he would sponsor. During my presentation to the board, I focused my attention on the president and with the help of the director, we secured the board's approval. The program then proceeded smoothly and, from time to time, I reported to the director in order to keep him informed of the progress—as well as to maintain our relationship.

This case represents the essence of the proper introduction, working with a sponsor, and reaching the appropriate person in the top level of the organization to get things done. I later noticed that every major decision in the project had to go back for the president's approval. The president even had to sign the letter inviting members to the seminar, in order to demonstrate the program's importance to the company, so that they would know they had to attend. If a person was invited by the president, they had better show up in the program or meeting without a question.

Now, test your skills in negotiating with Indonesians by answering the following quiz:

1. You think your Indonesian partner is stalling during negotiations. You should:
   a. Remind him of the deadline dates.
   b. Remind him of the airline ticket you will give him if he follows through.
   c. Remind him how much you rely on him.
   d. Ask him if you can help in solving the problem.

Some Indonesians will stall or become silent while negotiating. This simply indicates that a decision has not been made or even that the answer is no, but they don't want to be rude. This is certainly a problem, and your role is (d) to help solve it. You need to support them and find out how you can help in order to proceed further.

2. You are planning a training program in Indonesia for March 21. It is now February 21, but you haven't received a confirmation. You:
   a. Send faxes giving them February 25 as the final deadline.
   b. Send faxes indicating how difficult it is for you to meet your deadline.

    c. Send faxes reminding them that the program's date is approaching.

    d. Call them directly.

It is important to maintain ongoing communication with Indonesians in order to determine the status of your project. Frequent phone calls (d) to the project manager will give you insight into the situation. Remember that any delay is indicative that there is a problem in making a decision. The boss did not sign as yet.

3.   You have quoted your client a price of $1,000 per computer system package. He sent you a fax stating that the price is too high. You:

    a. Ask him to prove his claim.

    b. Respond with, "Sorry, that's the best we can offer."

    c. Remind him of your computers' new technology.

    d. Ask him what is acceptable.

You should seek information on your competitors with whom your client is dealing. You can then use this information to (c) emphasize the superiority of your system and how it can enhance their business. A small discount will be a good gesture that may convince him to rethink the deal.

4.   You are making a presentation to an Indonesian businessman for 1,000 calculators. He is reluctant to buy all 1,000 of them. You offer:

    a. Dinner at the Hilton hotel.

    b. To let him try one for a week.

    c. A 20% discount if he submits an immediate order.

    d. One free sample.

A free sample (d) will get your foot in the door. Keep your offer of a discount for later, after a nice dinner. Remember that Indonesians appreciate a win-win situation; there are no losers in Indonesian business.

5.   If Indonesians can't meet your expectations, they may blame it on:

    a. Government regulations.

    b. Natural disasters.

    c. The boss.

    d. God.

Indonesians rarely say no directly. They may blame a delay on (a), (b), (c), or even the budget. If you have room to compromise, this is the moment to work with them in order to overcome the problems and arrive at a mutually beneficial deal.

Encountering Indonesian Negotiators

	They	**You**
Group Compositions	The senior manager negotiates first, followed by middle executives.	Match your staff levels to theirs.
Establishing Rapport	Create harmony through social rituals, small talk. May give false impression of interest, agreement.	Obtain introductions through references, avoid initial conflicts, visit, and offer token gifts throughout negotiation.
Information Exchange	Informal, ad hoc; commitments and arrangements are vague.	Be more definite than they are. Communicate constantly through telephone calls, visits, etc.
Persuasion Tools	Stress future business opportunities, large profit margin, personal gain.	Emphasize gain for self and group; everybody must eat from the cake. Surprise key personnel with tangible rewards.
Decision Process	A spokesperson recommends you, an influential person then sponsors and lobbies for your proposal; finally, a decision maker approves it.	Identify: 1. A strong reference 2. An influential person 3. The decision maker at each stage
Decision Makers	An influential person with strong power behind the scene is key.	Persuade middle manager, who then persuades senior manager.

Working with Indonesians

When supervising Indonesians, it is important to remember that they value cooperation, group harmony, family, reputation, and spirituality. Make an effort to get to know them and learn about their environment. Be friendly, but do watch your social distance. Build two-way communication. If their personal problems are affecting their work, pay attention and offer your support. Above all, show trust in them and do not look down at them as your subordinate.

Answer the following quiz to test your skills for supervising Indonesian workers:

1. You want to motivate an Indonesian worker to stay late to finish an important project. You:
   a. Order her to stay to 8:00 p.m.
   b. Stay with her until she is finished.
   c. Promise her lunch the next day.
   d. Remind her of the managerial position that will be available soon.

Indonesian workers look up to you as a mentor who will take care of them. The worker will appreciate your concern if you (b) stay with them for a few hours. Buying the worker lunch the next day (c) is another way to show your appreciation for the extra effort. A pat on the back will inspire them after completing the job.

2. If an Indonesian disagrees with his boss, he will:
   a. Keep quiet because he shouldn't challenge the boss.
   b. Talk with him after work.
   c. Talk to the boss' supervisor about the disagreement.
   d. Openly discuss the matter with him.

If an Indonesian worker disagrees with an American manager, the Indonesian will probably remain quiet with a polite smile, as the worker values harmony over conflict. The American manager, on the other hand, expects a challenge from the Indonesian. Americans see open discussion as a step toward problem solving. Disagreements and conflicts with managers in Indonesia are handled somewhat differently from the common American strategy of openly discussing the matter with the manager. Indonesian business culture purports that if you disagree with your manager, you may talk to your manager's boss about the disagreement during a more relaxed time, such as lunch or coffee.

When working with or training Indonesian workers, criticizing them in front of their peers will make them lose face and damage their relationship with you. Indonesians are usually coached one-on-one by their immediate supervisors. This is a role that may prove difficult for American managers, who are accustomed to giving direct input. Most Indonesians are also not inclined to value openness, self-reliance, group achievement, or risk taking, so give fair and appropriate rewards and acknowledge their individual accomplishments.

In general, the greatest source of difficulty for Americans interacting with Indonesians will probably lie in the area of differing values placed on individual achievement, directness, risk taking, and independence. American expressions of individualism often include behavior that might be considered rude, intrusive, or arrogant from the Indonesian perspective.

Training Indonesians

If you will be conducting training sessions to Indonesians, you should keep the following in mind:

Keep class size to 15–20 participants.
Provide handouts before training begins.
Be relaxed and not too fast-paced.
Speak clearly and with enthusiasm.
Provide many examples and case studies with group discussion.
Use a lot of visual aids.
Provide translator if necessary.
Provide breaks with snack and for prayer.
Include jokes and humor.
Provide certificate of completion.
Provide comfortable seats for seniors.

Don't explain too quickly.
Don't give pop quizzes.
Don't go more than two hours per session.
Don't use rigid material and presentation.
Don't show disrespect for religion, tradition, or culture.
Don't forget to ask questions.
Don't forget prayer time.
Don't present passive training and boring situations.
Don't be too heavy on preparation and homework.
Don't hold too large groups.

Motivating Indonesians

The following are important factors that will motivate Indonesians to keep your project on schedule:

Money/Salary/Bonus	Avoid too much responsibility
Good work facilities	Don't change jobs too often
Suitability of work	Avoid offensive or public embarrassment
Giving expectations	Avoid references to background or family
Compliments and	Avoid looking like a liar
recognition	Avoid individually focused criticism
Group-focus	Don't use heavy handouts
Future promises	Don't use unclear directions
Clear instructions	Avoid shouting, blaming, and punishment
Relaxed situations	Avoid insensitivity to religion
Low-profile behavior	

Social Etiquette

Remember the following tips to maintain a good relationship with your Indonesian partners:

- Indonesians value group harmony and relationships.
- Show respect for and address seniors and elders by the proper title, such as Pak Warso or Pak Buddi.
- Exhibit your friendly and cooperative attitude.
- Point out where you come from, what island, and who you know in Indonesia.
- Upon completing a job with Indonesians, your counterpart will appreciate a token gift.
- Indonesians will welcome the idea of lunch or dinner to discuss business issues. They may expect you to pay the bill, however, even if they have initiated the invitation.
- Your personal references are weighed more highly than your technical capabilities.
- Be generous in your tipping to waiters, room service attendants, and taxi drivers. Your foreign currency has large value in Indonesia.
- Most Indonesian taxi drivers will leave the amount of the tip up to you.

Summary

Keep the following key points in mind when dealing with Indonesians: Greet people with smiles, respect, and a friendly attitude. Show respect for the boss or senior person, and show kindness toward subordinates. Avoid highlighting your position of power, or acting arrogant or self-centered. Respect government officials, and the importance of ceremonies, seniority, and formality in the Indonesian culture. Remember that relationships, reputation, group harmony, and cooperation are more important during negotiations than are product prices or even technological advancements.

Identify senior persons who can recommend you and your services to an Indonesian business community. Also, identify and work smoothly with internal lobbyists who will influence the decision on your proposal. Don't be misled by immediate positive feedback. Indonesians often say what they believe you want to hear.

Deals with Indonesians are made only after the boss signs; don't be surprised by last-minute changes or even cancellations. Remember to remain patient, but communicate with them constantly. Keep communicating openly to know the status of your deal, as well as to continually motivate and support their efforts. And don't forget that Indonesians expect everybody to share the fruits of a joint endeavor.

Good luck on your next deal with multicultural Indonesia!

Mastering
the Thai Wai

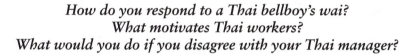

How do you respond to a Thai bellboy's wai?
What motivates Thai workers?
What would you do if you disagree with your Thai manager?

Doing business with Thais can be a pleasant experience if you
understand their deep culture and understand their verbal and nonverbal communication. Although most Thais look like Chinese, there are
unique differences in their values and communication patterns.
Through recent history, Thais have never been under the influence of
western cultures—as others have in Asia. They value and respect the
Monarchy system and their kings.

In this chapter, you will test and master your skills in dealing with
Thais. You will learn how to approach and deal with the Thais' business
environments, and also learn how to conduct phone calls, write to
them, and conduct business meetings and presentations. This chapter
will also take you through the process of successful negotiating with and
persuading your Thai partners. Managing Thai workers can be a frustrating experience if you do not master special skills in doing so. Also
included are a few social etiquette tips that will enhance your business
success and open the door for you in Thailand with a high wai.

Test Your Skills in Dealing with Thais with the Following True-or-False Statements

___ 1. Open and direct criticism is always welcomed in Thailand.
___ 2. Flattery is usually avoided when communicating with Thais.
___ 3. Generosity is a sign of an important person.
___ 4. It is bad manners to open a gift in front of the giver.
___ 5. Monks are the most respected and important people in Thailand.
___ 6. A Thai wai is a way to say "hello."
___ 7. In formal business meetings, Thais prefer to wear black suits.
___ 8. Pointing with fingers is acceptable to get the attention of Thais.
___ 9. Touching the head of your friend's teenage son or daughter is a good sign of caring.
___ 10. The Thai king must "wai" first at a monk if they encounter each other.

Answers:

1. F; 2. F; 3. T; 4. T; 5. T; 6. F; 7. F; 8. F; 9. F; 10. T

Personal Tale: Can You Wai?

During my first attempt to introduce my management training seminars in Thailand, I asked a professor friend of mine for an introduction. He kindly passed on to me the name of a professor at a leading Thai university. I wrote to the professor and after about a month I received a positive response to host my training program. They had a new management training center that was to open soon and I would be a guest speaker. In the meantime, I could conduct my program.

Price negotiation did not go too smoothly and I had to give a special discount as they claimed that they were a nonprofit organization and would have to charge participants very low fees. I took it as a good entry for me and went with the contract to establish a relationship and make a market entry into Thailand.

Upon arrival in Bangkok's Hilton hotel, I was greeted by a bellboy who gave me a wide continuous smile and a high wai (putting both palms together and holding them toward his chest). I was not sure how to respond so I reciprocated with another, higher, wai and continued this with everyone I met in the hotel staff on the way to my room. I enjoyed receiving wais, but most of the Thais were looking back at me with surprise—in addition to a smile. Later on, I learned that the wai is usually given to a more senior person.

My training program went well and I was even introduced to and had dinner with the rector of the university and his senior staff. This indicated to me the Thai value for establishing relationships, cooperation, and seniority. I also noticed the ceremonial nature of doing business in Thailand and their accommodation and hospitality to foreign guests. One of my hosts even took time during the weekend to escort me to some of Thailand's existing tourist places like the crocodile farms and the early-morning floating-boat market. This is usually not the case if I conduct training at any American organization. The Thais were very polite, having continuous smiles on their faces, and in harmony with everyone around. Although the streets of Bangkok were almost always crowded by cars and motorcycles, I rarely came across a serious accident or a fight. They push for being first on the road but at the end they take care of each other. The Thai wai was something new for me and I had to learn its meaning and value in dealing with the Thais. On the last day of my stay and while I was greeting my host, I made a wai to her and I was very happy that she looked at me with a smile and said, "Farid, you have mastered the Thai wai." This understanding of the Thais gave me the chance to come back for more business.

Thai Cultural Values

During management training workshops with Thai managers, we asked participants to prioritize 20 values common among many cultures. These values were group harmony, competition, seniority, cooperation, privacy, openness, equality, formality, risk taking, reputation, freedom, family security, relationship, self-reliance, time, group consensus, authority, material possessions, spiritual enlightenment, and group achievement. We also asked the same questions to groups of Arab and American managers. The following table presents what these three groups indicated were their top five values from this list.

Thais	Americans	Arabs
Seniority	Equality	Seniority
Reputation	Freedom	Spirituality
Cooperation	Openness	Reputation
Authority	Self-Reliance	Family
Relationship	Cooperation	Authority

As noted in the Thai priorities versus those of Americans and Arabs, a culture clash will clearly exist between Thais and Americans more than perhaps between Thais and Arabs. Seniority, reputation, and authority are high values for both Arabs and Thais but not with the Americans. This is in contrast to the American top values of equality, freedom, openness, and self-reliance.

In a business meeting, an American manager, with openness and self-reliance, will most likely have a culture clash with a Thai who looks for a senior person to lead and make final decisions. These differences will have an impact on most communications, negotiations, persuasions, and daily business activities between Thais and other cultures. As the table indicates, to succeed with Thais, you must respect Thai seniority, adhere to its authority and keep your reputation on line. Following this, you must work with and build a network of cooperative relationships. Furthermore, keep the following in mind when dealing with Thais:

- **Thais value the kingdom and serve the king.**
  Thais are generally patriotic people. While they are a developing nation striving to balance industrialism with an agrarian history, their political system has been in place for centuries. Citizens of Thailand value their system, and the king is the main core of it. Be certain not to disrespect the monarchy. Thais who criticize the king openly may receive severe punishments. But despite this reverence for the king, the democratic element of Thai politics is always present. The dual nature of the Thai system, since the country is in some ways a factioned democracy and in other ways a monarchy, in some ways resembles the British system of parliamentary monarchy. It is called constitutional democracy.

- **Respect for seniority is a top Thai value.**
  Thai status is more often related to earned religious merit, such as being a monk; high positions in business or government; education level; age; and the place in one's family. Remember this, especially when dealing with government and corporate officials. You will find, for example, that if you are an expatriate manager working in Thailand, your employees will ask you to help them solve their problems and alleviate their concerns. In this way, they are showing you their respect for your seniority, authority, and reputation by asking you for your help. If you are dealing with a senior Thai, show respect to them as well.

- **Most Thais are polite, nonhostile, and accommodating.**
  Politeness is valued highly in the Thai culture, especially when dealing with foreign guests. As a foreign manager working in Thailand, chances are you will be politely respected and liked by your staff and your Thai supervisors. Thais have a history of working with each other harmoniously, and this tendency toward communal growth and achievement will not suddenly stop with you. In fact, you will probably find yourself invited to many Thai social occasions and functions. Be sure not to offend your cohorts, however. Just because they are friendly and accommodating does not mean that they will easily take a snub. The old rules prevail: treat others the way you would like to be treated yourself. Try to reciprocate their politeness, smiles, and accommodation in a friendly manner and you will be in for great treats.
- **Thais are soft-spoken.**
  In speaking with Thais, do not act or speak like most Arabs or South Americans with high tones of voice and body language. This will put off your Thai partners. Thais are soft spoken due to their value of harmony and accommodation. While with an American, for example, you may be used to a friendly argument to get your point across, your Thai worker will definitely be more inclined to resolve conflict indirectly and in a peaceful manner. The tendency to argue with you will be less prevalent, so be careful not to misread what your Thai employees are saying to you. You will have to read between the non-verbal and verbal lines in order to know their true opinions. If you raise your voice at someone in your team, you will be out of the group's musical note!
- **Thais are not very materialistic.**
  As reflected in the teaching of Buddha and presented in a Thai monk's nonmaterialistic life, most Thais are less materialistic than others. Therefore, the materialist imperatives one sees evident in historically capitalist countries—such as the United States or even in the changing former countries of the Soviet Empire—are essentially absent. But don't fool yourself into believing that you will easily pull a fast one over a Thai businessperson. Doing so will only cause you eventual pain when you realize that your Thai partner, following the dictates of the Thai culture and background, is just as astute as you are. They are just guided more by spiritual feelings than by material demands.

Meeting Thais

Let us now see how ready are you to meet your next Thai partner with the following quiz:

1. A Thai "wai" can mean:
   a. "Hello."
   b. A show of respect to a superior.
   c. An expression of anger.
   d. An expression of inequality.

The wai is putting both palms together and holding them toward your chest. The wai is very important in Thailand. It is not simply a way of saying hello without saying a word. It is merely an action of respect and expression of inequality between people, overusing it devalues its meaning. Wais are appropriate to give to monks, the king, elders, and bosses. Handshakes are usually between equals. The inferior always initiates the wai. The superior may or may not return it. Watch for the "wai" level of the hand toward the head. It indicates the level of respect to others. The king does not wai his subjects unless they are monks. Do not wai servants, laborers, children, or other people of an obviously lower social status than your own.

2. A Thai smile can be used to:
   a. Excuse a small inconvenience.
   b. Thank someone for a small service.
   c. Return the wai of children.
   d. All of the above.

A Thai smile can be used as a powerful way to excuse oneself from embarrassments to others. It can be also used in appreciation for good service at a restaurant or shop. For children, a wai is not expected but a nice smile on the face will make that child happy for some time. A Thai's smile shows friendliness, not friendship. A smile or a wai is usually the correct gesture for repairing minor breaches of etiquette. It can also be used to excuse conduct that will require elaborate explanation and possibly monetary compensation. A smile can also demonstrate your embarrassment and defuse a potentially explosive situation. This is explained in the following personal tale.

During one of my trips to Thailand and while walking on the streets of Bangkok, I noticed that a man on a bicycle had accidentally hit a pedestrian. At that time, I expected a fight and an argument to start. I sped up to watch the expected fight. Instead, I saw the man on the bicycle stop and humbly give the other person a high wai. Immediately, the person that was hit nodded his head with a smile back accepting the apology and each went on his way. A crisis was defused within a couple of minutes because of the wai and a smile!

3. You should address Han Kittichanan, your Thai business person, by:
   a. Khun
   b. Khun Han
   c. Than
   d. Nai

Adults (Mr., Mrs., Miss) should be addressed as Khun followed by the person's first name, unless a title is used. Nai is used for businesspeople, and Than is reserved for dignitaries or monks.

Choose the most appropriate way (a, b, c, d, e) to respond to a Thai person in each of the following situations:

1. You have received some change from your taxi driver.
2. A monk gives you water and food.
3. You were greeted by a smiling hotel boy who opened the door for you.
4. A thank you from a street seller after you bought something from him.
5. Your maid saved your son from a wandering snake in the house.
6. A stranger in the street showed you the hotel you were looking for.
7. An immigration officer stamped your passport upon entry at Bangkok airport.

   a. No reaction
   b. Smile
   c. Smile and nod
   d. Verbal thank you
   e. Wai

Answers:

1. a or b; 2. e; 3. a or b; 4. b or c; 5. d; 6. c or d; 7. d or e

The first meeting with a Thai businessperson is usually for introductions only: do not go directly into business matters. Business cards are not as important as in other cultures and are usually used for reference. Thais will assess your relative status by your education, social connections, wealth, wage, occupation, age, family, car and house. They usually care less about your race, religious affiliation, friendliness, or even your ability to speak Thai.

Remember that Thai protocol begins and ends with a smile, which is particularly effusive in Thailand. The image of foreigners (called Farang) is of tall, hairy people who keep their eyes only on the bottom line. Thais show their respect and humility by not being at a higher level than a senior person. The culture rule requires that you lower your body slightly when passing between or in front of a seated senior adult.

In social encounters with Thais, the socially inferior person takes on a physically inferior position. The top of the head is the most important part in Thai culture, while the feet are the least important and dirtiest part. The worst insult is to point at a Thai's sacred head with your lowly foot. Do not touch anyone's head, even those of young children, as a way of caring as some cultures will allow.

Thais usually greet someone with the word "Sawaddee," an equivalent of "hello." Younger person greets first (seniority). Ask about each other's background (relationship). Avoid direct eye contact (threatening attitude). Use polite words only—no slang. Do not criticize directly, or ask each other's age. Do not comment on physical appearance or point fingers at other people.

In meetings with Thais, you must exhibit leadership, have set objectives, be prepared, encourage participation, maintain harmony, and assign and secure commitments. Elder or senior Thais will usually start conversations and younger Thais will follow their lead. Younger Thais compliment older Thais. After introductions, younger Thais excuse themselves for the time being and thank their elders, and "wai." Thais expect direction, as well as generosity, from their boss and they tend to be low-risk takers. Refrain from touching in ways that may be common to most South Americans or Arabs. Hugging, hand shaking, and friendly slaps on the back, are not necessary or desired when dealing with Thais. Point as little as possible. Thais dress in strict accordance to rank and place in society.

On the Phone with Thais

As director of purchasing for a Mexican textiles distributor, Richard Ortiz had recently heard rumors regarding a Thai manufacturer who was going out of business and selling his stock at astonishingly low prices. Richard saw the possibility of amassing huge profits if he could arrange the purchase of a large amount of the product. Realizing that time was of the essence, Richard called the Thai company and asked to speak with the head of sales. The secretary informed him that as the company was going out of business, the staff had been reduced and the person he was to talk to was the owner himself, who was out at the moment. The secretary took Richard's number and told him she would have the owner call him upon returning.

When the Thai owner called back, Richard was in a meeting with his boss. His secretary took the call. Richard had informed her that the call was extremely important and that she was to keep the Thai on the line at all costs. She was to interrupt the meeting with the boss in order to get him on the line, which she did.

But the meeting was on a different floor of the building and the secretary had to call the boss' assistant, who then had to fetch Richard. Understandably, the logistics of the process took a while. By the time Richard returned to his office, it had been over five minutes since his secretary had taken the call.

Richard picked up the receiver and found no one on the other end of the line. The Thai had hung up. Richard called back, but was informed that the Thai owner would be busy for the rest of the day. By the end of the week, when the owner was finally contacted, all of the products had been sold. Richard had lost a great opportunity. He learned the hard way that Thais don't like to be put on hold.

- Thais don't normally conduct business over the telephone.
- Thais use the telephone to introduce themselves or to make appointments.
- Telephone conversations start by saying "Sawaddee."
- The person who answers the telephone will identify the company and then will ask to whom the caller wishes to speak.
- Give your name and your company's name.
- Conclude by once again saying "Sawaddee."

Do's

- Answer politely.
- Be willing to provide information.
- Identify yourself.
- Take messages.

- Use short, clear, and simple language.
- Talk softly.
- Use recorded music when putting a caller on hold.

Don'ts

- Be rude.
- Simply hang up if unable to provide information.
- Keep the caller waiting.
- Speak quickly and loudly.

Writing to Thais

To give you an insight into Thai culture and how to enhance your written communication with them, following are examples of business letters sent by middle managers in Thai corporations.

Dear Dr. Farid,

I am sorry for not writing to you sooner. I was out for a minor oper-ation and was busy with everything. I received the book, Multicultural Management: New Skills for Global Success. *Thank you so much. It is very good. How is everything with you? This year we have very few courses in English. The management has cut down the training budget for staff abroad. They only allow the staff to attend courses that con-cern their technical skills.*

When you come to Bangkok, please come to our office and have lunch with me. Thank you again for everything including the book. You are very kind.

Hope to see you soon.
Yours sincerely,

M. D.

Here is another letter:

Dear Sir,

May I have this opportunity to introduce myself? My name is RP, Corporate Affairs Division Manager in charge of the training for our organization's staff members.

With regards to your proposed program budget, I very much appreciate your offer; however, as we mentioned in our fax to you, the fee exceeds our standard fee. We recognize your program as a valuable course for us, so we are now assembling 15 participants to prepare for September 14 - 15 and would like to ask for a special fee of $10,000. We will also host your stay in Bangkok.

Please fax me directly if we can reach a satisfactory agreement on this offer so that we can set the final program outline.

Thank you very much. I'm looking forward to hearing from you.

Sincerely yours,
RP

And one more:

Hello Dr. Farid,

Sorry for not replying sooner. We had two religious holidays last Tuesday and Wednesday. Thank you very much for your message. I have not yet seen your new book on Multicultural Management 2000. *I certainly would appreciate it if you would send me a copy to my home. Should you be visiting Thailand in the near future, please let me know.*

Cheers,

Dr. S

From the previous letters, you can note Thai politeness—an apologetic and peaceful approach. No threats, demands, or directness. They refer to authority, seniority, and appeal to your generosity and spirit of compromise. They show their accommodation and hospitality all the way. In following up with them, you can remind them of the issues and ask politely for the return of your request. Be patient and persuasive, but persistent; smooth sailing will do it. You should definitely not exhibit a threatening attitude. Following are further tips and taboos to keep in mind when writing to Thai contacts. Remember the following:

Do's

- Use titles with names.
- Open by explaining the reason for writing.
- Use polite, formal language.
- Use many adjectives.

- End the letter with "respectfully."
- Emphasize corporate rather than individual identity.

Don'ts

- Abbreviate.
- Use casual language.
- Immediately get to the point.
- Use the same word repetitively.
- Write short sentences.

Conducting Meetings and Presentations

If you are a foreign manager working in Thailand, you will have to adapt to the Thai culture in conducting meetings and presentations. Here are insights on some of these differences and how to overcome them.

You Should:	Because Thais:
Be a leader	Mostly look for a leader
Be on time	Sometimes are late
Set objectives	May stray from the agenda
Be prepared	May come unprepared
Encourage participation	Sit quietly until invited
Maintain harmony	Avoid conflict
Make commitments	May like to postpone

- **Thais do not respond to or expect open questions, especially in formal meetings.**
  Thais are relatively soft-spoken by Western standards, and maintain this trait during business meetings. If you do not follow this norm, you might find yourself quite embarrassed when your Thai colleagues fail to respond to your inquiries. Direct your question to individuals, preferably first to a senior person, rather than to the group. Try to engage other participants to initiate team discussion. If you think someone does not fully understand, repeat yourself using different sentence patterns, but do not raise your voice. Your success will stem from having your audience engaged with you. Otherwise, you will look like you are talking to yourself without true feedback and no solid commitments to follow up on.

- **Prepare for the subject and make announcements early.**
Preparing for your meeting should be second nature (although we all have experienced meetings in which an unprepared peer fumbled around trying to make up for a lack of content), but take careful note of giving early announcements. You may find yourself alone in a room if you try to schedule a meeting with little advance notice. Colleagues may not even be in the office the day of the meeting or presentation. Present the agenda and the topics at the beginning of the meeting. This is most certainly true when making presentations to potential clients and also when conducting meetings with your employees.
- **The leader of the meeting presents the subject.**
As a result of this cultural norm, do not delegate presentation duties to anyone below you in rank. If you are the senior person, your ideas will be expected to be presented by you alone. Expect little participation from meeting members, even during opening discussions. This echoes the first tip of this list, that Thais do not ask many questions during meetings. Thais do not like to be singled out. They also do not offer much feedback openly, so don't be offended or discouraged. Superiors sit in front, inferiors in back. Remember not to point to someone with your finger and especially not with your foot.

Persuading Thais

- **In one-on-one conversations, Thais will be open with you if they feel that they are trusted.**
Trust is always a key to success in business, and this is quite true in Thailand. Once you are trusted, you will find the rewards of your trust. You may begin to learn a lot about other players in a negotiation, or, if you are managing in Thailand, you may find out some of the inside information that will allow you to meet the needs of your employees and be a more successful manager. Thais want to socialize first. Americans can be seen as compulsive about logic, facts, and precise figures. Thais are more concerned with general goals, human relationships and harmony. Your seniority and reputation, as well as your generosity, will open the door for many successful deals for you. Be honest and speak your mind. Be yourself and people will respect you for it. Learn the Thai smile and relax. You will get there.

- **Don't get into an open conflict with a Thai; show your dissatisfaction indirectly.**

   An open conflict is an easy way to give deals, in their early stages, a turn for the worse. As mentioned, most Thais are nonresistant, non-hostile, and accommodating. Avoid doing or saying anything to cause offense. Be generous and do as most Thais do, smile and take it easy. Thais may withdraw from aggressive situations. While an aggressive style may work with Americans, it most likely will fail with Thais. The American used-car salesman who overtly pushes for an immediate sale would probably go hungry in Thailand. To enhance your success with Thais, you should never do or say anything offensive or make them lose face, especially in public.

- **When negotiating: propose, follow up, compromise.**

   When negotiating with Thais, you must propose, follow up, be patient, and compromise. Don't forget that you want to make a sale. There is nothing wrong with prodding your partner into making a decision, as long as the prodding does not overstep the Thai bounds of accommodation, nonhostility, and compromise. And be sure to give time for decision making. They have to present a proposal to the boss who will make the final decision after staff consultation. Keep your line of communication open to resolve any apparent delay in harmony. These steps may be universal to virtually all negotiations, but when dealing with Thai partners, take special note of the last verb: compromise. The ability to compromise will win you your Thai clients. Compromise is what Thais look for in long-term relationships, and offering it to them may very well allow you to win a new client that will stick with you for a long time to come. If you give in a little at the beginning, it will show your generosity and will place you in the boss's shoes.

- **Encourage Thais to be more risk takers.**

   Some Thais may like to postpone decisions. You have to make sure that this inclination does not hurt your business. As a result, your presentation or proposal to prospective Thai clients or partners should emphasize the concrete returns of their investment. Expect a lot of discussion if certain areas of your proposal are by nature risky. Try to make them trust you, by presenting yourself as a partner seeking long-term relationships and that you can be depended on. As a superior, show them that you will take care of them should any problems occur. They need to view you, not only as a partner, but also as a tutor and patron.

Encountering the Thai Negotiators

The following table presents some guidelines on how to encounter the Thai negotiators.

	Thais	You
Group Composition	2–3 Middle managers.	Bring 1–2 higher level managers for a more respected position.
Establishing Rapport	Set a tone of respect, accommodations, soft tone.	Accept their style, but take a leadership position.
Information Exchange	Give lead to others to propose, reveal little; may sound passive.	Be generous in your initial information but ask for similar ones.
Persuasion Tools	Will build on your leadership, seniority, being generous in concessions. Use time through ceremonies, such as dining and visits to temples.	Display your expertise and credibility. Trust will take care of attitude to gain their concession.
Decision Process	Engage in fewer bargaining processes until expected compromise is reached.	Be patient and willing to compromise. Encourage their risk taking by trusting you.
Decision Makers	Senior manager makes decision.	Identify and focus on decision makers and make them feel that they can trust you.

- **Dealing with government organizations**
  Most Thai government organizations have vertical hierarchical systems designed to fulfill cultural needs for authority and conformity. Most problems are passed up the ladder for resolution by the person expected to know all aspects of the organization's operations: the boss. The patron or superior provides protection, influence, and favors. The subordinates provide services and personal loyalty to the patron. A powerful patron may have several clients, but a client has

only one patron. A Thai of lower status does not usually offer unsolicited opinions. A manager may not be able to get any opinion at all from him/her. Relationships between superiors and subordinates are formal and authoritarian. Bosses are expected to be benevolent and paternalistic. They will spend a lot of time at employees' weddings, birthday parties, and funerals. A Thai boss may delay a decision until a problem resolves itself, especially if the decision would cause confrontation or disagreement. Thais would rather lose time than face. Once a decision has been made, it may be difficult to implement. Most Thais are not willing to be led too far too quickly. Thais are more concerned with human relations and general goals than Americans, who can be compulsive about logic, facts, precise figures, and bottom lines.

Working with Thais

Take the following quiz to test your knowledge of Thai business culture:

1. You are in charge of an important project in Thailand and found out that the project is behind schedule. You have summoned the Thai manager and his team for a review. You would:
   a. Tell them openly that if they do not meet the deadline they will be all fired.
   b. Ask them collectively to explain the reasons for the delay.
   c. Point out to the manager and ask him for explanation.
   d. Praise the team for overcoming the last problems and point out the great opportunity ahead of them if they team up to complete the project on time.

Considering your past knowledge about Thais, one must not openly single out or criticize a Thai publicly, especially a manager. Do not even present a threatening attitude or firing; otherwise, everyone will strike the next day. As mentioned earlier, Thais receive open criticism as a form of violence because it destroys social harmony. You probably want to start with praising them for past accomplishments (d) and then open a forum where you can listen and guide them to overcome problems that come up. Show your leadership and readiness to listen to them and affirm your support to their proposed action to overcome any stated problems.

2. If a Thai superior is criticized by an employee, she/he will most
   likely:
   a. Respond by removing the source of criticism.
   b. Offer nothing to the person criticizing him.
   c. Demote or transfer of the criticizer.
   d. All of the above.

Never openly criticize your boss. The boss will probably try to
remove the sources of criticism but later you will find yourself being
transferred to the back door of the organization. If you have a complaint, you should take time to explain it to the boss on a one-to-one
basis and seek their input to overcome your problem. If you make the
Thai boss happy, you will be more than happy, too. Remember, the
boss has many employees but you have only one boss.

3. A successful foreign manager in Thailand must try to:
   a. Become popular with workers and subordinates.
   b. Encourage teamwork.
   c. Show the workers how to do their jobs.
   d. Know how to criticize by praising and punishing through
      kindness.

All of the above are important criteria for a successful manager in
Thailand. Helping your employees and encouraging teamwork, giving
10 praises and one complaint and making everyone like you. They will
have Thai wais and smiles for you all the time. Be friendly by all means,
but without expecting to become close friends.

In training Thais, keep to a time schedule. A training schedule
should not exceed daily working hours. Training materials should be
simple; use pictures, graphs, local examples and case studies. Allow for
informal group discussions as Thais like to work in teams. Question
individuals directly in order to check their understanding. Use an off-
site training environment, especially for executives to keep them far
from daily job disturbances. Ask them to put all telephones and pagers
off to minimize outside disturbance.

Thai workers would expect generosity and gratuity from the senior
person. In return, they will serve you with loyalty. They expect that
decisions are made by the manager. Before assigning tasks to your Thai
workers, take the time to learn their strengths and weaknesses. They
expect clear direction from the boss and you must give them time to
respond to you. Give them recognition for jobs well done. Provide

good working conditions, give them more authority, and offer them a bonus plan if profits are high. Offer entertainment, leisure, and sports activities to enhance their team work. Praise workers who perform well during group meetings. Thais love flattery.

Motivate by showing respect—they will then respect you as a senior person. Remember, generosity is the sign of an important person—don't be mean.

A praise note signed by the big boss and copied through the hierarchy channel will make your Thai subordinates motivated for a long time. Thais will work hard when the benefits are obvious and immediate but will seldom work hard for deferred rewards. They do not work efficiently unless they are happy with the work situation. They view work as a social function.

If you have to criticize a Thai, avoid public confrontation at all costs. See the person yourself. Pick the best time for the talk, preferably when things are going well, never when you are angry. Balance any criticism with praise. Be indirect and diplomatic, and offer suggestions if possible. Be nice at all times and buy lots of cream cakes for everyone. Being nice, rather than asserting your authority, nearly always pays off. Since workers are considered junior members of the corporate family, few are fired. The best way to handle Thai employees is to be sincerely interested in them and their families, socialize outside of business hours, listen patiently, criticize privately, train carefully, use intermediaries to save face, and fire someone only as a last resort. Above all, show respect for your employees. Thais consider their personal lives as the center of their identity. They think and talk about their personal lives when they are on the job.

Social Etiquette

1. You and your family have just enjoyed a good dinner in a Thai restaurant. The waitress has brought you back small change. You pick it up and leave a tip. She looks at you with a smile and gives you a "wai" gesture before picking up the tip. You should:
   a. Stand up and return the wai.
   b. Ignore her and leave.
   c. Smile and continue talking to your dinner guest.
   d. Put another 50 baht on the table.

Remember that Thais respect seniority. Do not wai back. In this situation, a smile may deserve an extra 10 baht and a smile back from you while leaving. You will be assured that your hot and spicy Thai soup will be ready for you as soon as you visit again.

2. You are sitting in a crowded bus with your five-year-old son in a funride through the streets of Bangkok. An old man gets into the crowded bus and finds no empty seat. You should:
   a. Ask your son to give up his seat.
   b. Look through the window and do nothing.
   c. Give the old man your seat.
   d. Take your son on your lap and give the man your son's seat.

As mentioned before, generosity is highly valued in Thailand. Ignoring the situation may not look like a good idea. It is best to give up your seat and invite the old man to sit in it. You will be assured to get a wide smile and a high wai!

Here is further social etiquette that may earn you many wais:

- If you invite someone to your house, they expect to eat there.
- Do not wave your hands in an attempt to make yourself understood.
- Do not clap, snap your fingers, or hiss at wait staff. The correct way to get their attention is to beckon, palm down, moving the fingers rapidly toward yourself.
- A speedy taxi will slam on its brakes if you glance in its direction.
- When receiving a gift, set it aside to open later. Gifts are to be opened in private and not in front of the giver.
- Thais do not usually acknowledge gifts sent by mail or messenger, so deliver them in person.
- Legs should not be crossed when sitting on the floor or in a chair in the presence of a monk.
- Only wear black at funerals. Do not wear them in business or social functions.

Summary

The people of Thailand are courteous and soft-spoken. Their country is a growing agrarian state slowly accumulating the capital and resources of an industrialized nation. When doing business with Thais, you will certainly not encounter as many barriers as you would if dealing with Japanese, and fewer governmental restrictions will materialize than when working with the Chinese. It is still easy, however, to make cultural mistakes. Remember to respect their culture in every way. Be generous in dealing with Thais. You are looked upon as a boss. If you are in doubt, just ask them how and why, and do not assume. They will be most happy to inform you about their lovely culture. Compare what you have learned about Thais with other cultures in the book and pick the main differences to keep in mind during your next encounter with your Thai partner and friends.

Flattering the Arabs

7

When is it appropriate to accept an extravagant gift from
an Arab client?
How much time should you plan to spend on your first trip
to an Arab country?
How do you persuade your Arab client to accept your offer?

Major large organizations such as Mobil Oil, GE, IBM and others
have been relatively successful in the Middle East because of their early
entry into the Arab market. It took these companies many years to
establish a foothold in the Arab world. With expanding opportunities
for many other large, medium, and small size enterprises in the Middle
East, however, and with a new generation of business executives leading Arab companies, the need for a new look at how to succeed with
today's Arabs is necessary. This chapter will guide you through Arab
business and social values, and show you how to master your negotiations with Arab business partners.

Test Your Skills Dealing with Arabs

Answer the following true-or-false statements using your current
knowledge of Arab business culture.

___ 1. In general, Arabs do not like bargaining.
___ 2. Religion has a significant impact on most decisions in the Arab culture.
___ 3. Compliments and well-presented flattery are generally ignored.
___ 4. Most Arabs value eloquence.
___ 5. Arab businesspeople separate business from personal friendships.
___ 6. Your work experience will be enough when dealing with Arab businesspeople.
___ 7. It's courteous to shake hands every time you meet your Arab friend.
___ 8. Social status and distinctions are very important in Arab society.
___ 9. Expressions of open disagreement are desirable.
___ 10. Gifts should be opened in the presence of the giver.

Most Appropriate Answers:

1. F; 2. F; 3. F; 4. T; 5. F; 6. F; 7. T; 8. T; 9. F; 10. F

Mr. Bell Meets with Arabs: A Cautionary Tale

The following tale exemplifies the cultural challenges facing businesspeople trying to enter the Arab market and illustrates the reasons for their frequent failure (no matter how high the quality or how low the price of their products). John Bell, a sales manager for Watermovers, a mid-size U.S. producer of irrigation supplies and equipment, had traveled to Cairo for the first time. His mission was to introduce a new product line to Hassan, president of Sinai Utility, thereby establishing a market for Watermovers in the Sinai desert.

An hour before his 9 a.m. appointment with Hassan, Bell called the Egyptian executive's office to confirm his appointment. Hassan's secretary politely welcomed him, and said that she would call him back as soon as her boss arrived in the office. By 10 a.m., however, Bell had not been contacted, so he called the office once again. This time, a different person answered the phone and informed Bell that Hassan was still in a local marketplace, and would call him back right away. Finally, at 11 a.m., Hassan's personal secretary called to inform Bell that Hassan would be happy to have tea with Bell the following morning at 10 a.m. A disappointed Bell hung up the phone, frustrated that he had wasted an entire day and had nothing more significant to show for it than an appointment for morning tea.

The events of the next day were to prove equally frustrating for Bell. When he arrived punctually at 10 a.m., he accepted a cup of coffee from Hassan's secretary. After keeping Bell waiting for 15 minutes, Hassan finally entered the lobby, accompanied by two Western businessmen. Hassan greeted Bell with open arms, but Bell was unsure whether this was an invitation for a hug or a handshake, so he responded with a conservative offer of his hand.

Hassan invited his three visitors into the office and offered them all coffee. Bell refused the offer, saying that he had just drunk two cups, and was now ready to give a presentation of his company's new product line. Time was of the essence. Still unprepared to discuss business, however, Hassan asked Bell about his trip—in particular about his impressions of Cairo's world-famous Egyptian Museum. Bell responded by saying that it had been a long trip from America, and that he had stayed in his hotel the entire first day to rest after the 20-hour flight from the United States.

Hassan surprised Bell still again when he then began to ask his other Western guests about the prices of their products. When the discussion turned to the subject of Bell's products and his company's potential commission, the American remained uneasy with the setting. He had expected a one-on-one meeting, and it made him uncomfortable to discuss such matters in the presence of other businesspeople.

Bell's mood hardly improved when Hassan informed him that he could make a more formal presentation in two days to both Sinai Utility's technical director and marketing manager. Disappointed by the unexpected delay, Bell was finally beginning to understand that he would have to slow down when discussing matters of business in the Arab world.

Two days later, Bell arrived at Hassan's office fully prepared for a 9 a.m. meeting with the Egyptian company's technical staff. When he entered the company's conference room, though, he was surprised to discover 20, mostly young, Egyptians awaiting his presentation. Bell had expected only three or four people!

The presentation went poorly. Bell began by discussing his company's background for 15 minutes. When he showed some of Watermover's products, the crowd moved in so close to him to look at the products that he became uncomfortable; he had expected the technicians to study the technical manuals he had provided, rather than to cluster so tightly around him. Moments later, he was shocked when a young Egyptian with a Ph.D. from University of California at Berkeley questioned him on product specifications Bell had neglected to study.

At the end of the presentation, Bell was escorted into Hassan's office and asked to sit beside the president. Still hopeful, Bell asked if the Egyptian would like to place an order. Hassan responded courteously, "*Insha Allah* [by God's will], we will do some business." Unfamiliar with this common Arabic phrase, Bell was uncertain whether this meant yes or no.

When the meeting ended, Hassan told Bell that his company would write soon with "some good news." The American smiled and left the office elated at the prospect of an important contract despite all his frustrations. Not surprisingly, however, several months passed and Bell had yet to hear a word of response from Sinai Utility despite two written requests. It became obvious that he was not going to hear anything from the Egyptian company.

What went wrong? Bell's chances of succeeding with Sinai Utility would have improved had he been aware of the following:

- Commitment and time schedules are looser in the Arab world than in the West. Bell would have done well to leave ample time in his schedule for inevitable delays.
- Establishing rapport with an Arab requires a longer period of time and much more small talk. If at all possible, Bell should have been prepared to talk at length about the Egyptian Museum, or if he couldn't make a visit, he could have spoken about Arab culture and society with sufficient sincerity to establish a rapport with the Arab executive.
- Although Arabs tend to communicate with more than one executive in business meetings, this in no way diminishes their desire to show warm hospitality and generous accommodation to each executive. Had Bell been prepared for this, he would have maintained his good spirits and not further alienated Hassan.
- The younger generation of Arab businesspeople are often educated in the West and can be expected to ask detailed questions about the products their companies may buy from the West. Consciously or otherwise, Bell went to Egypt expecting a less rigorous inquiry into the quality of his products and their suitability to local conditions than he might have expected in the United States. His surprise at the quality of the questioning only magnified the damage caused by his lack of technical preparation.
- In Arab countries, closing a sale takes place in an informal setting, thus requiring more time and energy to consummate than in most Western societies. A contract may be agreed on at midnight after a long dinner party, for instance.

Arab Cultural Values

Let us further examine how some of Mr. Bell's cultural clashes can be explained. In our management training sessions, we asked groups of Arab, American, and Thai managers to list their top five values. The following table presents the responses of these three groups.

Arab	Americans	German
Seniority	Equality	Time
Spirituality	Freedom	Competition
Reputation	Openness	Privacy
Family	Self-Reliance	Openness
Authority	Cooperation	Reputation

In order to succeed in your dealings with Arabs, you must show respect for the seniority of the father, boss, and leaders of the country. Bosses again will use their authority to dictate what they believe is the way to go, and their reputation will be on the line if they fail. Others will depend on the boss, who therefore often has to make decisions with minimal information.

These values will clash with those of most Americans. On their first encounter, the Americans' sense of equality and freedom will clash with the Arabs' emphasis on seniority and authority. American self-reliance will clash with the Arab dependence on the boss. On the other side, note how the German desire for punctuality and timeliness will clash with Arabs who believe they have plenty of time to spare. The German value of privacy will oppose the Arab value of hospitality. Keep these differences in mind when you initiate your next encounter with Arabs.

An American attending a business conference, for example, is likely to introduce themself to an Arab businessperson, then quickly walk off to talk to other executives, declining invitations to have some coffee during the break. The American doesn't have enough time for more than a brief chat with anyone; their direct objective is to make as many contacts as possible. Arab businesspeople are put off by this behavior because Arabs place a high value on building personal relationships; they want to get to know someone fairly well before discussing business matters. Arabs hold a much longer-term view of time; they don't shun spending months or years on building personal relationships and trust.

Even the "simple" subject of physical distance can create misunderstandings. An Arab executive may well stand closer to you than would an American or a German. While this is the Arab's way of expressing personal warmth and hospitality, most Westerners and those from other cultures will retreat, because they feel their comfort zone of personal space has been invaded. As also pointed out, Arabs emphasize spirituality as one of their high values. For instance, when dealing with Arab Muslims, one must understand the basic pillars of Islam and how these influence Arab beliefs, behaviors, and decision-making processes. There are five pillars of Islam. First, one must believe that God exists and that Mohammed is his last prophet. The second pillar is that Muslims must worship God by performing five daily prayers. When dealing with Arab Muslims, you must show respect for their spirituality and allow them to perform their duty toward God during these times of prayer. Some Westerners may find it frustrating when Arabs ask for a break to pray.

The third pillar is the fast during the month of Ramadan. Muslims will sustain from water, food, and smoking from dawn to sunset during this month. During this month, most business activities in Arab countries slow down. Therefore, do not push your business too much during Ramadan. Most workers will leave work early to break their fast at sunset with family and friends.

The fourth pillar is to share some of their income with those who need it (Zakat). This is similar to a government tax, but it is the responsibility of every Muslim to give it to the needy in his community. The fifth and last pillar is to perform the Haj by visiting the holy city of Mecca in Saudi Arabia. This is required only once in a lifetime. Again, many businesspeople will be involved in the Haj and business may slow down during this time.

Meeting Arabs

In your personal meetings with Arabs, be sure to employ extravagant flattery. Arabs are used to hyperbolic praise and are not embarrassed by the sort of talk that would make most Westerners blush. They may not necessarily believe such praise, but nevertheless enjoy and expect it.

Try the following quiz on Arab business culture:

1.   Your Arab acquaintance asks, "How are you doing?" She expects you to respond with:

a. "I'm having a bad day, but happy to meet you."
b. "Fine, thank you."
c. "Sorry, but I'm in a rush."
d. "I've been sick all day."

When asked how you are, you should answer honestly (a) and, in return, inquire after the person's well-being, finally asking "What do you do?" This may open the door for many other business opportunities and expand your contacts among other Arab business executives. Flatter them back and you will be delighted with their accommodation. Don't respond automatically with the American answer, "fine, thank you."

2. Upon exchanging business cards with an Arab executive, he will most likely:
    a. Ask you to explain the meaning of your name.
    b. Admire the quality of your business card and title.
    c. Look at your title to see if you're an important person in your company.
    d. Ask what you do.

Arabs will find a way to show their eloquence by (b) admiring the color or quality of your business card or your title. Remember, you must reciprocate by remarking on their importance within their own company and society. Of course, they will look seriously at the title presented on your card and pay respect by referring to you appropriately, i.e., as Dr. Farid, or Mr. President. When Arabs are being introduced in public, their names are preceded by their accumulated titles: Prof. Dr. Engineer Farid Elashmawi.

3. When talking with an Arab, you should:
    a. Stand a foot away from him.
    b. Stand two arm lengths away.
    c. Stand one arm length away.
    d. Avoid making eye contact.

Don't be surprised by the close proximity of Arabs to other people (a). Try to accept this as a way of showing hospitality; they might even include physical contact, like patting your back. Accept Arab hugs and reciprocate, for this is a positive show of friendship. Arabs will also use direct eye contact as a way of showing their admiration and attentiveness. Don't be shy about reciprocating with a pat on the back at the appropriate moment in the discussion. Some Arabs can walk in the street hand in hand as a show of close, but not sexual, friendship.

4. When meeting with an Arab executive for the first time, you should:
   a. Hand your business card to him immediately.
   b. Wait for him to hand his business card to you.
   c. Just shake his hand without exchanging cards.
   d. Wait until the end of the meeting to give him your business card.

Don't rush to exchange business cards with Arabs as you are expected to do with the Japanese. Proceed with the exchange of information in order to first get to know the person. It's a good sign when (b) the Arab offers a business card to you first. The Arab is certainly interested in following up with you. In Arab culture, business cards don't have the same intrinsic value as in the Japanese or other cultures. However, if an Arab doesn't offer you a card, (d) give your own card to them at the end of the meeting.

On the Phone with Arabs

David McDonald, Director of International Marketing of Global Business, is preparing for his visit to Amman, Jordan, after a three-month negotiation with Mr. Abdullah, the director of International Imports. David is calling Abdullah to confirm his meeting with him next week.

David:	Abdullah, this is David McDonald from Global Business.
Abdullah:	Yes, David, it is very nice to hear your voice. Where are you calling from?
David:	I am in New York.
Abdullah:	Oh, you must be suffering from the snow storm that is sweeping across your lovely city.
David:	Thank you, Abdullah, but we are fine.
Abdullah:	When are you coming to our country?
David:	That is why I am calling. I will be in Amman next Sunday.

Abdullah:	We will all be waiting to meet you when you come and I will send my driver to pick you up from the airport.
David:	No need, Abdullah, I can rent a car or take a taxi.
Abdullah:	No, no, David, you are our guest and, by the way, do not forget the five samples I asked you about and also the computer for my son Amr.
David:	I will bring three samples only and the computer may be difficult for me to bring.
Abdullah:	Please, do your best and, *Insha Allah,* you will manage. Is your family coming with you?
David:	No, I am afraid they will not be able to join me as my son is still in school.
Abdullah:	I also plan to introduce you to my friends in the ministry and invite you to dinner with my family. But I hope you can give us the extra samples and the 20% discount I asked you for.
David:	I will do my best, Abdullah. I have to go now.
Abdullah:	Okay, have a safe landing in Amman.

The American has just one objective in mind: to confirm his visit. Abdullah exhibits his accommodation and hospitality but, in return, is negotiating with David for more free samples and an extra 20% discount. He pushes for this stating that he will introduce David to other businessmen. David intended his call to last under a minute, but it lasted much longer, and now he is left wondering what he will do about the free samples and Abdullah's son's computer.

In another situation, Mohamed, an Arab businessman, called a Swedish computer company to get a quote for 10,000 computers. Excited by the possibility of such a large sale, and the call from the Arab client, the Swedish salesman, Ulf, gave the Arab his bottom price. Mohamed told Ulf that the price of each computer was very attractive, and that he would contact him later in the week. Mohamed called him a few days later, and Ulf was astonished to discover that he only wanted to purchase 10 computers. Mohamed also requested that each computer be discounted by an additional 25 percent.

Ulf should not have given his bottom price to Mohamed. If Ulf had known that Arab buyers often exaggerate the quantity of products they wish to purchase in order to discover the seller's bottom price, he would have quoted a higher price.

Take the following tests to challenge your own cultural knowledge:

1. If you call your Arab partner, he will probably first:
   a. Ask when you will issue a letter of credit.
   b. Ask how your family is doing.
   c. Ask what he can do for you.
   d. Say that it's good to hear from you.

Don't rush to get down to business on the phone. Remember that hospitality is a key cultural value. Your partner will probably (d) say that it is good to hear from you and ask about your family, even if this partner has never met them. This is a sign that the Arab cares about you and, thus, your business. The Arab will probably move on to business by saying, "by the way, where is my order?"

2. At the end of your conversation with an Arab client, you should:
   a. Hang the phone up before he does.
   b. Allow him to hang the phone up before you do.
   c. Ask him if he needs anything else.
   d. Thank him for his continuous support.

If an Arab calls you, it is wise to (b) wait for the Arab to hang up first. Arabs don't appreciate it when a door is shut in their face. If you elaborate and thank Arabs for their continued support and offer to help them, their family, and their business in whatever way possible, they will certainly call you back.

3. You telephone an Arab client in Kuwait, but get his answering machine. You should:
   a. Hang up.
   b. Leave a message asking him to return your call.
   c. Call back later.
   d. Leave a detailed message.

It is important to leave a message that you missed your client, but you should (c) call back later. Your client will expect you to initiate the long-distance call, as he or she is the one paying you. Personal relationships are still important when conducting business in Arab countries. Leaving a message and expecting a call back is still not as common as in America.

4. When negotiating with an Arab client over the phone, you should promise:
   a. The lowest price.
   b. Free samples of your product.
   c. An all-expense-paid trip to California.
   d. All of the above.

Arabs will expect many free samples, the lowest price, and even an all-expense-paid trip to California to visit your company's headquarters. They expect to be treated like a king or queen at a five-star hotel with a red carpet. Consider this when figuring out your overhead costs. But remember, once trust is established, you may have an agent with a lot of connections that will protect you from future competitors.

Writing to an Arab

1. The salutation in your letter to Engineer Mohamed Saleh, Ph.D., the managing director of your Arab client should be written as:
   a. Dear Dr. Mohamed,
   b. Dear Mr. Saleh,
   c. Dear Mohamed,
   d. Dear Dr. Eng. Saleh,

Arabs will precede their names with every title imaginable. Don't fall into the informal American habit of addressing Arabs only by their first names. The most appropriate answer is (d) to use a respectful title in front of their first name to show both respect and friendship.

2. Persuading an Arab supplier in writing, you should mention:
   a. The deadline for submitting the quote.
   b. The commission he will receive on the deal.
   c. The problems that will occur if they don't make an immediate decision.
   d. That he will lose you as a client if he doesn't act immediately.

Avoid giving Arabs an ultimatum. Their time frame is probably different than yours. Focus on (b) the commission on the deal, and on the future benefits of dealing with you. Any problems are yours to resolve. Start persuading the Arabs from the beginning of the deal and don't ever wait for the last minute to ask for concessions.

3. What will speed up the delivery of a late shipment from an Arab supplier?
   a. Giving them a two-week ultimatum.
   b. Thanking them for their continued cooperation.
   c. Promising to secure another order with them.
   d. Asking the manager for a personal favor.

You may start by asking (d) for a personal favor and promising to place another order with the supplier if an extra effort will be made to speed up this delivery. Be sure to thank the supplier again eloquently if you receive a response, which will open the door for future cooperation.

4. The written correspondence of the Arabs tends to be far more lengthy than that of other countries because they:
   a. Want to ensure that you understand their request.
   b. Like to practice writing English.
   c. Have plenty of time on their hands.
   d. Try to fill their letters with as much flattery as possible.

Written correspondence with Arabs may seem unnecessarily long. Arabs usually start and end their letters with compliments and flattery. Adapt this style of your writing to a lengthier Arab style, or they may feel you are too abrupt.

Following is an example of an appropriate letter to an Arab businessperson:

Dear Prof. Dr. Eng. Abdel Salam Eldaly:

I was very happy to have met you yesterday. I hope that you and your family enjoyed your visit to California and arrived back home safely.

Our business discussion was very fruitful to expand our business relationship with you and your esteemed company. I look forward to receiving your first order, which will be delivered on schedule as I promised you.

In the meantime, please let me know if we can help you in your other bids to the government agency you mentioned.

Please accept my personal greeting to you, your family, and staff until we meet again very soon.

Sincerely,

Mike Bernard
VP International Marketing

Use of titles, greetings, flattery, and business expectations are all important when writing to Arabs.

Enhancing Relationships with Arabs

1. You are visiting the office of your potential Arab client for the first time. You should:
    a. Bring him a gift from your country.
    b. Wait until your second trip to give a gift.
    c. Give him a gift after he signs the contract.
    d. Send him a gift after you return home.

Arabs don't expect a gift from someone they don't know or have a relationship with. An appropriate time to give a gift would be (b) during the second visit, after a relationship has been established. The most appropriate gift would be something that can be displayed in the office or at home. Do not expect that it will be opened immediately.

2. During business discussions with an Arab businessman, he admires your Rolex watch. You should:
    a. Take it off and offer it to him.
    b. Offer to give it to him if he speeds up clearing the goods through customs.
    c. Thank him and, in return, admire something else of his.
    d. Bring him a similar one next time.

Arabs will show their eloquence by admiring the color of your tie, the style of your clothes, and the quality of your watch. They don't mean to imply that they would like it, so you should (c) thank them and, in return, admire something of theirs.

A German friend of mine told me the following story. He was once in a meeting with a wealthy Arab businessman and he noticed that the Arab was wearing a $5,000 Rolex watch. He remembered to admire the Arab's style, so he said, "Salleh, you're wearing a great watch." Salleh in return, took off the watch and handed it to the German, saying, "please, please, have it as I have another one like it." The German, remembering his notes about not refusing a gift from an Arab, kindly accepted the watch. An hour later, the German invited Salleh to lunch and, as they were getting in the German's Mercedes Benz 500c, Salleh, with a wide smile, said, "I really like your Mercedes." The German was choked and wondered if he would have to give his new $50,000 Mercedes to Salleh in return for the $5,000 Rolex! To avoid confusion such as this, be careful the next time you admire or accept a gift from an Arab!

3.   Your Arab business partner calls you from the Middle East to inform you of his visit to your office next week. He will expect you to say:
   a. "I will be waiting for you at the gate."
   b. "I will send the company limousine to pick you up."
   c. "My secretary, Nancy, will be waiting for you at the hotel."
   d. "Do you need any help at the airport?"

According to Arab hospitality, your partner will probably expect you to offer to help them with arranging transportation from the airport—thus, you should ask (d) if they need help with transportation. They would do the same for you by having their Mercedes and chauffeur waiting for you at the Cairo airport. Accommodation is highly valued in the Arab culture.

4.   As you enter an Arab office, your host offers you a cup of Arabic coffee. You just had two cups earlier, however. You say:
   a. "Thank you" and don't drink it.
   b. "No, thank you; I had many drinks this morning."
   c. "Your Arabic coffee makes me very nervous."
   d. "Thank you," and accept the coffee, taking small sips.

The Arab will offer you a cup of coffee as a demonstration of hospitality and sharing of common things that will lead to the discussion of business. Even if you had just drunk some coffee, you should (d) accept the coffee, take a sip and drink it slowly. The Arab will understand. If you and the Arab are smokers, you should reciprocate by offering them a cigarette from your own country.

5. While dealing with an Arab businessman, you notice that he is stalling his decision to make a purchase order. He is doing this because he:
   a. Wants to see if you will give him a gift before the deal is closed.
   b. Must check your references before making a decision.
   c. Sees stalling as a good method for bargaining over the price.
   d. Is waiting for the details of his personal commission allotment.

The best answers are (b) and (c). The Arab decision-making process takes longer, and is based on trust and intuition. Arabs may not seek as much technical information as compared to Japanese. They may also use time as a way of pressuring you to make a discount. Be patient when it is time for a decision with Arabs.

6. You are in an Arab businessman's lounge for one hour, nervously waiting for his arrival. His secretary notices and asks if you are enjoying visiting the city. You respond:
   a. I don't have time.
   b. I have seen many places like this before.
   c. I'm on a business trip.
   d. I enjoy seeing the historical places.

Don't be surprised at the hospitality and accommodation of Arab administrative staff while you are waiting for the boss. The secretary may strike up a conversation with you, inquiring about your country or the places you have visited in the city. Use your eloquence and show your admiration of their history and important places (d). This will put you at the head of the line waiting to see the boss. A nice gift to the Arab gatekeeper will help you open the gates for many businesses.

Establishing rapport with Arabs is an important process and can take much time. You will need to show generosity, maybe invite the boss and a couple of the executives to a dinner. They will think highly of you and you will have the opportunity to build friendship and trust. You will need to leave plenty of time in your schedule for delays and small talk, also to deal with matters that show up on the spur of the moment! Do not be frustrated if you did not have a one-on-one meeting with the Arab, and that your meeting was interrupted several times.

Arab executives are trained to deal with more than one issue at a time. They almost never stick to a set schedule. This aspect of the Arab business culture will be discussed further in the next section.

Conducting Meetings and Presentations

Sorry, the meeting is delayed

Stephen James, an American automobile spare parts dealer, wanted to expand his business to include the Middle East. He knew of several Ford dealership groups in the region and planned a trip to make presentations in Egypt, Jordan, and Lebanon. His assistant made appointments for him with the procurement manager of each corporation, allowing for two days in each city.

James first flew to Cairo. He arrived on Sunday night and rested well for his confirmed appointment with Mr. Sallim, the procurement manager, at 9 a.m. on Monday. At 8 a.m. James called Sallim's office for directions, but was told by the secretary that Sallim was out of the office for a couple of hours. They would need to reschedule the appointment for later that afternoon.

James called after lunch to confirm the appointment and was told that Sallim had been called to an urgent meeting with the Ministry of Transportation that would last the rest of the day. The secretary rescheduled the meeting for 9 a.m. the next morning. Frustrated by the delay, James spent the rest of the day in the Hilton hotel bar sharing his concerns with other foreign businessmen.

Fearing another delay, James decided to go directly to Sallim's office the next day. He did, only to learn that Sallim had yet to arrive. The secretary offered him some coffee to cool him off. When Sallim did arrive, at 10, he was with two other American salesmen. James was introduced to Sallim and the others, and the four gathered in Sallim's office. Sallim continued his discussions with the other Americans.

After these talks, which lasted until noon, Sallim invited everyone to lunch. The lunch was enjoyable, but lasted until 2:30 p.m. When Sallim and James finally returned to the office, they began discussing their possible joint venture. Soon after they began, however, Sallim was interrupted by telephone calls and his employees, who discussed some problems with him. By five o'clock, James and Sallim had yet to settle their affairs.

Sallim told James that he had an important dinner to attend, and asked James to return the next day for lunch so that they could settle the logistics of their plan. James didn't know how to proceed. He needed Sallim's business, because the Arab owned 10 dealerships throughout Egypt. In order to meet with him again, however, he would have to cancel his trip to Jordan and change his air travel plans.

James should have known about the Arab time frame. Most Americans will adhere to a definite schedule and plan. Arabs tend to take more time meeting their contacts in order to establish a trust-based relationship. In addition, Arab managers are trained to handle many issues at a time. James would have been in a better position if he had allocated more time for his trip and focused initially on establishing a friendly relationship with Sallim.

The following tests illustrate different business situations in dealing with Arabs:

1. You are in an Arab businessman's office making a short presentation. Another guest suddenly enters. You should:
   a. Ignore the guest's entry and continue your presentation.
   b. Ask your host for a new appointment at a different time.
   c. Wait until your host asks you to continue.
   d. Politely ask the guest to excuse himself, then continue the meeting.

Most Arab secretaries will allow newcomers to meet with their host as soon as they arrive, especially if they are close friends. This presents an uncomfortable situation for foreign guests, who normally expect a one-on-one meeting with the Arab host. In this case, be patient and get acquainted with the new guest, who may be able to open doors for new business opportunities. Thus (c) wait until your host asks you to continue the discussion, even in the presence of the new guest. Most Arab businesspeople are able to conduct meetings with more than one guest at the same time.

2. You are making a technical presentation to Arab clients. You could expect:
   a. That questions will only be asked by the senior person.
   b. That no one will ask questions because you are their guest.
   c. Some generic questions about the subject.
   d. Detailed technical questions about application.

Most Arab audiences will probably wait for a while before interrupting you with questions in respect for you as a guest. Their first questions will usually be (c) generic questions about the subject, and then move to (d) more detailed questions. Give attention to the senior person in the meeting, as well as to the technical staff, who will probably give their opinion to the senior managers in order to help them with their final decision. Most of the other attendees will just sit back and listen to the dialogue.

3. You are entering the office of your Arab host. In the room are several other members of the staff and guests. You should:
   a. Greet them loudly.
   b. Shake hands with your host and ignore the others.
   c. Open your arms and wait for your host to give you a hug.
   d. Shake hands with everyone in the room.

Arabs are warm and hospitable people. Handshakes and even hugs among acquaintances are expected. A warm handshake and a pat on the back with those whom you've already met (d) will be appreciated. You can also (c) give your host a hug. Don't be surprised by the high and emotional tone that the Arabs use when they meet. This reflects their emotional appeal and feeling about the others.

4. You are conducting a presentation to Arab executives in hope that you will be selected as the project manager. They will be most interested in:
   a. The name of your graduate school.
   b. Your current and past titles and the number of people who work underneath you.
   c. Your salary history.
   d. Your accomplishments in the last two years.

In order to position yourself and your credibility among Arabs, you must highlight (b) your title, e.g., Dr., ex-Minister, etc. as well as the size of your department. To them, this is a reflection of a credible and respected person. The name of any school you've attended in the West (a) will add to that credibility. On the other side, most Americans will look for your past accomplishments.

5. You are conducting a presentation to an Arab firm. You start by:
   a. Apologizing for not speaking Arabic.
   b. Asking everyone to introduce themselves.
   c. Thanking them for their time, interest, and cooperation.
   d. Telling them they must make a firm commitment by the end of the meeting.

It is appropriate to (c) thank your audience. There is no need to apologize for not speaking Arabic nor to ask everyone to introduce themselves, as they probably already know one another. It is your job to know the background of the senior members in the meeting. Don't push for a decision at the end of the meeting, as decisions are usually made behind the scenes.

6. In a meeting with an Arab businessperson, you are expected to:
    a. Wait until the end of the meeting to state your position on the deal.
    b. Explain your position immediately.
    c. Express your ideas openly and rationalize them aggressively.
    d. Maintain the harmony of the group.

It is usually wise to wait until the end of the meeting before stating your position on the deal. However, you should start working toward your position and try to sense the Arab response as you go along. Try to maintain harmony and avoid emotional situations. Most Arabs will not put all of their cards on the table from the beginning, but will put them down one at a time, as negotiations proceed.

Persuading Arabs

10,000 sprinklers

Although product features and price are important factors when dealing with Arabs, sensitivity to cultural differences and Arab business conduct will also contribute highly to your success with Arab partners. The following examples show what can go wrong if you are not aware of the Arab way of doing business.

David Anderson, a salesman for a large sprinkler system company in Chicago, was thrilled to receive an urgent fax from an Arab distributor in Jeddah, Saudi Arabia, requesting prices on 10,000 sprinkler heads. David quickly faxed his Arab client with a discounted price on the sprinklers. The Arab's fax had been titled "Very Urgent," so David assumed the sale might be completed by the end of the month.

At the end of the month, however, no return message from the Arab had arrived. David waited. Finally, two weeks later, the Arab faxed a request for 50 free samples of the sprinkler head, claiming that he wanted to show them to his potential clients. David, eager to close the sale as quickly as possible, sent the samples by overnight mail. His boss had been hounding him about the apparent sale. Two weeks passed without a word from the client, though, so David called. He was told that the Arab purchaser was out of the office. A week later, the Arab finally contacted David. "Mr. Anderson, it's good to speak with you. Thank you for the samples. We are interested in purchasing 500 sprinklers. Can you give them to us at a 20% discount from the price you quoted earlier?"

As you can imagine, David just about dropped the phone into his Chinese lunch! Five-hundred sprinklers with a 20% discount from the 10,000 price quote! If David had been aware of Arab price negotiation strategy, he would have been in a better position to secure his ultimate goal. Most Arabs will lead you to believe that they are interested in a large order. They will then pin you down to your lowest quoted price.

Red carpet, please

Another example: Mark Thomas was unaware of his own biases when he invited Sheik Mohammed Al-Zahir, a high-level executive from Kuwait, to visit his hotel construction firm in Houston. Thomas invited the executive in the hopes of finalizing contracts for hotel construction in Kuwait following the successful outcome of the Gulf War.

When Sheik Mohammed arrived at the airport in Houston, he found no one waiting for him, even though he had faxed Thomas his arrival plans. Mohammed called Thomas, who told him that there was a regular shuttle that can take him to his hotel. Thomas said that he would meet the Sheik at his room in two hours for dinner. Thomas's casualness astonished Mohammed, who had expected a limousine. He was even more perturbed when he had to pass up the first two shuttles because his family, including his wife and six children, couldn't all fit.

When Thomas arrived at Mohammed's hotel room, the executive suite, he was surprised to hear the voices of children coming from the room. He had not expected Mohammed's children or wife, and had to change the dinner reservation from two people to nine. Mohammed didn't like the fact that his family was limited to the few items on the Chinese menu that weren't prepared with pork or pork fat. As Thomas had expected to discuss business that night, he had already made other plans for the following day. He had to change these plans when he recognized that Mohammed was not going to discuss business in front of his wife and kids. Thomas also had to ask his executive assistant to change her plans while Mohammed was in town, since Mohammed expected someone to show his wife and children around Houston and to take them shopping.

The meetings with Mohammed did not go as well as could be expected due to Thomas's social mistakes. On the final day of meetings, however, Mohammed indicated that upon his return to Kuwait he would fax Houston with a positive response, *Insha Allah* (God willing). After three months, though, Thomas still had not heard from Sheik Mohammed, and cursed himself for his cultural ignorance.

24-hour deadline or out

Richard Larson, an American businessman, wanted to sell a large quantity of automotive repair parts to his Arab client, Mohammed Al-Salaami. Richard faxed and phoned his client several times, but Mohammed still had not decided if he would make the purchase. Eager to close the sale, Richard invoked a 24-hour deadline for Mohammed to make his decision. Mohammed was greatly offended by the deadline, and took his business to a Japanese firm.

Why did Richard lose this deal? Because he did not understand Mohammed's cultural influences and inclinations. Mohammed delayed the transaction in order to establish trust and to investigate Richard's references. This is practiced commonly by Arab businesspeople. Arabs strive to create personal friendships with their business acquaintances.

Richard Larson's failure shows us how cross-cultural business deals are often complex and difficult to execute. Price advantages, quality services, and reliable products cannot ensure success in the diversity of today's global economy. Businesses must be able to work effectively within a multicultural environment. Cultural competency is the most important skill to employ while working with Middle Eastern organizations.

Test your knowledge with the following quiz:

1. You are visiting Egypt to present your company's proposal for a joint venture. You want to discuss this deal with the president of the company. When and where should you do so?
   a. At the company president's office the day after you arrive.
   b. During dinner after a visit to his office.
   c. At the president's house.
   d. During an open seminar to the company manager on the first day.

It would be appropriate to respond (a) or (d) if you were meeting with an American, but not if you were meeting with an Arab president. Here you must use restraint; business matters are simply not discussed in the first meeting. You should wait until you have had a chance to establish a rapport. After informal discussions at both the president's office and during dinner (b), it may be appropriate to open the subject, when the president will be most receptive to such discussions. You should, however, not open the subject while visiting the president's house unless, of course, the president initiates it. Recognizing the different values placed on time in the various countries will help avoid frustration or misunderstandings. Getting through this stage smoothly is vital to ensure success in the next stage.

2. You want to close the sale by the end of the day to Arab managers, so you:
    a. Invite the negotiating team to dinner at the Hilton Hotel.
    b. Ask the senior manager to sign the order immediately.
    c. Ask the technical director to give you his personal account number.
    d. Offer a special discount if they make their decision before the deadline.

The final decision is usually made during informal meetings or at the dinner table (a). At this time, you should be ready to close the sale with (d) any special discounts which you have not yet discussed. Arabs will appreciate a symbolic gift in response to the negotiations.

3. You deadlock on the price agreement of a product with an Arab client. You:
    a. Take a break to collect your thoughts.
    b. Give them an ultimatum.
    c. Ask your go-between to mediate.
    d. Offer them an additional 10-percent discount.

Price negotiation is a lengthy process in the Arab culture. It usually won't be discussed until a firm rapport has been established and mutual interest has been clearly defined. A go-between (c) will usually mediate between the two sides and come up with a compromise in order to keep either side from losing face.

4. You have just received a fax from an Arab dealer requesting a quotation for 10,000 computers. He is actually interested in:
    a. 10,000 computers.
    b. Your ability to deliver a large order.

    c. 100 computers.

    d. Your bottom price.

If you received the fax from an American or a German company, the concern would probably be about your ability to deliver a large order. If you received a fax, however, from an Arab or Chinese dealer, (c) and (d) are the correct answers. Telling an Arab or Chinese your bottom price will probably cut into your profit margin.

In Arab countries, negotiations take place on a one-to-one basis. Aside from slowing down the information gathering process, such an arrangement also requires a personal connection between the two potential partners before business can be discussed. Arab management is looking for evidence that it can trust the foreign businessperson.

    5.   For the past six months, you have been discussing a joint venture with a Saudi Arabian government agency. During your last visit, your counterpart invited you to visit a local historical site for the day. While you were touring the site, the government official started discussing prices. This was his way of:

        a. Strengthening his personal rapport with you.

        b. Showing pride in his country's historical tradition.

        c. Persuading you to cut prices.

        d. Obligating you to invite him to your country.

What's really happening? After six months of discussion, you should already have a well-established personal rapport with your Arab counterpart. While the official has probably chosen the historical site out of pride, the fact that the official is discussing prices should indicate that they have motives beyond simply showing you around the attractions of their country. Now is the time to negotiate prices.

    6.   Tom, from Western Steel, was closing a deal with an Arabic partner, and was frustrated for quite a while that certain persuasion techniques that had proved so successful elsewhere were getting him nowhere with potential clients. He soon discovered that the most effective method of persuading the other team was to:

        a. Maintain a sense of technical superiority.

        b. Act arrogantly, so they would not attempt to intimidate him.

    c. Work as a team member.

    d. Show willingness to compromise.

The first two answers would be effective techniques had Tom been negotiating with an American company. Answering (c) would have been a good approach for negotiating with the Japanese. However, neither (a), (b), or (c) would have brought much success with an Arabic businessperson. It is important when working with Arabs to show that you are willing to compromise. This will often bring negotiations to a swift and positive close.

Encountering Your Arab Negotiators

Consider the following table during your negotiation with Arabs:

	Arab	You
Group Composition	Junior managers first followed by seniors.	Bring in senior level managers first to show power position.
Establishing Rapport	Accommodating, flattering, make you feel at home.	Accept their style, but don't get trapped into their accommodation and flattery.
Information Exchange	Mix personal with business information to establish personal commitments.	Give at the begging but hold until you receive commitments or you will end up giving it all free.
Persuasion Tools	Build on established relationships. They negotiate by making you feel guilty or obligated to make a concession. Utilize a go-between to mediate.	Display your personal support and trust. Stay firm on your initial offer until a concession is made first.
Decision Process	Engage in an extensive bargaining process until final compromise is reached.	Be patient and enjoy the process but be ready to compromise at the end. Reach out to decision makers.
Decision Makers	Senior manager makes final decision based on recommendation from technocrat.	Identify and focus on establishing personal relationships with decision makers.

Working with Arabs

Tea, anyone?

Franz Kerr, a German-born executive, was transferred to Syria, where he managed his company's manufacturing plant. During his first week on the job, Franz noticed that his employees socialized and drank morning tea for 10 to 20 minutes, which led many to start work well after the official 8 a.m. starting time.

Accustomed to punctuality among employees, Franz posted a notice on the bulletin board informing Arab employees that their wages would be docked if they did not begin promptly at 8:00 a.m. Soon thereafter, however, Franz began to notice his employees shirking their responsibilities and becoming less productive throughout the day. They seemed to resent his very presence. Franz's mistake was that he failed to recognize that he needed to accommodate his Arab employees' desire to socialize at the beginning of each shift: it was their culturally traditional warm-up before turning the computer on!

Please help me, father

Similar conflict is likely to occur if there is a disagreement in the workplace, since Arabs take a very different view of how to manage conflict than Americans. If an American worker disagrees with a manager, the American is most likely to discuss the matter directly with that manager. This is because Americans value social equality and believe that frank discussion can solve many difficult problems. In Arab countries, however, an employee who has a disagreement with their immediate supervisor (American or otherwise) may well decide to appeal to a higher authority—the manager's boss, who traditionally maintains a fatherly role among the employees. If the immediate supervisor is American, this surprise can generate even greater ill will.

Pop quiz

Training and motivating Arab workers can also be a new experience to many Western managers. When working or training Arabs, don't criticize them in front of their peers; coaching is best done one-on-one by the immediate supervisor.

In another scenario, Sally Walters had been selected by her Total Training organization to manage the transfer of an important new telecommunications technology to Jordan. Since the technology was not too complicated, she believed that she would be able to complete the transfer process within a month's time.

Upon arriving in Amman, however, she immediately encountered her first problem. She noticed that the training facilities and equipment were not up to par as in the U.S. She asked the facility coordinator if anything could be done, and was assured that more modern equipment would arrive within a week. Sally changed her schedule somewhat and believed that if she motivated her students to work a little harder they would be able to meet the deadline she had made.

The students, though, were not easily self-motivated to learn. After her first week, Sally noticed that the students were continually beginning their work late. While the class was scheduled to begin at 7:30 a.m., the students did not attend the class until 8:00 a.m. From 7:30 to 8:00 a.m., they met in groups at the cafeteria and drank their morning tea and ate pastries.

She also noticed that many students requested a break at noon in order to make their daily noon prayer, but they didn't return until 12:30. And, by 2:30, they were ready to go home for their main meal. Unfamiliar with the typical Arab daily schedule, which ends at 3:00, Sally had planned her training activities with Americans in mind. She was used to the 8 a.m.-5 p.m. schedule.

After another two weeks of struggling with her students, Sally decided to measure their performance. On the next Monday morning, she gave them a pop quiz. The results shocked her—all the students received below-average grades. She asked a friend why the results were so low. The friend said her students probably weren't reading the manuals she had given them—they learn better by watching trainers perform the correct procedures.

Sally then realized that her whole style of teaching was inappropriate. Her first two weeks of teaching had been fairly useless. It would not look good on her next review when her supervisor asked why she had to stay in Jordan a month longer than she had planned. Proper awareness of the cultural baggage that her students would bring with them and an understanding of her own biases would have prevented such a situation.

Here is another quiz that will help you during your next assignment in Arab countries:

1. You are working for an Arab company in the Middle East. You notice that your Arab subordinate receives many guests for social purposes. You should:

a. Tell him that this is a work place and guests are not permitted.

b. Leave the room when his guests arrive.

c. Greet his guests and welcome them to the office.

d. Report him to his manager and file a complaint.

Arab offices are considered one's home: a place to meet with friends and acquaintances. Don't be surprised if your subordinate or co-worker receives frequent guests while at work. Due to the Arabs' sense of hospitality, they cannot refuse to see visitors. They usually entertain their guests with a cup or two of coffee or tea, or even cigarettes. Join them for a short time in order to (c) welcome them. You might even meet someone who can help you in the future.

2. During your first month as a technical supervisor in an Arab factory you become acquainted with a few Arab managers. You should:

a. Prepare an American barbecue in your house and invite them.

b. Wait until your host's manager invites you to his house.

c. Ask your co-manager if you can visit his house and meet his family.

d. Invite them for a potluck supper at your home.

Arabs will initially be conservative with their foreign supervisors. They will try to establish a line of communication and extend their hospitality to you. Don't refuse an invitation by one of the Arab managers to visit their house. However, they will probably (a) expect you to invite them to your house. Don't suggest a potluck supper, however, as Arabs will not expect to bring food.

3. You are supervising a group of Arab workers. You notice that they:

a. Work in harmony.

b. Compete against each other.

c. Stay late after work to catch up with work.

d. Go out after work together and play football.

Arabs don't work in a team or in harmony the way the Japanese do. They often have to leave early in order to run personal errands like shopping, picking up the kids, or avoiding the traffic. Sports facilities at work are not common in the Middle East. On the other hand, Arabs do (b) compete against one another in order to earn individual respect from their boss in the hopes of a promotion.

4. If a problem arises on the factory floor, an Arab worker will often:
    a. Ignore it and continue working.
    b. Call his supervisor for advice.
    c. Fix it himself.
    d. Meet with his colleague to fix the problem.

Arabs may (a) ignore a problem in the beginning, and then (c) try to fix it themselves. The Arab will probably (b) go directly to the boss for advice rather than asking a colleague. Arabs appreciate and value one-on-one coaching more than learning in a group.

5. You are managing your American company's office in an Arab country. Local employees might see you as:
    a. Coming for vacation and to play golf.
    b. An expert in the field and trying to help them.
    c. Aggressive and demanding.
    d. Spying on behalf of the U.S. government.

Arabs expect foreign supervisors to be (b) experts in their field. You should demonstrate your technical competency from day one; otherwise, you will lose their respect. They might see you (c) as aggressive and demanding if you adhere to your time frame and ignore their perspective. They may envy your extended vacation and expensive membership at the golf club. Don't get into discussions about politics or religion.

Social Etiquette

Now consider the Saudi businessman, Ahmed, who invited Pierre, a French businessman, to his home for dinner. Eager to display his appreciation for Arab culture, Pierre arrived at dinner wearing Arab attire he had purchased at the market. Pierre also brought a bouquet of flowers for Ahmed's wife. Ahmed and his family were very cordial to their guest, and Pierre departed believing he was close to finishing the business deal. The next morning, Pierre was shocked when he received a call from Ahmed's assistant, who informed him the deal has been postponed. Pierre went home later that day, baffled over what had gone wrong. He wondered how he would explain the failure to his boss. He made two mistakes: for Arabs, it is more appropriate to bring chocolates for the family rather than flowers for the wife. Also, it is not considered a compliment to wear Arab attire; Arabs feel that doing so is a sign that you are imitating their culture, which is not appreciated. Informal social encounters with your Arab clients can also damage your business productivity if you're not careful.

Try the following quiz to test your cultural skills:

1. You are invited to a wedding of an Arab worker. You should:
    a. Turn down the invitation because he is a worker and you are the expert.
    b. Tell him that you are coming but send flowers instead.
    c. Accept the invitation and go for a while.
    d. Go to the wedding and join them in the Arabic dance.

As a show of hospitality for a foreign guest, Arab workers will definitely invite you to their wedding. Send flowers or even accept the invitation (c). Go to the wedding for a while; you will certainly enjoy the exotic food and dance. A moderate gift for their house would be greatly appreciated.

2. You are having dinner with your Arab host at an exotic Arabic restaurant. You notice that they do not use a fork or spoon. You should:
    a. Do the same and use your hands.
    b. Say, "I am not comfortable eating with my hands."
    c. Ask for a fork and spoon.
    d. Use your hands, as well.

Some Arabs enjoy eating with their hands, especially when eating exotic dishes like lamb with rice or nuts. Don't hesitate to (c) ask for silverware or, if you prefer, follow their example and eat with your hands. You might even ask for their help in learning the technique. Be sure to wash your hands after eating in preparation for dessert.

3. You invite an Arab businessman to your American home for dinner. You should:
    a. Introduce him to your family.
    b. Ask your wife to prepare a good pork meal.
    c. Have a discussion with him about Islam and the Middle East politics.
    d. Serve good wine with dinner.

The Arab will appreciate being (a) introduced to your family, but will feel more comfortable talking directly to you. Most Muslim Arabs do not eat pork, nor do they drink alcohol. Talking about Islam or politics can be interesting, but be open-minded about their views and beliefs. Arabs are not accustomed to staying as late as typical American parties last, so they will probably leave early.

4. You have been invited to an Arab businessman's home for dinner. An appropriate gift is:
   a. A bottle of good brandy or wine.
   b. Have the local butcher send a cooked leg of lamb.
   c. Flowers for his wife.
   d. Chocolates for his children.

Don't bring food to an Arab's home. It is an honor for the Arab family to cook for you. They will probably prepare an elaborate meal with enough food for a week. Just bring some (d) chocolates for the children and bring some flowers for the family (not for the wife). Remember that Arab hospitality dictates that they will try to take care of you in their home.

5. You bring a small gift to an Arab businessman. He will:
   a. Open it as soon as you sit down.
   b. Thank you for the gift and open it after you leave.
   c. Ask his son to open it after dinner.
   d. Ask his wife to open it before dinner.

Most Arabs will (b) thank you for the gift and open it after you leave. It is considered rude to open a gift in front of others. Dinner has already been prepared and there is no need for the gift to be opened right away. If you bring flowers, however, they will be displayed in a show of appreciation for your consideration.

6. You are in Egypt on business. Noticing your admiration of a picture of King Tut on his wall, your client asks if you would like it. You should:
   a. Thank him and accept the picture.
   b. Tell him that company policy forbids your acceptance of any gifts.
   c. Thank him, but tell him that King Tut looks better on his wall.
   d. Thank him, then tell him to arrange to have it delivered to your hotel.

The Arab's eloquence and hospitality will offer you whatever you admire, but they don't mean it. Elaborate back by (c) admiring the item where it is. If you accept a large gift, you should be ready to reciprocate with a gift of equal value. Don't be surprised if the Arab buys a similar item and sends it to your hotel in order to solidify a relationship with you.

Summary

If you keep the following in mind, you will greatly enhance your business success with Arabs:

- Avoid rushing or pushing through your first business trip to an Arab country. Stay in the country for at least one week. This gives you adequate time to promote your products carefully. It is also helpful to express authentic interest in Arab culture during your visit. Don't begin discussing business until the subject is broached by your Arab host.
- Always greet and welcome the guests of your Arab client if you come into contact with them, and be sure to shake hands with everyone. Be patient with what may seem like excessive socializing during business hours; this socializing is very normal for Arabs. Arabs value courtesy and hospitality. Act differently in the company of Arabs than you would with the reserved Japanese or informal Americans.
- If an Arab offers you a cup of tea, accept it even if you do not want to drink it. This also applies to snacks and other beverages. Arabs offer snacks and beverages to display their hospitality.
- Do not accept a valuable or extravagant gift, like a painting or a Rolex watch. Such an offer should be answered with, "No thank you. It looks very nice right here." If you accept a valuable or extravagant gift from an Arab, they expect you to offer them something of equal or greater value.
- Understand that Arabs value authority and respect. If a problem arises on the factory floor, an Arab worker may be inclined to call a supervisor to ask for advice rather than fix it themself.
- Since most business decisions are made on the basis of personal trust, be prepared to show your partner strong references and recommendations. Serious business will not begin until you have established trust.
- When an Arab asks, "How are you?" take the time to prepare a detailed reply. When you ask an Arab the same question, be sure to take the time to listen carefully to the response. Make sure that you

return an Arab's hospitality and flattery. This is important to establish trust.

- When you receive a gift, don't open it in front of the giver, and when you give one, don't expect the recipient to open it immediately.
- Arabs bargain in order to establish rapport and future deals. Most decisions are made by intuition and supported by religious beliefs and commitments from an authority.
- Arabs don't argue with foreigners, and may withdraw from a deal if faced with disagreement.
- Respect the Arab's wish to keep family life private, and avoid discussing politics or religion with an Arab unless they initiate it.

These suggestions should help you avoid unnecessary cross-cultural mishaps. It can be easy and rewarding to conduct business with Arabs. Remember that the success of your business in the global market depends upon your ability to adapt to the multicultural nature of modern business. An American will say, "Let's do business, and we may become friends." But an Arab will say, "Let's become friends, and we will do business forever."

Discovering European Diversity

8

How do you establish rapport with the French vs. the Germans?
How to persuade a Swiss or a Dutch businessman for a price discount?
How do you start your sales presentation to the British vs. the Italians?

For the past 50 years, Europe has continually been one of the greatest markets for foreign products, while also exporting numerous goods. Its importance in the global marketplace is only bound to increase as the Euro replaces the currencies of the many nations that comprise the European Union. Indeed, many analysts predict that, in the near future, Europe may be the dominant force in the global economy. Whether selling goods to Britain or procuring goods from Germany, the first step toward successfully dealing with Europeans is to master the norms that affect business in the region.

Doing business with Europeans requires many skills: proper etiquette, a keen business sense, and the ability to read nuances of verbal and nonverbal communications, to name a few. In addition, the diversity of European cultures forces the foreign businessperson to acquire skills they possibly never had before. It might seem for many that dealing with all Europeans is the same. It is definitely not, however, as we will discuss.

This chapter will provide you with the uniqueness of several European managers, with whom we had the opportunity to work. It introduces the main values of the dominant European cultures and covers important topics, such as conducting meetings and presentations, and establishing relationships. As with each of the other chapters in this book, tests and comparison charts will provide interactive activities to enhance learning.

The following are some general questions to test your knowledge of the European business culture.

Test Your Skills in Dealing with Europeans: True or False?

Answer the following true-or-false statements using your current understanding of European business culture and norms.

____ 1. The Swiss business climate is very conservative and methodical.

____ 2. It is quite acceptable to call a Swiss businessperson at home after work for business reasons.

____ 3. Germans are expected to contradict and criticize their colleagues publicly.

____ 4. In Germany, compliments are expected and given for a job well done.

____ 5. In Britain, consensus is preferred to individual initiative.

____ 6. Gifts are normally exchanged at the first meeting with a British partner.

____ 7. Most Italian business meetings are unstructured and informal.

____ 8. Reporting lines in Italian organizations are very structured and clear.

____ 9. It is common to ask a newly met French person about their occupation, salary, and age.

____ 10. You may send a business gift to a French colleague's home.

____ 11. Most Dutch managers take work home and don't mind being called there.

____ 12. Autocratic management still exists in many Dutch companies.

Answers:

1. T; 2. F; 3. T; 4. F; 5. T; 6. F; 7. T; 8. T; 9. F; 10. F; 11. T; 12. T

European Cultural Values

During management training workshops with some European managers, we asked participants to prioritize 20 values common among many cultures. The following table presents what French, Germans, Swiss, Spanish, Russians, and Americans indicated as their top five values from the list.

French	German	Swiss
Self-Reliance	Time	Reputation
Freedom	Competition	Relationship
Openness	Privacy	Freedom
Relationship	Openness	Openness
Time	Reputation	Family

Spanish	Russian	American
Family	Family	Equality
Reputation	Freedom	Freedom
Relationship	Self-Reliance	Openness
Freedom	Openness	Self-Reliance
Openness	Material Possessions	Cooperation

As we can note from this table, self-reliance is valued highly by French, Americans, and Russians. It is no wonder that many conflicts among these cultures have existed, especially politically. France, for example, has always resisted the "American big brother." There are also other examples of self-reliance: In America, most children at the age of 18 must begin to finance their own living or, at the very least, pay for their own tuition. And Russians, under both the old and new political systems, have tried to take care of themselves economically.

On the other hand, the Germans, Swiss, and Spanish place an emphasis on reputation. This is reflected in German and Swiss high-quality products, while the Spanish emphasis is on family reputation and relationships.

Note where conflicts among these cultures may arise: The American's value of equality may conflict with Europeans who expect more respect for their titles, education, age, family background, and personal connections. An American handshake will put the other person on the same level, and the partner will have to prove their worth by showing that they can accomplish their tasks, obligations, and promises. If Bob Smith, the American executive, meets German Prof Dr. Schiffers, for instance, Bob may ask Schiffers to call him Bob, but Schiffers probably will not give that permission to Bob until later on, when business has proceeded further.

Relationships are selected highly by the Spanish, French, and Swiss but not by the others. Russians are the only group to select material possession, which may reflect the current status of their faltering economy. Finally, we note that openness has been selected as one of the top five by all of the above cultures. This is inherent in most westerners, but this may not be on the list for most Eastern cultures. This is shown in the openness of daily communications between most Western cultures.

The Diversity of European Cultural Values

The following table further presents the unique values of some of the European cultures that we have studied and that you must consider when doing business in Europe. Furthermore, when dealing with major businesses or governments, you must realize and deal with the centralization of power and decision making. Major decisions are usually made by powerful chief executives.

French	German	Swiss
French culture and history	Punctuality	Honesty
Novelty	Privacy	Hard work
Good manners	Perfection	Orderly
Centralization	Achievement	Formality
Individuality	Compartmentalized	Reliability

Italians	British	Dutch
Loyalty	Traditions	Independence
Dignity	Reserve and restraint	Equality
Pragmatism	Courtesy	Practical
Alliance	Dry humor	Autocratic
Charisma	Formality	Teamwork

In France, you must show your knowledge and appreciation for French culture and history. This will put you in a more equal intellectual position with your French partner and, if you speak the language, numerous doors will be opened for you. Speaking at least a small amount of French, in fact, is crucial when visiting the country. If you ask a French person for directions in English, for example, you will probably find yourself having to use your own map.

Throughout history, the French have appreciated and valued fashion, novelty, and good manners in every aspect of life. This is one of the reasons that Paris is known worldwide as a center of fashion, food, and culture, and why millions of tourists flock to France each year. The French use their intellectual and cultural knowledge to enhance their personality and individuality. If you are ignorant of French culture, you may be caught off guard in either a social or business setting.

On the other side of the continent, Germans will appreciate your punctuality when attending meetings, delivering goods, or joining a party. Punctuality shows respect and reverence for the client or partner, and ignoring this cultural norm will cause friction. Also, to Germans, privacy is appreciated and expected—their space is their own. Therefore, do not disturb a German manager unless you have an appointment and be sure to knock on the door before you enter. Perfectionism is also a trademark of German culture and German companies, and they expect the same from their partners or suppliers. Compartmentalized knowledge, or a "need to know only" mentality, is also part of German management for control of information. If you work in the accounting department, for instance, you need not know about marketing activities and vice versa. Achievement is a constant challenge to German people and those who they select to work with.

Located not far from Germany is Switzerland where you have to deal culturally with the Swiss Germans, the Swiss French, and the Swiss Italians. In dealing with the Swiss, try to find out your party's background. If you do, you will get ahead much faster and with more success than those who ignore these multicultural backgrounds. As noted in the table, honesty, formality, hard work, and reliability are also keys to succeed with the Swiss.

When dealing with Italians, you must show your loyalty and enhance your relationship by focusing on, and giving priority to, family, boss, company, and your own network of alliances. This will increase your assurance of support whenever you need it personally or in business. Your charisma and pragmatic approach will position you in a leadership position.

In contrast, when dealing with the British, one must adhere to their sense of tradition, formality, reserve and emotional control. The British, after all, are known for displaying courtesy, politeness, and restraint in times of high emotion and stress. However, you must also be ready to enjoy the British sense of humor and their jokes, which may not fit in with your culture.

When working with your Dutch partner, you usually start off on an equal footing, as with most American partners. You must be prepared, however, for their independence and lines of authority. Don't be fooled with the Dutch's teamwork, as decisions are still made by the boss, and most organizations are still run in an autocratic manner.

The above contrast shows the mosaic of some of the European cultures. Landing in and dealing successfully with each depends on how fast you can pick up the subtle difference in values that we have pointed out. Watch for how you have been approached, and how they have exchanged their business cards, broke the ice, conducted meetings, negotiated, and so on. All these reflect each culture's inherent values, which you must pick up as fast as you can before your competition does. Europeans will not tell you about their cultural values, but you will have to watch for it and recognize it before you clash with them and lose your opportunity for successful business deals.

Communicating Effectively with Europeans

As mentioned before, communicating effectively with Europeans requires an in-depth knowledge of their unique cultural values and social norms. Consider the following scenarios when you communicate with Europeans.

Dealing with British Counterparts

Dealing with British formality can be frustrating for many foreign business people. Let us examine the case of Ali Saeed, the marketing manager of an Arabian trading company. He had met Jane Bickard, the procurement manager of British International Services during her visit to Cairo, where they had the chance to get acquainted with each other's line of business.

During his tour of Europe, Ali stopped over in London with his family. The next day, he searched his wallet for Jane's address and stopped by her office to discuss any interest she might have in his company's products. Jane was very surprised and apologized to Ali because she was very busy. She advised him to confirm his visit weeks in advance. She then asked him to see her secretary for the soonest available appointment. Ali was very disappointed as he would have to wait for three days to be able to meet with her, which would be after his departure. He wondered what to do with the French perfume he had brought for her. He would have to come back to meet with her on his next trip.

The above case illustrates the cultural clash between the formality of the British and the expected hospitality of the Arab. Meetings with the British are usually scheduled well in advance and should have a clearly defined purpose. Among Arabs, one can stop by at any time for chatting and coffee.

How would you deal with the following scenarios?

1. You are meeting a British manager. You should:
   a. Hand him your business card before you start greeting him.
   b. Hand him your business card at the end of the meeting.
   c. Feel no need for a business card exchange.
   d. Follow what your partner does.

There is no set ritual for the exchange of business cards in Britain. Therefore, just (d) follow what your British partner does. In contrast, most Japanese will not talk seriously with you until the exchange of cards and, with Arabs, there is no need for an exchange of business cards.

2. You are beginning business discussions with your British partner. You should:
   a. First hand him an expensive gift from your country.
   b. Hand him a special gift with your company logo on it.
   c. Wait until the successful conclusion of the negotiation and then hand him the gift.
   d. Do not give any gifts.

Gifts given in business follow the cultural norms of the country. In Britain, gifts are neither given nor expected when conducting business, as they are in Japan or China. Giving an expensive gift may be perceived as vulgar. Appreciation for business is usually expressed by a dinner invitation to a luxurious restaurant.

3. When hosting a British business meeting, it is wise to:
   a. Discuss the latest royal family scandal as an ice breaker.
   b. Expect a few humorous jokes.
   c. Get down to business after polite conversation.
   d. Use casual English.

Business meetings with the British have to follow their cultural norm, as well. Watch your language and avoid slang whenever possible in verbal or written communications with British partners. Get down to business after courteous and polite introductions and conversion. Avoid bringing up any of the royal scandals unless the subject is raised by your partner. Expect and appreciate, however, their dry humor and jokes.

4.   When dealing with the British, you must exhibit your:
     a. Family background.
     b. Technical know-how.
     c. Individual creativity.
     d. Respect for traditions.

In your first encounter with the British, you must show your respect for their traditions, and be courteous and polite in order to be successful. Your individual creativity will be appreciated, but you have to finally adhere to the group's decision.

5.   During small talk with your British businessperson, you may:
     a. Slap him or her on the back or put your hand on their shoulder in appreciation for the joke he or she just said.
     b. Keep spatial distance between yourself and your business partner of an arm length or longer.
     c. Ask them what part of London they live in.
     d. Show your respect and keep your formality.

British will keep their distance for some time until they get to know you. Avoid body touching, and do not ask the British questions about their family, where they live, or how much money they make. Show your respect for their tradition and follow their formality.

6.   British business meetings are usually:
     a. Scheduled well in advance.
     b. Have a clearly defined purpose.
     c. Get into the business at hand after a few moments of polite conversation.
     d. End up with a consensus on action items.

All of the above are important criteria in conducting business with the British. Avoid coming late to meetings, calling for an urgent meeting to convene, or showing your creativity by stepping out of line.

7. Most organizations in Britain are described as:
   a. Multilayer with vertical chains of command.
   b. Decentralized in decision-making processes.
   c. Run in a military fashion.
   d. Follow a democratic decision-making process.

In Britain, most organizations have rigid multilayered levels with a chain of command given for each head of a division. Leaders have the principle responsibility for making important decisions. The board of directors is the center of power in many organizations. Networks of committees exist in larger companies and make the recommendation for senior managers' final decisions. You will also find that consensus is preferred to individual initiative, but often groups are reluctant to take responsibility for mistakes.

8. Most business contacts are centered on:
   a. Old-boy networks.
   b. Schools and university alumni.
   c. Family ties.
   d. Connections with the royal family.

These are all important ways to expand one's business contacts. Most British will use old-boy networks from schools and university alumni, business clubs, golf courses, family and, most importantly, any connections with royal family members. Try to fit yourself and company executives into these strong networks. Cold calls will usually be received politely and courteously.

9. You are hosted by your British partner for dinner. You should expect that:
   a. Drinks will be served before dinner.
   b. "To the Queen" is a toast made after the main course at a formal dinner.
   c. Salad is generally served before dinner.
   d. You can stay seated when "God Save the Queen" is played.

As mentioned, the British love and expect others to follow their protocol and tradition.

The male guest of honor is usually seated at the head of the table or next to the hostess. The female guest of honor is seated next to the host. Drinks are usually served before dinner. Salads are generally served with the food and not before, as Americans do. They love to toast to the Queen after the main course is done and remember to stand up when "God save the Queen" is played. Never lift your fork to start eating before your host does. Keep your hand on the table at all times during the meal. When the host folds their napkin, the meal is over. It is polite to leave a small amount of food on your plate, when you are through eating.

10.   If you are invited to a British home, you should:
      a. Bring white lilies as a floral gift.
      b. Bring a small but not expensive gift from your country.
      c. Have a 12-inch pizza delivered to your host's home.
      d. Arrive one hour after the invitation time.

You better not bring those lilies! These flowers denote death and usually are given at funerals. It is appropriate, however, to bring a small gift from your country or a bottle of a famous brand of whisky or wine. You can have the pizza delivered to an American home during a Super Bowl game. You should arrive on time but do not be late more than 30 minutes or so. Never drop in on someone in England without phoning ahead.

11.   During your shopping on London's famous Oxford Street, you must:
      a. Never cut in line, especially for a bus or to get on the subway.
      b. Never shout in public.
      c. Be willing to give up your seat on crowded city buses to an older person.
      d. Never display affection in public.

One should not shout in public, display affection in public, or cut in a waiting line. You will be immediately scorned by others. Giving your seat to an elder will be received by polite thanks and a show of appreciation by all.

These situations show some of the uniqueness of the British and how to successfully deal with them. If there are some things that you are not sure about, just ask them, but make sure that you enjoy their humorous jokes!

For a quick review, remember the following when dealing with the British:

- Formalities and protocol are extremely important.
- Meetings are scheduled well in advance and have clearly defined purposes.
- The British tend to get down to business after a few moments of polite conversation.
- Company organization is multilayered with a vertical chain of command. Leaders have the principal responsibility for making important decisions.
- The board of directors is the center of power in many companies, and networks of committees exist in larger companies.
- Consensus is preferred to individual initiative.
- Business is centered on old-boy networks. Schools, universities, and family ties are important.
- Quiet conversation is appreciated. Boisterous behavior causes embarrassment and is frowned upon.
- Gifts are normally not exchanged at business meetings or even after the successful conclusion of negotiations.
- When invited to someone's home, always present the hostess with a small gift upon arrival. Giving expensive gifts may be perceived as vulgar.

Dealing with German Counterparts

Budi Ibrahim, the Indonesian project manager of a joint venture between TeleMobil Indonesian and the German Global One, arrived in Frankfurt for a meeting with Dr. Wolf Gang, the German director of operations. On Monday morning at 9:30 a.m., Dr. Wolf Gang and his assistant were wondering what had happened to Budi who was supposed to be in for the 9:00 a.m. meeting. He should have called them to advise them of his delay. Punctuality is a German trademark. Finally, Budi and three of his staff arrived with an apology for missing the exit off the freeway on their way to the office.

Dr. Wolf Gang was wondering why Budi had brought these two extra guests. When the meeting was finally started by Budi, who was presenting the status of the project in Jakarta, Dr. Wolf Gang immediately interrupted him to ask about sources of the data he was presenting and questioned him about some of the facts. In turn, Budi looked back to his assistant for answers. Dr. Wolf Gang suspected that Budi had not done his homework before the meeting and thus was avoiding dealing with him directly. He expected the presentation to be full of numbers, facts, charts, and tables. Budi, however, just summarized the status and expected the German party to take him for granted. Disappointed, Dr. Wolf Gang had to cut the meeting short and hand it over to his assistant for a followup with Budi and his team.

Budi had ignored basic German values such as punctuality, facts, and top-quality products and presentation.

Try the following quiz:

1.   You are hosted by a German agent to meet his clients. You will:
   a. Wait for him to introduce you first.
   b. Introduce yourself and hand them your business cards immediately.
   c. Feel no need for the exchange of business cards.
   d. Hand them your business card at the end of the meeting.

Germans are very formal in personal introductions. Your business card must point out your title and degrees, such as Prof. Dr. Ing. Your host is expected to introduce you, after which you can go through the process of exchanging cards. Use German last names and appropriate titles until specifically invited to use first names.

2.   In Germany, most business meetings are:
   a. Run in a formal fashion.
   b. Scheduled weeks in advance.
   c. Used to gain trust with participants.
   d. Used to debate issues.

These are all important characteristics of German meetings. Be formal and follow the meeting agenda and the meeting leader. Do not call for an urgent meeting unless it is necessary. Germans come to meetings well prepared and expect others to do so, too. Initial meetings are to gain trust and to build credibility among team members. Be ready and expect hot debates among meeting members.

3.   You have been invited to present to a German team. You are expected to:
   a. Be punctual.
   b. Present material backed by facts, figures, charts, and tables.
   c. Respond aggressively to your challengers.
   d. Maintain harmony with the group and do not respond to arguments.

You will earn the Germans' respect if you do your homework well before the meeting. Present your work backed by all supporting data and means and be ready to challenge your counterpart with facts and figures. Be punctual and keep track of the meeting's stated time. Keep in mind that Germans may appear reserved and unfriendly in meetings. Gifts are normally not exchanged at business meetings, although a small, attractively wrapped gift may be appropriate at the end of a successful negotiation.

4. You are listening to a presentation by a top German executive and you disagree with his rationale. You should immediately:
    a. Leave the room.
    b. Point out his failings to the person on your right.
    c. Discuss your disagreement with him immediately.
    d. Leave the matter until after the presentation is over.

In most Asian cultures, even if you largely disagree with the presenter, it is appropriate to wait and raise the issue later on to avoid loss of face to the presenter. In German culture, however, you should be ready to defend your point of view to those who disagree with you. Among peers, it is okay and expected to criticize each other even in front of a foreigner. Never criticize your boss publicly, though. This was made clear to me when a German company representative was making a presentation to an Egyptian client's team and one of his colleagues interrupted him in a disagreement with one of the points he was presenting. This put the Egyptian team in shock, as it made them falsely assume that the German team was not united.

5. In dealing with Germans, you must be ready to respond to their:
    a. Competence.
    b. Ambitious nature.
    c. Hard bargaining practices.
    d. Punctuality.

Listed above are some of the main values of German business people. Business procedures and routine work are done strictly "by the book." Bosses are respected for being strong, decisive, and hard-working. A vertical hierarchy exists and organizations are methodological and compartmentalized. You are expected to know only what you need to in order to do your job. Cars, the size of an office, and holiday venues are all important symbols of individual German success.

6. In order to be promoted within a German organization, you must show your:
   a. Decisiveness.
   b. Ability to follow rules and procedures.
   c. Complimentary attitude.
   d. Imagination.

Being decisive is a value of a good manager. Being able to follow rules and procedures is a value of a good subordinate. You can be imaginative, but be ready for the questioning and challenges posed by both your boss and colleagues to define your idea until the end. Do your homework well before encountering Germans in debates.

7. You are working for a German boss and have done a good job in your last project. You will expect your boss to:
   a. Compliment you on your performance provided.
   b. Compliment you in front of your team.
   c. Do nothing since he believes that it is your responsibility to do a good job.
   d. Invite you to lunch.

Compliments are seldom given by German bosses. Even objective criticism isn't given or received easily. So, do not be disappointed if your boss does not compliment you on your hard work, especially if you are an Arab or an Asian where frequent compliments by the boss will fuel up your motivation to further excel. Remember to knock on the boss's door before entering to see them. Do not call a German at home unless it is an emergency.

8. You are invited to a German dinner party. It is appropriate to:
   a. Leave food on your plate.
   b. Drink before the host raises his glass.
   c. Smoke while the food is served.
   d. Leave your knife and fork crossed when you have finished eating.

Dinner attire should always be clean and neat. Don't drink at a dinner party until the host raises a glass. It is impolite to leave food on your plate. Do not smoke until dinner is finished and coffee is served, and ask permission before doing so. When you've finished eating, place your knife and fork side by side on the plate at an angled position on the right side of your plate. The honored guests are expected to make the first move to leave. Thanks is usually given in person or with a telephone call a day or so after the party. A man or a younger person should always walk to the left side of a woman. Compliment carefully and sparingly, since it may embarrass, or not please them. Stand when an older or higher-ranking person enters the room.

As a review, remember the following when dealing with Germans:

1. Punctuality is a German trademark. Call or write with an explanation if you expect to be delayed.
2. Briefings and presentations should be backed up by numerous facts, figures, charts and tables.
3. Germans may appear reserved and unfriendly until you get to know them better.
4. Germans are competitive, ambitious, and hard bargainers.
5. A vertical hierarchy exists in the German business culture. Corporate organization is methodological and compartmentalized. Procedures and routines are done "by the book." Communication within German companies tends to be from the top down.
6. Bosses are respected for being strong, decisive, and hardworking. Subordinates rarely contradict or criticize bosses publicly.
7. Objective criticism isn't given or received easily. Compliments are seldom given.
8. Gifts are normally not exchanged at business meetings, but small gifts may be appropriate at the end of successful negotiations. Bring a small, attractively wrapped gift.
9. Cars, the size of an office, and holiday venues are all important symbols of individual success.
10. Don't expect compliments or a quick friendship. Losing your temper in public, shouting, stepping out of line, entering a room without knocking, or calling a German at home unless it is an emergency is taboo.

Dealing with French Counterparts

Close to concluding a business deal with his prospective French buyer, Mr. Lee, the vice president of Singapore Power Technology, invited Isabelle Pujol and her staff to dinner at a major restaurant in Paris at 7:00 p.m. Lee hoped that this entertainment would help him close the deal. Rushing into the restaurant at 7:30 p.m., however, Lee complained that no one could help him with the right exit from the Paris subway. After a warm greeting and seating at the dinner table, Lee handed Isabelle a well-wrapped gift and asked her to open it. Isabelle, excited to find out what was in it, opened it carefully but, after examining it, she politely thanked Lee and set it aside. Lee wondered why she did not seem to like it. It was a Parker pen with his company's logo on it. Everyone in Singapore loved them.

While the French appreciate unique gifts, those gifts with company logos look impersonal and cheap to them. Isabelle, sensing the embarrassment of Lee, changed the subject and asked, "Please tell us about what you have seen in Paris during your visit: the Eiffel Tower, the Louvre, the night life?" Lee responded that he had been too busy promoting the new line of equipment of his company. Perhaps he would have more time on his next visit, after he had made some sales. Isabelle wondered about his knowledge of French languages, art, and even simple etiquette—and the chance of the success of their joint venture. Lee had not done so well: his French partner wondered about his sincerity and his ability to do business with her.

To see how well you will do with the French, take the following quiz:

1. In order to enhance the success of your business relationship with your French partner, you should show your appreciation and understanding of French:
   a. Manners.
   b. Fashions.
   c. Culture.
   d. Novel ideas.

A French person will bow and open the door to many business opportunities for you if you speak French, show appreciation for French wine and cheeses, follow French manners, debate well, and present novel ideas, as well as mention your visits and appreciation of French culture. If your French partner recognizes these values and behavior in you, your business dealings will be greatly enhanced.

2. In your encounter with your French businessperson, you are expected to:
   a. Be punctual.
   b. Offer a quick, light handshake before and after the meeting.
   c. Inquire about his/her family, even if you have not met them.
   d. Use first names immediately.

Punctuality for a business meeting in France is expected. Offer a quick, but light handshake after exchanging business cards and after closing the meeting. Do not ask a French person about their occupational salary, age, or family unless you have a well-established friendship. Use last names and titles unless invited to use first names, which would indicate that a closer relationship has been established. In France, only family and close friends call each other by first names.

3.   You are making a presentation to a French client. You should be:
    a. Informal and friendly.
    b. Pointing out your technical competency.
    c. Expecting a quick decision on your offer.
    d. Presenting him/her with a gift with your company logo on it.

Presentations to the French should be made in a formal and professional style that appeals to the conservative business values of the French. Technical competency is admired, and rivalry and competition are encouraged. While the French get down to business quickly, decisions are made only after long deliberations. Most French organizations are highly centralized and have powerful chief executives. A vertical structure with a rigid chain of command is the norm. Work gets accomplished through a network of personal relationships and alliances. Company loyalty is highly valued. Note that the French are world leaders in economic planning and you should take this into account when dealing with them.

4.   Your French partner has helped you to win a contract. You could reciprocate by:
    a. Sending him a gift with your company logo on it.
    b. Sending his secretary six red roses.
    c. Sending two bottles of California wine to his home.
    d. Personally handing him a high-quality and beautifully wrapped gift from your country.

Do not give a French partner a gift with your company's logo stamped on it. They consider it to be a cheap gift. A gift should be of high quality and wrapped beautifully. Never send a business gift to a French colleague's home. In France, red roses are for lovers only. Just personally hand them a gift from your own country with a word of appreciation. A gift to a French person will probably not be unwrapped immediately.

5.   You are invited to join a French person for dinner. You:
  a. Are expected to arrive on time.
  b. Can order a martini or whiskey before dinner.
  c. Expect that wine will be served before dinner.
  d. Are expected to taste everything offered.

Arrive 15 minutes or so late for social occasions but on time for restaurant meetings. Do not ask for a martini or a whiskey before dinner as most Americans or British might do. Wine is always served with meals. The host will offer the first toast. It is acceptable for women to propose a toast, too. Taste everything offered. Leaving food on your plate is impolite. In Asia, however, it is accepted. Do not discuss business over dinner but show a good amount of knowledge of French history, politics, and culture. Compliments may be appreciated but are usually received with denial.

The French also prefer intelligent and satirical humor and funny stories of real-life situations. Do not sit with legs spread apart, use toothpicks in front of others on the table or nail clippers, chew gum, or comb in public. Do not put your hands in your pockets when speaking to or greeting someone. Remember to send a thank you note or telephone the next day to thank the host.

6.   French advertising mainly focuses on:
  a. Simplicity.
  b. Images.
  c. Transmitting product information.
  d. Prices.

Most French advertisement, especially for consumer products, would focus and respond to French cultures of novelty, imagination, simplicity, and images. The French will mostly buy brand name products. Prices, quality, and other product features will come second.

7.   If you need to get directions from a well-dressed person in the Paris subway, you should:
  a. Ask if he speaks English before asking for directions.
  b. Get a taxi as it will probably be faster.

c. First greet him in French.
d. Say, "I am sorry but can you show me the way to Eiffel Tower?"

The French value their time, and are self-reliant and independent. If you do business with them or ask for help, you should first show appreciation for their culture by speaking at least a few French words. You do not have to be a master in French but a few words to greet or compliment them would impress your French counterpart. Many American tourists visiting Paris complain about the French being hesitant to help or respond to anyone speaking other than French. So, in this case you should greet them in French first and then ask for directions in your own language if necessary. Otherwise, you should get a taxi to take you to your destination.

8. Your French client has not returned your overseas calls to his office in Paris for about a month. The month is probably:
    a. January and he is recovering from the holidays.
    b. April and he is on spring vacation skiing.
    c. August and he is with everyone on holidays.
    d. December and he is busy for Christmas.

The French value their holidays and their time with friends and family. If you visit Paris in August, you will find out that most French people leave to the countryside at that time to enjoy their summer holidays. So, you have to be patient until they come back from their vacations. This also happens to a lesser extent during other seasons, such as Christmas and around New Year's Eve, and spring holidays.

Remember the following during your next encounter with the French:

- Punctuality for business meetings is expected. Offer a quick, light handshake before and after meetings.
- Presentations are made in a formal and professional style that appeals to the conservative business values of the French.
- Organizations are highly centralized and have powerful chief executives. A vertical structure with a rigid chain of command is the norm.
- Work gets accomplished through a network of personal relationships and alliances. Company loyalty is highly valued.
- Technical competency is admired, and rivalry and competition are encouraged.

- While the French get down to business quickly, decisions are made only after deliberation.
- Gifts should be of high quality and wrapped beautifully. A gift to the hostess will probably not be unwrapped immediately.
- Show a good amount of knowledge of French language, history, politics, and culture.
- The French prefer intelligent and satirical humor and funny stories of real-life situations.
- It is acceptable to arrive 15 minutes late for social occasions but you should be on time for restaurant meetings. Do not discuss business over dinners.

Dealing with Italian Counterparts

Mr. Kanaka, a Japanese vice president of finance, arrived in Rome to audit the books of the Japanese-Italian automotive joint venture. Sales had been good and profit margins were on the rise. On his first day in the office, he met with Frank Pizzaro who was to assist him. Kanaka knew about the Italians' love for expensive gifts, so he handed Pizzaro a well-wrapped gift that he had brought for him from Japan. Pizzaro looked at it and set it aside. Kanaka asked Pizzaro to go ahead and open the gift. Pizzaro again politely declined, explaining that the black wrapping, in Italy, would indicate that the gift was for a funeral.

The next day, Kanaka arrived at his scheduled 9:00 a.m. meeting in the office of Pizzaro. He was welcomed by the secretary who asked him to have a seat until Pizzaro was done with his guest. At 9:45 a.m., he was still waiting, wondering if Pizzaro was ignoring him. In Italy, however, foreigners are expected to be on time, but you may be kept waiting by your Italian colleagues. After several days, Kanaka was complaining about unclear reporting lines in the organization, and that he had to establish stronger relationships between him and other office managers to get the job done on time.

To learn more of the details of the Italians' unique culture, take the following quiz:

1. You are meeting with your Italian business partner for the first time. He will expect a:
   a. kiss on both cheeks.
   b. Firm handshake.
   c. Hug.
   d. Handshake with a slap on the back.

A kiss on both cheeks is usually expected from close friends, as well as a hug and a slap on the back. A firm handshake is appropriate until business relationships progress and move into close friendships, which most Italians will look for. When receiving a business card, look at the name and title carefully and do not just put in in your pocket and then ask what the person does, as Americans might do. Use last names and titles until invited to do otherwise. Maintain eye contact while talking, otherwise Italians might think you are hiding something. This is in contrast to the Japanese, who usually avoid direct eye contacts as it indicates a hostile attitude.

2. You are invited to meet with an Italian businessman at 9:00 a.m. in his office. He will:
   a. Definitely meet you at 9:00 a.m.
   b. Probably see you between 9:30 and 10:00 a.m.
   c. Invite you to his office while he is having a discussion with another party.
   d. Expect you at 9:30 a.m.

It is extremely impolite to break an appointment with an Italian. They expect you to come on time but they may not see you at the time of the appointment. Half an hour is an acceptable waiting time. Be patient for your meeting and take the time to get acquainted with your hosts' secretary and staff. Most Italian business is conducted in a friendly environment in an attempt to establish a trusting relationship between the parties.

3. You are making a presentation to your Italian clients. You must display your:
   a. Technical competency.
   b. Leadership.
   c. Charisma.
   d. Loyalty.

Making a good first impression matters deeply to Italians. Dress elegantly but conservatively. These are all important character traits that most Italians will look for and admire. Being loyal to the partnership, and leading it through your charismatic personality—as well as with your technical competency—will open the door to many businesses for you. Leaders are also respected for their ability to establish personal relationships, to fulfill commitments, and to cooperate well with others.

4. You are working in an Italian organization. You have noticed that:
    a. Pragmatism and improvisation are appreciated.
    b. Protocol and rules are generally ignored.
    c. Reporting lines are not clear.
    d. Personal alliances are a key to success.

These are important cultural traits in most Italian organizations. Establishing personal alliances within and with others is a very important network. Being pragmatic in performing your task will open the door to you for more opportunities. On the other hand, most protocol and rules are generally ignored in Italy, which is in contrast to British and German organizations, where reporting lines are very well defined and followed.

5. You are in Italy in an attempt to sell your products to Computer Magic outlets. You must start by:
    a. Making a formal presentation to the board of directors.
    b. Establishing a personal relationship with the sales manager.
    c. Sending a sample of your product by overnight courier to the director.
    d. Focusing on the old-boy network you have developed.

You must start by making a sound personal relationship with the Italian sales managers. Exhibit long-range relationships and loyalty. Being pragmatic and exhibiting your leadership and creativity will get you to higher levels and it could even get you a presentation to the board of directors. This may introduce you to the Italian old-boy network that would expand your business throughout Italy. Leaving a sample of your product or a homemade gift will help speed up the decision process in your favor.

6. You are discussing your proposal with your Italian partner. You will expect:
    a. A formal and well-structured meeting.
    b. That a decision will be made in the meeting.
    c. That a decision has already been made before the meeting.
    d. A friendly and unstructured meeting.

Most Italian business meetings are unstructured and informal. Decisions are generally made and agreed on privately before the meeting by senior managers. Use the meeting to further enhance your relationship, credibility, and ability to deliver what you promised in a pragmatic way.

> 7. You want to appreciate your Italian partner's business and so you want to give him a gift. You should:
>   a. Send him a K Mart saw chain to cut his house tree.
>   b. Give him a brand name chocolate box wrapped in black paper and a golden ribbon.
>   c. Send him a red envelope with cash money inside.
>   d. Give him a bottle of French or California wine or champagne.

Gift giving is common in business, but exchanges are generally not made at initial meetings. Italians are very generous gift givers. You will be embarrassed if you give a cheap or practical gift, such as the saw for tree cutting or office desk supplies. If you give flowers, an uneven number of flowers is acceptable, but not 13 as this is considered to be an unlucky number. Do not wrap any gift in black or tie it with a gold ribbon (a sign of mourning). A gift from your country, a local brand-name box of chocolates, or a bottle of drink would usually be appreciated. Make sure to send a thank you note after being entertained or given a gift.

> 8. You are being entertained at your Italian friend's house for dinner. You are expected to:
>   a. Arrive at the time specified in the invitation.
>   b. Take your shoes off when you enter the house.
>   c. Take small amount of food when served by the wife.
>   d. Keep your wine glass half full all the time.

Arrive 15 to 30 minutes after the time specified on the invitation. There is no need to take your shoes off as you would in most Japanese homes. Take a small amount of food when being served, because your hosts will always offer a second helping and it is impolite to refuse. Keep your glass almost full if you don't want a refill. The fingertips kiss means "beautiful." Use it to show an appreciation for food and your host will be pleased. Fun and flirtation are part of life in Italy. The "hand purse" (finger tips held together) indicates a question.

Now remember the following to enhance your success with the Italians:

- Make firm handshakes and eye contact before and after meeting. Friends may greet each other with a kiss on both cheeks.
- Establish a personal relationship with Italians; they like to deal with people they know and trust.
- Foreigners are expected to be on time, but you may be kept waiting by your Italians colleagues. It is extremely impolite to break an appointment.
- Formal presentations are made to display the leader's status, personality, and charisma.
- Leaders are respected for their ability to establish personal relationships, to fulfill commitments, and to cooperate.
- Pragmatism and improvisation are considered the keys to success; as a result, protocol, rules, and organization charts are generally ignored.
- Reporting lines in organizations are not clear. Organizations are built mostly on personal alliance.
- Italians are very generous gift givers. You will be embarrassed if you give a cheap gift. Exchanges are generally not made at initial meetings.
- Do not wrap a gift in black with a gold ribbon (a sign of mourning).
- Fun and flirtation are part of life in Italy.

Dealing with Swiss Counterparts

Mr. Park, the purchasing manager of New Fashion of Korea, is in Zurich negotiating the final sales of 1,000 Korean-made watches to a NewGen Swiss distributor. All specifications had been agreed on by the technical staff, and Park only had to negotiate the final price with David Benwell, the Swiss-Italian purchasing manager. Park originally stated terms that would give him a 40% markup. He finally settled, however, for a more reasonable amount. Mr. Benwell finally agreed on the offer but wondered if he could trust Park, who could have made 40% more profit before the negotiation began.

Price negotiation with some cultures can be frustrating. The Koreans will usually mark prices up at least 40% and would be ready to compromise. Swiss are hard but fair bargainers. Park did not recognize Benwell's Italian culture and thought that he could win him from the first round!

Test your knowledge of Swiss business culture with the following quiz:

1. You are hosted by a Swiss agent to visit a client. You will:
    a. Introduce yourself and exchange cards.
    b. Wait for your agent to introduce you first.
    c. Exchange business cards after the meeting.
    d. Just mention your name and title.

Upon meeting the Swiss, your host will introduce you to other executives. Exchange business cards immediately. Make firm handshakes and eye contact with everyone in the meeting. Use last names and appropriate titles until specifically invited to use first names. Academic and professional titles are used frequently. The Swiss are formal and courteous. Some small talk is acceptable before doing business. Once again, you may notice style differences in the culture of Swiss companies that may vary somewhat, depending on whether they are in German-, French-, or Italian-dominated areas.

2. Most Swiss companies prefer to do business with people who are:
    a. Honest.
    b. Hardworking.
    c. Reliable.
    d. Planners.

These are values that most Swiss companies admire, encourage, and reward. Punctuality in meetings and product delivery is also highly valued. Call or write with an explanation if you expect to be delayed.

3. When conducting business with Swiss organizations, you should be:
    a. Impersonal.
    b. Task oriented.
    c. A strong bargainer.
    d. Expecting quick friendships.

Do not expect quick friendships when dealing or working with the Swiss. Friendship is built over time and only if you fit within their values. Personal relationships develop only after successful business negotiations. Do not show off your strong Arab or Chinese bargaining attitude with the Swiss. Be fair and soft in your dealings and they will settle with you. Do not mix personal affairs with business matters, as most Swiss separate the two. The Swiss are formal and courteous. Some small talk, however, is acceptable before doing business.

4. Swiss business organization culture can be described as:
    a. Conservative.
    b. Methodical.
    c. A consensus decision-making process.
    d. Comprising fast-decision makers.

The Swiss business climate is very conservative. Decision making is slow and methodical, and discussions are cautious and sometimes pessimistic. The Swiss are hard but fair bargainers. Do not haggle with them. If you earn their respect, they will open doors for you.

5. You are communicating with your Swiss counterpart for business deals and need urgent information. You should:
    a. Call him at home any time.
    b. Wait until the next day and call him at his office.
    c. Send him an e-mail at home.
    d. Call him at home but not after 8 p.m.

The Swiss are impersonal and separate their life from business matters. Therefore, it is not acceptable to call a Swiss at home. Do so only in an emergency situation with an apology. It is better to wait until the next day and save that call for a real emergency. Do not even bother a Swiss with an e-mail at home.

6. After a successful business and personal relationship has been developed with your Swiss counterpart, he invites you to his home. Now, you should:
    a. Consider this an honor.
    b. Ask for a tour of the house and show your admiration for Swiss watches on the walls.
    c. Arrive on time.
    d. Stay past midnight to show your appreciation for his wife's dinner.

It is an honor if you are entertained in someone's home, but don't ask for a tour. Bring a small, attractively wrapped gift. Gifts are normally not exchanged at business meetings, but small gifts may be appropriate at the end of successful negotiations. Whiskey, cognac, or a good pictorial book are good gift choices. If the host proposes a toast, don't drink until after it is proposed. It is polite to propose a toast after dinner. Keep your hands on the table during the meal, not in your lap.

It is polite to leave food on your plate. Ask for permission to smoke at the dinner table. Leave a party no later than midnight.

7. Your Swiss business partner has invited you for a Saturday lunch and a visit to the market. You may:
    a. Show your bargaining skills with the street vendors.
    b. Ask him personal questions about age and earning power.
    c. Speak your mind, be honest, and enjoy the day.
    d. Request a tour of his or her house after the shopping trip.

Do not get into personal matters with your Swiss associate until you know them personally. Even if you are invited to their house, do not ask for a tour. The Swiss value their privacy and may be less open to sharing their space than others. The Swiss are not strong bargainers, so do not show your skills in settling purchases on the streets of Zurich. Just speak your mind, and be direct and honest in your interactions.

8. You are wandering on a street in Zurich, and you have noticed that some locals are looking at you with angry faces. You have been:
    a. Littering in public.
    b. Stretching and slouching.
    c. Putting your hand in your pocket while talking with your friend.
    d. Pointing your index finger at your head.

These are all taboos to do while visiting with the Swiss. Refrain from these, and you will receive a good welcome from your host in the office, shops, restaurants, or even on the streets of Switzerland.

Here, again, are tips in dealing with the Swiss:

- Punctuality is highly valued. Call or write with an explanation if you expect to be delayed.
- Upon meeting the Swiss, your host will introduce you to other executives. Exchange business cards immediately. Make firm handshakes and eye contact with everyone after meetings. Use last names and appropriate titles until specifically invited to use first names. Academic and professional titles are used frequently.
- Business meetings are impersonal, orderly, well planned, and task oriented. Presentations must be well-prepared and detailed.
- The Swiss are hard but fair bargainers. Do not haggle with them.

- The Swiss are formal and courteous. Some small talk is acceptable before doing business.
- The Swiss business climate is very conservative. Decision making is slow and methodical, and discussions are cautious and sometimes pessimistic.
- Gifts are normally not exchanged at business meetings, but small attractively wrapped gifts may be appropriate at the end of successful negotiations.
- At dinner, the host proposes the first toast. Don't drink until after it is proposed. It is polite to propose a toast after dinner or to leave food on your plate. Ask for permission to smoke at the dinner table.
- Business is discussed over meals.
- Do not litter in public, or ask a person's age, job, or family status. Do not expect quick friendships.

Dealing with Dutch Counterparts

Paulo Pizzaro from Brazil was in the Netherlands to finalize his terms of agreement with Fons Brown, general manager of Speed International. Pizzaro was very happy that Speed International had accepted his offer for two containers of Brazilian coffee every month. The negotiations and the decision-making process had been ponderous, but fast-paced. Fons invited him for dinner in celebration of signing the contract and also invited Mr. Tons, the vice president.

Over dinner, Pizzaro started asking Tons about his family and how his wife was managing her new business. He also inquired about Tons' age and the time that he would be retiring. Tons politely listened, then moved the discussion on to business terms and stressed the importance of Pizzaro keeping his committed delivery dates. The rest of the dinner time went smoothly but Pizzaro was wondering what he had done or said to make Tons very quiet.

Do you know the answer? You will find out as you read through the following quiz:

1. When meeting your Dutch partner for the first time, you should respond by saying:
   a. "Hello."
   b. "It is nice to meet you."
   c. "It is nice to meet you. My name is Dr. Farid."
   d. "My name is F. E. Ashmawi."

Most Dutch will approach others by the example in (d), stating their initial and then last name. You can reciprocate in the same manner or in your own culture's. If a Dutch person gives you their first name, you are being granted permission to address them with it. You may add titles such as Dr. or Professor. Offer a warm handshake and make eye contact.

2. Most Dutch prefer a business partner who values:
    a. Equality.
    b. Frankness.
    c. Independence.
    d. Ambition.

All of these are values that most Dutch admire. Start with respect and on an equal base with your partners. Being frank, with ambition and a sense of independence and risk taking, will give you the Dutch support for a long time.

3. You are making a presentation to a prospective Dutch business partner. You should:
    a. Get right down to business.
    b. Be practical and factual.
    c. Not expect much participation.
    d. Not ask for an immediate decision.

Punctuality is expected at business meetings. Your presentations are expected to be practical and factual. Ideas should be researched, well thought out, and clearly presented. The Dutch tend to get right down to business. Taking your jacket off in an office is acceptable. In a meeting, the chairperson sets the tone as to whether jackets should be on or off, however.

4. Most Dutch organizations are run in:
    a. An autocratic management style.
    b. A consensus management style.
    c. A participatory management style.
    d. A militaristic management style.

Autocratic management still exists in many Dutch companies. New organizations, though, are moving toward horizontal and participatory management. Dutch companies are frugal and profit oriented. The decision-making process is ponderous, but negotiations may be fast paced. Successes are attributed to the team, not to individuals. Commitments are honored, and individuals are held accountable for decisions.

5.   If you are working in a Dutch organization, you are expected to:
   a. Take work home.
   b. Not mind being called at home for business matters.
   c. Not promise anything that you can't deliver.
   d. Work well with your team.

Most Dutch managers take work home and don't mind being called there, but usually not after 9 p.m. Do not promise anything you can't deliver. You must try to fit yourself within your team as soon as possible.

6.   You are meeting for the first time with a Dutch prospective business client. You should:
   a. Invite him to a French restaurant.
   b. Present a gift to him after lunch.
   c. Discuss business during lunch.
   d. Compliment him on his Italian suit.

The Dutch love French restaurants. Gifts are exchanged in business only once a close and personal relationship has developed. If this is already established, you can present a gift upon arrival. It will be opened immediately. It is appropriate to discuss business during lunch. You should respect people's privacy by not asking personal questions. Also note that food is not an important part of the Dutch social culture as it is in many other cultures. Socialization often occurs over coffee. Do not give personal compliments before you know someone well.

7.   You are invited to your Dutch friend's home for a party. You should:
   a. Arrive one hour after the invitation time.
   b. Expect that the party will go on until the late hours.
   c. Expect that your gift will be set aside to be opened the next day.
   d. Mention a joke about the Dutch royal family.

The Dutch are punctual, even to parties, so do not be more than 30 minutes late or you will miss the opening fun. Parties may go on until the late hours. Bring a gift which will be opened immediately. Bread usually isn't served at dinner. Do not make a joke or a derogatory comment about the Dutch royal family. And remember not to call the Netherlands "Holland." Holland is a region in the Netherlands.

Now, focus on the following tips which will help you secure business with the Dutch:

- Most Dutch will give you their first initial and last name. If they give you their first name, they are granting you permission to address them with it.
- Upon greeting, offer a warm handshake and make eye contact. State the Dutch person's last name, instead of "hello."
- Punctuality is expected at a business meeting. Meetings are frequent and usually followed by decision making. The Dutch tend to get right down to business.
- Presentations are expected to be practical and factual. Ideas should be researched, well thought out, and clearly presented.
- Autocratic management still exists in many Dutch companies. New organizations, though, are moving toward horizontal and participatory management.
- Dutch companies are frugal and profit oriented. The decision-making process is ponderous, but negotiations may be fast paced.
- Successes are attributed to the team, not to individuals. Commitments are honored and individuals are held accountable for decisions.
- People's privacy is to be respected, so do not ask personal questions. Do not give personal compliments before you know someone well.
- Food is not an important part of social culture. Socialization often occurs over coffee. It is appropriate to discuss business during lunch.
- Gifts are exchanged in business only after a close and personal relationship has been developed. If you present a gift upon arrival, it will be opened immediately.

Summary

Although Europeans have created a common business market, we have discovered that dealing with them requires close attention to their unique cultural differences. Keep in mind the British formality and tradition; German punctuality and thoroughness; French intellectuality, fashion, and manners; Italian charisma and loyalty; Swiss privacy and quality; and Dutch autocratic management style and ponderous decision-making process. If you keep these European values in mind, you will certainly have the upper hand in competing and dealing with the diverse European community. If you succeed, you will definitely enhance your own cultural values to take along with you on your global journey.

Looking Behind the Chinese Facade

How would you secure a meeting with the mayor of Shanghai?
Why are Hong Kong Chinese always in a hurry?
How would you persuade a supplier from Taiwan for a
price discount?
How can you keep up with today's managers from Singapore?

These are examples of the many questions most businesspeople dealing with the Chinese often ask. More than new technology and capital will be needed to attain success in establishing business alliances and operating joint ventures with the Chinese. The cultural competency of negotiators and operational managers will play a significant role in your company's Chinese market growth.

Although this chapter will focus on the mainland Chinese, some differences in dealing with the Chinese from other countries in the Asian region such as Hong Kong, Taiwan, and Singapore will also be explored. The cultural influence of the British and the Americans on the behavior of the Chinese negotiators will be pointed out.

The chapter will start by testing your current knowledge in dealing with Chinese businesspeople. It will then focus on the Chinese cultural values and differences among the Chinese from these countries. Mastering the process of personal introduction, writing to the Chinese, conducting business meetings and presentations will also be discussed in detail. A section on enhancing your relationship with the

Chinese, and what you need to do to persuade and successfully contract with them will be presented, as well. You will also learn how to manage Chinese workers, as well as socialize with the Chinese. All of this will help you succeed in your next interaction with Chinese businesses and partners.

Test Your Skills in Dealing with Chinese: True or False?

Answer the following true-or-false statements to test your skills in dealing with the Chinese:

___ 1. Laughing is one way that the Chinese may show nervousness or social discomfort.

___ 2. Discussing one's income is taboo in China.

___ 3. For the Chinese, a signed contract is a set of specifications that can be changed by parties.

___ 4. Chinese on-site negotiators have the authority to make final commitments.

___ 5. When Chinese negotiators encounter opposition, they tend to keep restating their original argument.

___ 6. In China, harmony is promoted by de-emphasizing individual needs and desires.

___ 7. The Chinese tend to be good at compromising during business negotiations.

___ 8. If a Chinese person asks if you have eaten, then that person is inviting you for a meal.

___ 9. You must present a gift of higher value to a Chinese manager than to the manager's staff during an award ceremony.

___ 10. You must maintain your credibility and build long-term relationships with Singaporeans to earn their business.

___ 11. Singaporeans conduct their business at a faster pace than the Chinese.

___ 12. Singaporeans look for tangible references before conducting business with their new partner.

___ 13. In Hong Kong, maintain your original offer. If they want your product, they will eventually give in to your price.

___ 14. Most Singaporeans take few risks and are afraid to lose.

___ 15. Competition is at the top of what most Taiwanese value.

___ 16. Most Taiwanese must spend time after work with their boss to review their progress.

___ 17. In Taiwan, working together as a group is not as important as working as an individual.

___ 18. You should indicate your lowest-accepted price as soon as possible when negotiating with the Chinese.

___ 19. Most Chinese expect gifts to come in pairs and money in even numbers.

___ 20. Time is more highly valued in China than in Hong Kong.

Answers:

1. T; 2. F; 3. T; 4. F; 5. T; 6. T; 7. T; 8. F; 9. F; 10. F; 11. T; 12. T; 13. T; 14. T; 15. T; 16. F; 17. T; 18. F; 19. T; 20. F

Personal Tales

Please help!

While I was attending and speaking at an international conference in Singapore, I was introduced to a Chinese director of a local management association in Shanghai. He noticed that I lived in California and so asked me if I could do him a favor and carry a small gift to his wife who was studying at the University of California at Berkley. In a show of cooperation and trust, I accepted and ended up carrying $100 worth of gold jewelry and other small items for his wife.

He appreciated my help and, in two months, he wrote to me inviting me to speak at a local conference that he was preparing. Initially, I took this to mean that he would pay for my travel and local expenses since I had accepted without charging him any fees and had also helped his wife. Later on, I discovered that his invitation was not as I had expected, however. He expected me to pay for my airline flight, to pay the $500 conference fees, and to receive no compensation for my speaking services.

He only offered me local accommodations at a three-star hotel, and was willing to take care of my food bill. I recognized how the Chinese imagine foreigners, especially Americans and Europeans, as rich millionaires who should donate their time and resources to help China. They expect that foreigners should come to China with the technology, expertise, and money and that the Chinese will provide the land, labor, and hopefully the market.

As this was my first trip to China, I negotiated a waiving of the conference fee and arranged my travel plans to stop by China during another Asian trip. In the end, it was a worthwhile effort, as I met with and was introduced to many local officials in appreciation for my coming and helping to make the conference a success. I also made friends with my Chinese partner, and did not let our cultural differences hinder our business relationship.

John Smith goes to China

John Smith, the marketing manager for the American company Global Mobile Telephone, planned to introduce his product into mainland China. Based on his experiences in Singapore and Taiwan, he responded to an opportunity to present his product in one of Shanghai's annual exhibitions. After one week in the show, having given out 100 product samples and 10,000 brochures to exhibition visitors, he was confident of receiving a flood of orders upon his return. Three months later, however, he had received only two inquiries for technical information and no orders. He wondered what went wrong. This process had always produced orders in America and in other countries where he had made product introductions.

The reason for Smith's lack of success was his application of American cultural values and past experience in other Chinese markets, such as Hong Kong and Singapore, to introduce his product into mainland China. As an American, engaging in the development and marketing of new products, risk taking, entrepreneurship, and taking advantage of new opportunities were strong motivations. He assumed that the very same things would be valued by his prospective Chinese buyers; he failed to recognize and understand China's core business culture, however.

In order to achieve a successful market entry in mainland China, one must first verify whether or not a compatible government policy exists for a new product or service that a foreign supplier wishes to introduce. For example, is it an approved policy to invite a foreign supplier in a joint venture to sell mobile telephones? If the foreign businessperson does not take this step to investigate relevant governmental policies, Chinese managers will only show a hint of interest in the product, no matter how useful or marketable it is.

Once the businessperson has verified the existence of a compatible policy, along with its details, the Chinese partner will insist on a joint venture. The partner will define it differently from Westerners, however, who tend to construct joint ventures as a matching dollar-to-dollar and resource-to-resource endeavor. According to the Chinese concept of a joint endeavor, the foreign supplier will supply the technology, money, and equipment, while the Chinese will match those contributions with land, labor, and the promise of a potential market. Westerners are frequently unaware of this Chinese outlook toward joint ventures, which unnecessarily prolongs the negotiation for market entry. Perhaps Smith failed to verify the existence of government policy regarding his new product in the market.

Chinese Cultural Values

The Confucian ethic is in the heart of most Chinese cultural values. Historically, the core cultural teachings that compose Confucianism have been extremely normative for all Chinese subcultural groups, regardless of the country they live in. The attitudes that have been significantly influential in their world view include total loyalty to a hierarchical structure of authority, duty to the parent, strict order, and descriptively defined forms of conduct between children and adults, in the roles of husband and wife, and trust between friends.

Most Chinese who immigrate to other nations carry and preserve these principles, while adopting other values from their new country. These values from the Confucian ethic have also markedly influenced Singapore, Hong Kong, Taiwan, and even Western countries where, in a similar adaptive process, the Confucian ethic has been combined with additional values that reflect the unique history and challenges of each country.

The cultural revolution and, more recently, the move toward the open market have deeply influenced mainland Chinese culture. In the case of the Chinese in Hong Kong and Singapore, there has been a significant impact by the British system; American culture has also impacted the Chinese in Taiwan and recently in Singapore.

During our research, Chinese business managers from China, Singapore, Hong Kong, and Taiwan were asked to prioritize 20 common values. As with our other groups, these values were group harmony, competition, seniority, cooperation, privacy, openness, equality, formality, risk taking, reputation, freedom, family, relationship, self-reliance, time, group consensus, authority, wealth, spirituality, and group achievement. The six top values selected were as follows for the groups studied:

Priorities of Values Among the Chinese

China	Taiwan	Hong Kong	Singapore
Equality	Competition	Competition	Relationship
Freedom	Family	Relationship	Family
Family	Reputation	Reputation	Openness
Group Harmony	Seniority	Time	Cooperation
Cooperation	Authority	Wealth	Freedom
Competition	Wealth	Authority	Equality

As shown, the Chinese managers that we interviewed from China, Hong Kong, Taiwan, and Singapore each hold distinct cultural values that reflect their base Chinese values and divergent historical encounters with Western culture. The variance in values reflects diverse patterns of social change, economic policy, and political history. Westerners must attune themselves to the impact of these diverse values if they hope to establish business relationships and take advantage of opportunities in the Chinese market.

You may want to compare these finding with other cultures presented in this book. Although traditional Chinese business values—such as family security, relationship, cooperation, and competition—can be observed in most of the four groups, their relative priorities differ and are balanced by elements contributed by various Western cultures with whom they have had close dealings in their respective histories.

In China, for instance, managers show high value for equality which is reflected by the current social system in the country. This should not be confused with Americans who also highly value equality in the sense of equal opportunity. The Chinese also value freedom, which may indicate a desire for change in the current system. Family security, group harmony, and cooperation follow up in the Chinese values.

It is interesting also to note that competition comes at a lower rank in China than in Taiwan and Hong Kong where many work opportunities and social services are not guaranteed as in China.

In Taiwan, competition is highly regarded, a reflection of the Chinese emphasis on hard work. The Taiwanese also put emphasis on reputation or loss of face, seniority, and respect for authority. These are best understood as a reflection of the fact that Taiwan is a small country that survives under strong leadership. Family security is also still highly regarded. Although Americans have been in Taiwan for decades with their technology, few American values have been adopted by most Taiwanese.

Hong Kong Chinese also place high value on competition due to their local free market condition. British culture has influenced the Chinese in Hong Kong through their high values on reputation and authority. The value of family is listed in all the Chinese groups except for Hong Kong, which has such a fast-paced competitive urban environment that the family has been placed at a lower value than it has been with other Chinese.

In addition, this is the only Chinese group to list time as one of their top priorities. The value of time in Hong Kong was made very clear to me during a trip there in 1996. While taking a taxi ride, I noticed that the driver was unusually speedy. When I pointed this out to him, I found out that he held two jobs as he needed to make more money. He explained that he had only a few more years to make enough money, in case things did not work out when China took control of Hong Kong. People in Hong Kong had to take advantage of their time, he said.

In another case, I was in the Hong Kong airport waiting for my next plane and decided to spend some time looking at a watch in one of the tax-free shops. I asked one of the sales girls, "How much is this watch?" She replied, "$200." I asked if I could try it on and to my surprise, she waved her hand at me, signaling "Go away!" Apparently, she recognized that I was not a real potential buyer and was wasting her time. For her, time was money. She then turned her attention to a Japanese prospect. She had noted that he was the real buyer!

In Singapore, you will still find that family, relationships, and cooperation are highly valued. The relatively low rating of competition in Singapore may well result from the fact that Singaporean Chinese have been forced to adapt to a society of extreme ethnic diversity—with relationships valued higher than competition. Singaporeans lived for a long time in a more diverse society of Malaysian, Indian, and Chinese influences, and are thus more open to new cultural elements. Furthermore, Singapore recently has acquired some American cultural elements—such as being more open, equal, and free in the American sense—as a result of the modernization process and open-market society. It represents a new society that embraces a Western culture but still maintains its Eastern values. It is a society with great potential for global success as reflected in Singapore's fast-growing business environments.

As you can see, not all Chinese have the same values. They all subscribe and come from a core set of Chinese values but are also influenced by the society and cultures that they have grown in. So, next time you meet a Chinese person, try to find out if they are a Chinese from the mainland or from another country. Most likely, they will have been influenced by a secondary culture.

Meeting the Chinese

Meeting the mayor

After his first trip, John Smith, the marketing manager for the American company Global Mobile Telephone, learned the importance of establishing a formal relationship with Chinese government officials. He then attempted to meet with the mayor of Shanghai.

Take the following quiz to test your own business sensibilities:

1. To approach the mayor, Smith should:
    a. Find someone who is a good friend of the mayor and ask for an introduction.
    b. Send a fax directly from his company to the mayor's office asking for a meeting.
    c. Have his marketing manager call the mayor's secretary for an appointment.
    d. Send a formal letter to the Foreign Affairs Office of Shanghai requesting a meeting.

Based on his experience in Taiwan, he would probably choose (a). In Singapore, approaching a company or the government (b) would be acceptable. In America, (c) would be sufficient. In dealing with the Chinese government officials, however, you must adhere to (d) first, going through the channels to obtain a formal introduction—but then you may have to utilize the strategy in (a) for a good reference.

2. After corresponding several times, Smith has acquired his long-awaited meeting to discuss his joint venture with the mayor of Shanghai. He then wondered how he could open the conversation. The topics that should be discussed during the first encounter include:
    a. The history of China.
    b. Current developments in Shanghai and new investment policies.

    c. His company's accomplishments.
    d. The mayor himself.

The opening subject of discussion with the mainland Chinese is a very sensitive matter. Among the Chinese, it is usually begun by hinting at a mutually beneficial relationship in the future. This sets up a framework to begin negotiations. The process is initiated by getting agreements from their counterparts to agree on a long-term general goal that will benefit both parties. Once this general framework has been agreed upon, the scene is set for both sides to compromise on any details involved in the general commitment.

Therefore, the correct answer is (b), to show interest in the long-term goals of the city, and in very broad terms, the development of a business relationship. Talking about yourself and your company's accomplishments would probably be more impressive to your American counterparts. Asking the mayor to talk about himself would probably embarrass him and his colleagues.

Let us also look at the following quiz:

1.   In introducing yourself to a Chinese business partner, it is acceptable to say:
    a. "I'm pleased to meet you."
    b. "Have you eaten?"
    c. "Are you busy?"
    d. Any of the above.

All of these are acceptable ways to break the ice and to begin a conversation with your Chinese counterpart. "Have you eaten?" (b) does not indicate that you are inviting them for a meal; rather, it is a general way to ask about their well-being. It comes from the Chinese old days when food was a scarce commodity and people asked each other if they had enough food to eat.

2.   You should begin discussions with your business partner by talking about:
    a. Religion.
    b. Mutual benefits.
    c. The weather.
    d. Politics.

Avoid discussing politics and religion unless it is opened up by your host. You should usually begin by emphasizing (b) the mutual benefits of the business you are discussing. If you run out of conversation, it is always acceptable to talk about (c) the weather!

3. One of the leaders of the Chinese delegation has a continuous smile on his face. This means that he is:
    a. Nervous.
    b. Embarrassed.
    c. Amused.
    d. Any of the above.

A smile from a Chinese person might indicate (d) any of the above. You must watch other signals carefully in order to distinguish between these three possibilities. Don't take most Asian smiles for general agreement.

Following are some tips and guidelines to enhance your first personal meeting with the Chinese and your entry into the Chinese market:

- The Chinese don't like to do business with strangers, so be properly introduced. If you can't get introduced, offer as much information as possible about your company and what you hope to accomplish.
- Connections are extremely important. They are required to get business matters processed quickly and smoothly through official channels. Look for any possible connection with Chinese counterparts who might act as catalysts for developing trust.
- Approach the Chinese in a formal way, but do not ignore getting business through local contacts or friends.
- Start your discussions by emphasizing mutual benefits and long-term relationships. Present your company as a potential supplier of capital and technology, with long-term interests in the Chinese market.
- *Guanxi* is a name for a network that binds people through the exchange of favors rather than through expressions of sympathy and friendship. Favors are paid for with return favors. Don't ask for impossible favors and don't accept any unless you are prepared to reciprocate. In any relationship, the number of favors done by each party must equal those of the other.
- Names are very important—the Chinese only use first names with close relatives and friends. Greet your business partners with their title and family name. Remember that family names come first in Chinese.

- The Chinese tend to shake hands very lightly. A handshake can last for 10 seconds or more. The more it lasts, the warmer your friendship will have gotten. They may also tend to stand closer than most Westerners are used to in a show of good friendship.
- Class distinctions are strong and must be obeyed. You must show respect to those in superior positions. The Chinese are conscious of and place a high degree of status on hierarchy.
- When dealing with lower-ranking persons, don't act superior and don't be too informal. Do not treat people as junior in rank when their official status in an organization is higher—this can cause them to lose face.
- Be aware that there is no word for privacy in Chinese. People are watched and suspicious events are reported.
- Public displays of affection are uncommon, except among members of the same sex. Do not touch members of the opposite sex, elderly persons, or your superiors.
- Everyone from your company should speak with one voice—show a united front and not a random collection of individuals.
- Do not be alarmed by Chinese habits such as smoking cigarettes indiscriminately, staring at foreigners, belching, spitting in the street, and laughing at mishaps.

Be also aware of the following nonverbal messages:

- The Chinese are very comfortable with silence, which may indicate politeness (paying attention) or a way to buy time during negotiations.
- Roundabout language is used to say no: "inconvenient," "under consideration," or "being discussed." Another Chinese tactic of refusal is to simply not deal with a request at all.

The following are also nonverbal messages of Chinese anger or being in an uncomfortable situation:

- Blank facial expressions, with no smiling.
- Impatient nodding and smiling.
- Periodic glancing at a clock or watch.
- Not questioning anything.
- Avoiding eye contact.
- Answering your requests with cold silence.
- Waving a hand in front of face.

If you notice these signals, you should slow down. You are going too fast or conducting a hard sale.

Written Communication

In written communications with the Chinese, formality is of the utmost importance. These are some of the favorite phrases commonly used by Chinese, "China is a big potential market," "we look forward to a mutually beneficial relationship," and "let us stand together, hand in hand." Use them and you will get ahead with them.

Here is an example of a letter I received from China:

Dear Dr. Farid Elashmawi:

Thank you for your kind reception during my visit to San Francisco and for your telephone call to me.

With regard to the joint venture consultant company, I have had no special discussions with the relevant department. Here are some suggestions:

1. You can establish a branch of your company or a representative office in Shanghai to initiate the business and to lay a path for further development.

2. We will set up a joint venture company, putting a certain amount of investment into it by both sides.

I know that you will have no opposition to the above suggestions; what is important is for the company to have a place of business, so that a market research investigation can start as a first step.

I am sorry not to have replied to your letter sooner. Very happy to have you as a friend, whose intelligence and abilities are outstanding. I believe that you will succeed and that our corporation will be in full blossom in the near future.

Yours,
Hong Jun Lu

Can you pick up the Chinese values from the letter? Read it again. Thanks is included, along with an acknowledgment to hospitality. Hong Jun Lu also stressed joint venture partnership, along with consulting with connected friends at the government and providing logical procedures according to government policy to initiate business. There was a show of appreciation for capability, seniority, and knowledge. Finally, humbleness and apologizing were included.

If you have been communicating with the Chinese, take a moment and re-read their letters to you with a cultural eye in mind and you will discover that what they want is directly stated. If you are writing to a Chinese person soon, include these cultural values within your letter and you may get a contract.

Conducting Meetings and Presentations

Mr. Smith gets closer to making a sale

Mr. Smith finally attracted the mayor of Shanghai's interest in his project and was referred to the mayor's staff for a detailed discussion. A month later, after the staff had determined that the project fit within the city plan and policy, Smith was asked to return to Shanghai and to present the technical aspect of his project. Now he wondered where the presentation should be held. Should it be at his local office? In the mayor's conference room? At the Sheraton Hotel conference room? In a restaurant during dinner?

Finally, he decided to do what he did in Singapore: offer to hold his presentation in the government office conference room, with government officials as hosts. He was extremely disappointed when he received a reply from the mayor's office saying that they were not available for a meeting with him as he proposed. He immediately picked up on the hint given to him about the best place to hold his meeting. He thought it would be more appropriate to invite the Chinese negotiation team members to one of the five-star hotel meeting rooms. He was now happy that the meeting was confirmed and that 20 members would be attending from the mayor's office. He had to ask for a larger room.

Smith wondered about the time at which his presentation should begin and end. Based on a presentation in Hong Kong he had given a month earlier, he was confident that he could conduct the meeting between 9:00 a.m. and 5:00 p.m., so he scheduled his one-day meeting for those times. To his surprise, most of the participants were available at 8:00 a.m. to welcome him and were waiting for their boss to arrive. Smith was ready by 9:00 a.m. for his presentation. He should start by mentioning:

a.   His last trip to China and how many friends he had made.
b.   New developments he has noticed during his visit.
c.   The improved U.S. policy toward China.
d.   His interest in a long-range mutual and beneficial relationship.

Smith should first bring up his own accomplishments of achieving $1 million in sales last year in Hong Kong, as well as his keen interest in moving fast with the current project in China. He should also indicate that U.S. policy toward China is passing through a difficult time, but assume that the outcome would lead to further cooperation. Soon after he noticed more interest from his audience, he should start with option (d) followed by (b).

His presentation went well until 12:00 p.m. because, by that time everyone was ready for lunch, which took them until 2 p.m., toasting and enjoying the special Chinese dishes that Smith had asked the hotel to offer. It was now the afternoon session, and Smith had to work hard to get his audience's attention after the big eight-course lunch. To his disappointment, all were ready to leave by about 4:00 p.m., before he had the chance to complete the presentation he had planned for 5:00 p.m. They were not accustomed to the time frame of most Western business meetings. He later realized that he did not need to go into the technical details as he had planned.

The next day, Smith wondered which arrangement would be best for the first business dinner. Would he insult his Chinese hosts if he invited them again to dinner on his expense account? Recalling his trip to Taiwan, where he was invited, along with his team, for dinner by his Taiwanese hosts, he decided that the best approach was to wait for their invitation. Just to test the alternate possibility, however, he invited the mayor's staff for dinner as his guests. To his surprise, the Chinese delegation had been expecting it and accepted eagerly. Later, he was again surprised when the Chinese insisted that, on the last day, they act as hosts for the formal dinner together as a farewell to him and his team.

In China, the foreign businessperson coming in to present a product or service is expected initially to host the Chinese to make their presentations. You are expected to approach them in a formal and respectful manner in this social context. When they host you on the last day, they feel that you are obligated to come back and reciprocate the honor for future business dealings. They expect you to be their host on the first day, and then they insist upon entertaining you on the last day.

Smith had also wondered what to talk about during the first dinner. Should he discuss his work and family, how many cars he owned and how big his house was, his travel experience around the world, the current inflation in China, or perhaps, current human rights issues and the move toward democracy in Hong Kong? After trying to converse about all of the above, he discovered that they were mostly interested in his work and family. The other subjects were just received with a polite smile. At this stage of the relationship, it was appropriate to talk more personally and informally, whereas formality was essential at the beginning.

The above is in total contrast in meeting with managers in Hong Kong or Singapore, where meetings can be held in the company offices. You can be met by one or two persons or by a manager. Meetings are generally short and to the point. You can present yourself, explain the purpose of the meeting, and have a fair and open discussion. Ceremony is at a minimum and decisions are usually received within a short period of 1–3 weeks from the meetings. Sometimes, the meetings are followed by lunch to further enhance the relationship. Payment can be shared or reciprocated in future meetings. You can expect an open and direct discussion of the topics under consideration.

Following is another quiz to consider:

1. Where should you seat the head of the Chinese delegation?
   a. By the door so that he doesn't have to walk far.
   b. Sitting with a beautiful painting behind him.
   c. Facing a beautiful painting so that he can enjoy it.
   d. At the head of the table.

In China, the guest of honor or the highest-ranking person will sit (b) in front of a beautiful painting.

2. When you start a meeting with the Chinese, you should first:
   a. Introduce yourself briefly.
   b. Thank the participants for coming and state the meeting's purpose.
   c. Introduce the Chinese co-chairman.
   d. Introduce the VIPs to the participants.

Introduce the Chinese co-chairman (c) first, followed by (d) the VIPs. Then (a) introduce yourself before (b) thanking the participants for attending and stating the purpose of the meeting.

3. A Chinese businessman might respond to your proposal by saying, that possibly they could reach an agreement on your proposal. This means:
   a. Yes.
   b. Probably.

     c. Probably not.
     d. No.

"Maybe" in Chinese culture will usually mean "probably not" or "no." No Chinese person has the authority to give a confirmed yes until the big boss has agreed—after a lot of discussions with the other managers. Nothing can be taken verbally; everything should be confirmed in writing.

    4.   In closing a formal meeting, it is best to:
       a. Say a few words of thanks to the participants.
       b. Give a brief summary of the meeting.
       c. Present your own views and recommendations.
       d. Give a short summary and ask the co-chairman to say a few words.

In closing a meeting, it is appropriate to (d) summarize briefly and then offer the co-chairman the opportunity to say a few words. You must then (a) thank the participants for attending. Formal meetings usually start by the boss saying a few words to motivate participants for cooperation and finally end with thanks for participants.

    5.   A senior Chinese official wishes to end the meeting. He expresses this by:
       a. Thanking you for coming.
       b. Offering you more tea.
       c. Standing up.
       d. Summarizing what has been said.

If the Chinese wish to end a meeting, they will probably (b) offer you more tea rather than standing up or thanking you. At that time, you must be ready to conclude the meeting and summarize the discussion.

Tips for Conducting Business Meetings with the Chinese

- Hire your own interpreter and use them to gain maximum benefit. Avoid using their interpreter who, in turn, may be used to negotiate against you.
- Arrive prepared and present yourself in a professional manner. Your handouts, such as product descriptions and company brochures, should be in English.

- They may ask you for a list of the names and positions of your team members. You should seek the same to identify the level of responsibility and decision makers.
- The first meetings will be formal and usually go slowly.
- Provide background information about your company in time for the Chinese to study it. This will speed up formal discussions with you. Giving them this information may very well be one of the keys to completing the sale.
- Initial meetings with foreigners are usually held in conference rooms of major hotels, and not in their own offices. There will be designated seating for the senior participants.
- Arrive on time and be prepared to break the ice with small talk, but not jokes.
- Only senior members on both sides are free to talk; junior members must wait for specific invitations. Never put anyone, especially senior members, on the spot by openly disagreeing with them.
- Do not interrupt the Chinese leader, even if the leader is making a mistake. Instead, take note on what is said and mention it to them later, preferably outside of the conference room. Be prepared to listen to bland introductions by leaders and drink a lot of Chinese tea.
- Make your presentation formal and don't use humor. With some cultures, humor may be used as an ice-breaker; with the Chinese, however, it is definitely taboo. Your presentation should be free of technical jargon. Remember to give them the technical data weeks in advance. Your presentation is meant to actually make the sale. The shorter the presentation the better.
- The Chinese do not like surprises and will tend to work out their position before the meeting. They prefer to know what will be discussed ahead of time.
- Do not be secretive with your information. This will make the Chinese suspicious and reluctant to do business with you. Remember, trust and honesty are important to the Chinese. You must satisfy their values and needs in order to be considered a partner. You cannot make the sale depending on your price or on new technology alone.
- The Chinese traditionally believe in doing things carefully and meticulously. They examine every detail, strive to clarify every point of discussion, and have no strict deadlines to meet.
- Take notes on what your Chinese partners suggest. This lets them know that you are taking their advice and opinions seriously. It shows them respect, and will also give you the information you need when lengthy discussions begin.

- Be willing to answer any questions. This should be obvious, yet often presenters are either unwilling or unprepared to answer their Chinese clients' questions. Asking many questions on issues that have already been responded to, however, can be interpreted as mistrust.
- Business agreements will only proceed when it is obvious to the Chinese party that they will lead to common interests.
- At the end of the meeting, summarize the discussion. Ask for a contact person for future negotiations.
- Expect and allow for an average two-hour break for lunch after a three-hour morning meeting.
- It is important to recap what has been agreed upon after each meeting.
- Teams tend to be larger than some cultures expect.
- Recognize and follow the firm's hierarchy. Chinese managers do not make quick decisions.

Persuading the Chinese

Mr. Smith negotiates with the Chinese

After spending almost $500 making the Chinese delegation happy during dinner, Mr. Smith was confident that his presentation the next day would bring him a spectacular order. Smith now had to close the sale and discuss the price.

He had these options:

a.   Present his price and offer them three days to accept it.
b.   Present testimonials from his clients in Taiwan and Hong Kong which demonstrated their satisfaction with his product.
c.   Ask the group leader to state his view of the offer.
d.   Finish his presentation with a statement that stressed their long-term mutually beneficial relationship.

To his surprise, none of these were good options. The group leader, Mr. Chen, immediately asked him for a special discount to guarantee long-term success. To Smith, this was the hint that the Chinese were really interested in his product after long discussions on technical matters.

Since he was authorized by his board of directors to give a 10% discount, Smith immediately offered it to sweeten the deal, which the

Chinese received with appreciation, but without firm commitment. They asked him to reconvene with them the next Tuesday for further negotiation. Smith was so happy and confident that he immediately faxed his boss in California with the good news of the large order soon to be finalized. Smith spent the weekend beside the Sheraton Hotel swimming pool, drinking and celebrating the order which he expected next week. He thought the team accepted his offer and discount.

The following Tuesday, Smith met with the Chinese. To his surprise, half of the team had been replaced by older, more senior managers. When he began to discuss the order, he was informed by the new senior negotiator, Mr. Lee, that he could not accept the given discount on the order, and would need another 10% discount to take his offer to Beijing.

"What about my agreement with Mr. Chen?" Smith asked. The Chinese negotiator explained that Chen was only the junior negotiator, whereas he, the senior member of the team, would be the one to take his offer to Beijing. Without any further authority to discount, Smith had no option but to remain silent. He recognized that he had failed to identify the level of seniority/authority of the negotiation team.

Having given up everything he could discount, the client offered him more tea, a signal that the meeting was concluded. Smith went back to the Sheraton wondering how he could justify his $5,000 expense account during his one-week stay at the Sheraton in Shanghai and the loss of the big order he had promised.

Negotiating in the Street

Here is one of my own perennial examples of how price negotiations are handled in China. During a recent visit to Taiwan, I decided to buy a shirt and observed the interaction closely. Upon walking into a retail clothing shop, I asked the clerk, "How much is that shirt?" The clerk replied, "Twenty-five dollars." I then countered with $5, thinking we could settle for $15 or $20. The angry owner, however, almost threw me out of his shop.

I had to leave that store and, through repeated experiments at making counter-offers at another store, I learned that at the beginning of the negotiation you should never make counter-offers. The Chinese consider counter-offers that are far less than their own price to be insulting. Secondly, never reveal your lowest price. Once you do, your Chinese counterpart will raise you a dollar or so, and the bargain will be stuck at that level.

The strategy is to refuse each succeeding offer the Chinese negotiator offers you, claiming that you simply cannot afford it, until the negotiator can lower the price no further. You can even walk out of the negotiating room or store. In my shirt-buying experiment, I finally obtained an identical shirt for $16 by using the two basic strategies of refraining from making counter-offers and never naming my lowest price.

Consider the following quiz:

1.   You are promoting your company's product to Chinese government officials. You should mention that your:
     a. Product is the cheapest.
     b. Price is not the cheapest, but the product is of the best quality.
     c. Customers are of the utmost value to you.
     d. After-sales services are the best in the industry.

The Chinese will look for foreign investors to supply technology and capital. They will entertain your projects if they feel that both of these will be provided. They will look first for the (b) best quality and then for the (d) after-sales service. The Chinese will always produce items at the cheapest possible price.

2.   During negotiations with the Chinese, they'll be most concerned with:
     a. Maintaining government policies.
     b. Reducing the price of your offer.
     c. Compromising with you.
     d. Providing jobs for their people.

Government policy (a) must always be adhered to by the Chinese negotiator. Price negotiation is a win-lose situation to the Chinese—they will not compromise.

3.   To be accepted as a partner in a venture with the Chinese, you must show:
     a. Creativity.
     b. A desire to make the deal mutually beneficial.
     c. Leadership abilities.
     d. Technical know-how.

The Chinese will look for a partner who focuses on (b) mutually beneficial relationships. Technical know-how (d) and providing new technology creatively (a) are also strong assets.

In negotiating with mainland Chinese, there are several factors that are important to keep in mind. The group composition of the negotiators will be middle- to high-level managers, depending on the stage of the negotiations. Negotiators will receive instructions from superiors throughout the negotiations, and will demonstrate a formal style. They will establish rapport by hinting at the long-range mutual benefits, and will try to persuade you to meet their terms by stressing benefits over the long range and how large their market is. The decision process will involve their seeking formal approval from the department head and their adherence to strict policy.

To respond effectively to their style of negotiating, it is crucial that you identify the level of the negotiators at each stage and who the decision maker is. Ultimately, it is the top-level manager who finally decides. When the Chinese hint about long-term benefits, reciprocate and show that you share their vision, but focus on results, step by step.

In response to their suggestions that you will gain a large market and plentiful business connections, stress their gains in technology and capital investments, exportability and expanding overseas markets of their own, such as bringing in foreign currency. Focus on their point of view and economic needs. If there is an opportunity, influence lobbyists. Allow for their need to reach a consensus and obtain approval. Be patient and ready to compromise, but never indicate your final terms or your lowest price.

Another way of understanding the unique mainland Chinese negotiation style is to contrast it with that of other Pacific Rim groups. In terms of persuasion tools, as mentioned, the Chinese will hint about long-range benefits and their large market and seek formal approval from the department head, who adheres to strict policy. In contrast, other groups reflect other dominant themes and values in their own negotiations. Indonesians engage in a three-stage process in which a spokesman initially recommends you, then an influential person within the company sponsors you and, finally a decision maker, whom you may never meet, approves your transaction. They stress future business opportunities, but emphasize the large profit margin to be earned, as well as the personal gain of each participant.

The Japanese consider consensus to be essential; a recommendation from a "sponsor" will be approved by the top manager. Koreans engage in a bargaining process until a compromise is reached and will integrate you into their own interpersonal process through ceremonies, such as visits to shrines, while Americans will press for immediate decisions or the loss of the opportunity. They also ensure that facts back up the business arrangements discussed before making a formal commitment.

Tips for Enhancing Your Relationships with the Chinese

- Relationships are important to the Chinese. If they bring business to you, they expect you to reciprocate their efforts.
- You must maintain your credibility continuously, and build long-term relationships with Singaporeans.
- Be willing to spend some money on your Chinese client. If they are visiting your country, show them a good time. Above all, don't be cheap. A visitor to San Francisco, for example, may expect a room in a nice hotel, along with a tour of the city and the Golden Gate Bridge. A nice dinner after the tour may bring you one step closer to a deal. To the Chinese, your success as a host will be an indication of your potential success as a partner.
- Establishing and promoting friendship is key to successful business dealings with the Chinese.
- Sometimes face can be given, earned, taken away, or lost.
- The Chinese look for tangible references before conducting business with their customers.
- The Chinese will not discuss details until they feel that you are committed to a long-term relationship. Trust and mutual obligation are key factors in determining whether or not the Chinese will decide to do business with you.
- The Chinese may be silent, which can be awkward for Westerners, but their silence does not necessarily indicate an opposition to questions and discussion. Ask pertinent questions and be prepared to back up any suggestions you may have.
- Do what you can to reward your Chinese partners. Introduce them to any government connections you may have that will help their careers. They will do the same for you. This is especially true if your partners do business with your native country often. Also, they may very well reciprocate these rewards and introductions with valuable rewards and introductions of their own.
- If government policy changes, you too may have to change your requirements in order to maintain your business status. Remember to be open to change; if you work with your Chinese partner, unexpected conflicts can usually be resolved.

- Discount the enthusiastic Chinese statements about future prospects and their own power.
- Singaporeans conduct their business very quickly. Try either to match their fast pace or to slow them down.

Characteristics of the Chinese Negotiator

The Chinese basic assumption in negotiation is that logic leads to the right conclusions. They will often:

- Form reasons, draw conclusions, and apply them in negotiation.
- Argue in favor of or against one's own or another's position.
- Direct, break down, divide and analyze.
- Put things into a logical order.
- Weigh the pros and cons.
- Make identical statements.
- Use linear reckoning.

They often use the following key words and phrases: *because, then, consequently, therefore, in order to.*

In responding to these, you must in turn:

- Use logic.
- Look for causes and effects.
- Analyze the relationships between the elements.
- Be patient.
- Analyze pros and cons of various options.

The following table summarizes the contrast in negotiating with diversity of the Chinese in the Pacific rim region. Keep these differences in mind during your next encounters with each of these groups.

	Mainland	Singapore	Taiwan	Hong Kong
Group Composition	Middle- to high-level manager, depending on stage of negotiations.	Middle manager takes charge.	Junior and middle managers.	Middle and senior managers.
Rapport	Long-range mutual benefits.	Relationship and reference.	Credibility and reputation.	Semiformal until a relationship is established.

	Mainland	Singapore	Taiwan	Hong Kong
Information Exchange	Formal with high expectations for capital and technology.	Semiformal, emphasis on immediate mutual benefit.	Cautious, slow.	Fast, time pressure, follow procedures.
Persuasion Tools	Capital, technology, export potential.	Afraid to lose, "Kazo."	Price conscious.	Immediate benefit.
Decisions	Adhering to policy directed by middle managers.	Fast, low risk-taking.	Top-down.	Fact-based, low risk.
Decision Makers	Top management.	Middle management.	Top management.	Top management.

Countering the Chinese Negotiation Team

Following are further tips on how you can encounter the Chinese negotiators:

	Chinese	You
Group Composition	Middle- to high-level manager, depending on stage.	Identify the level of negotiators at each stage, and the ultimate decision maker.
Establishing Rapport	Hint about long-range mutual benefits.	Reciprocate but focus on results, step by step.
Information exchange	Use formal style. Have high expectations for investment funds and technology.	Give gifts, participate in social activities; give, but ask for fair return.
Persuasion Tools	Stress long-range benefits, their huge market, business connections.	Emphasize technology gain, capital investment, exportability, the market.
Decision Process	Seek formal approval from department boss, adhere to strict policy, instruction from superiors.	Allow for their need to reach consensus. Never indicate bottom price; compromise.
Decision Makers	Top-level manager decides.	Focus on the boss's point of view, their economic needs. Influence lobbyists.

Further Tips for Negotiating with Chinese

- At the beginning of negotiations, the Chinese will hint about the need for long-term business relationships characterized by friendship, understanding, and mutual dependency. Once they do this, stop them and ask them to define the details before you proceed.
- Losing face is a major cause of lost deals, often for overzealous Western negotiators. The Chinese will keep their feelings mostly hidden, and you may want to learn to do the same, even if this is not your usual bargaining style. Avoid showdowns. Causing the Chinese to lose face will not help your chances for success.
- Know which negotiating points are important to your Chinese counterparts and do your best to accommodate these factors.
- Accommodation has an amazing way of bringing you closer to closing a deal. The Chinese are sharp negotiators. However, don't accommodate so much that you are stuck with the short end of the stick.
- The Chinese may stress mutual interests rather than compromise, but they think of winners and losers. Maintain your original offer. If they want your product, they will eventually give in to your price.
- In Chinese organizations, decisions are made by a process of consensus involving people at several different levels of management.
- Singaporeans analyze all details and possible outcomes of their deals.
- Many Singaporeans take few risks and are afraid to lose. They are satisfied with a small but guaranteed profit.
- Expect the Chinese to ask at the last moment for an extra enticement to be thrown into the deal. Keep your sweetener to the end.

Contracting with Chinese

In contracting with the Chinese, watch for the following:

- Be careful when contracting with the Chinese. Generic contracts may get you into trouble because they may be out of date concerning certain policies of the Chinese government. Only sign a contract that is designed specifically for you; a generic contract should not be accepted.
- Don't sign on the dotted line until you are certain of every move your Chinese partners will make and how your place in the market will be affected by government policy.
- A signed contract is seen as simply one incident in a series of many in a long-term relationship. The main purpose of a contract is to establish a positive relationship that will continue indefinitely.

- Expect and be willing to renegotiate contracts. To the Chinese, contract signing is the beginning of the relationship and so changes are expected and acceptable to them.
- If the policies of the Chinese government change significantly between the signing and completion of a contract, they will ask to renegotiate.

Working with the Chinese

The following quiz will give you an insight into improving your relationships with Chinese workers:

1. During your first week as a general manager in China, it is appropriate to:
   a. Invite your staff to lunch to discuss your business plans.
   b. Photograph yourself with your arm around your new secretary.
   c. Take a group picture with yourself sitting in the middle.
   d. Pay a visit to the mayor's office.

A group picture with you in the middle (c) and paying a visit to the mayor's office (d) are fine. Inviting your staff to lunch to discuss your business plans (a) is an excellent way to introduce your ideas and personality to them, as is often used in the United States. Photographing yourself with your new secretary (b), especially if the secretary is a woman, will be seen as too overt for a new manager. You may not last as a manager for a long time.

2. Chinese workers are motivated primarily by:
   a. Competition among themselves.
   b. Social recognition.
   c. Money.
   d. Promotion within the company.

Being promoted within a company (d) is a means of social recognition (b), which will in the meantime bring them (c) more money and power. Being a boss is highly valued and sought out by most Chinese.

3. Your Chinese chauffeur has made an extra effort to help you get to your destinations every day on time. You want to recognize him at a dinner party. You should:

a. Ask the hotel manager to deliver a boxed dinner to him in his car.
b. Invite him to dinner with you and the other delegation members.
c. Ask the hotel manager to serve him dinner at a nearby table.
d. Give him 10 dollars so that he may purchase his own dinner.

In the Chinese social system, it is appropriate to invite staff members and even your driver to share a meal with you (b). The driver is considered part of the team. It would not be a bad idea to later give the driver a small gift from your country or company in appreciation of the extra efforts.

Tips for Working with the Chinese

- Be patient and polite when working with the Chinese. Maintain surface harmony at all times. Never do anything to cause public unpleasantness or embarrassment.
- Having face means having high status and prestige in the eyes of one's peers. It is a mark of personal dignity.
- Achieving friendship will lead to a smoother business relationship based on mutual obligation and trust.
- Lies may be told to avoid disrupting social harmony or to keep a guest from losing face.
- The Chinese do not question or try to change the social order. They bow to authority and believe that group membership is more important than individuality.
- The actions of individuals reflect on everyone in the group.
- Consensus is desired above all else. Debate continues until a consensus is achieved. The leader's decision is final. Individuals must accept and act on this decision regardless of their personal opinions.
- The regard in which one is held by others, or the light in which one appears, is of vital importance. Causing someone to lose face by failing to treat them with respect or by publicly criticizing them will result in loss of cooperation and even retaliation.
- Praising a worker to their superior will give a Chinese more face and will be greatly appreciated.
- The Chinese often use intermediaries to carry unpleasant news, offer trial ideas, and serve as back channels for information.
- The Chinese are obligated to relatives, friends, neighbors, classmates, and coworkers, but no one else. Philanthropy is almost

nonexistent and the Chinese tend to show little respect for public or commonly held property.

- Don't tell jokes, especially political jokes, in the workplace.
- Ask for permission before photographing anyone.
- Do not show anxiety or impatience in the early meetings and don't be pushy or aggressive in hopes of speeding up the work.
- Chinese workers are likely to return to previously discussed topics and go over them again.

Be aware of Singapore's diversity: Singapore is populated by Chinese, Malaysians, and Indians—and each group has its own way of doing business.

- Senior managers can be as young as 40–45 years old, working managers are 30–40, and working staff are from 20 on up. You must learn to work with each of these levels of age.
- Singaporean office managers don't seek personal financial gain from your business. They often try to impress their bosses rather than seek good deals.
- Singaporeans respect their bosses: everyone strives to become one.
- You must be ready to deal with young, vibrant, energetic individuals who are very well-educated.
- Singaporeans conduct their business very quickly. Try to match their fast pace, or slow them down.
- Singaporean businesspeople have been influenced by American values of directness.
- Singaporeans still value relationships, networking, and adhering to authority.
- The decision-making process is much faster than that on the mainland, along with the execution of projects.
- Relationships are important to Singaporeans. If they bring business to you, they expect you to reciprocate their efforts.
- Singaporeans analyze all details and possible outcomes of their deals.
- You can approach a Singaporean company solely on your technical merits. Closing the sales, however, will again require establishing a trusting relationship.
- Singaporeans are satisfied with a small but guaranteed profit. They may seem to be afraid to lose.

Social Etiquette

Here is a quiz regarding various social encounters that you may face:

1. If you invite a Chinese person to lunch or dinner, he will probably say, "No, thank you." This means that:
    a. He does not want to accept your invitation.
    b. The Chinese don't mix business with pleasure.
    c. He is being polite by refusing your first invitation; offer again.
    d. He does not want you to pay for his meal.

The Chinese often refuse first offers. It is the polite way of saying yes (c). You must repeat your offer once or twice; they will certainly accept it. Be generous in the selection of food and be a good host in serving them.

2. When invited to a Chinese home for dinner, you should:
    a. Bring some food typical of your country.
    b. Bring a gift.
    c. Bring nothing.
    d. Have a local delicacy delivered.

A gift from you will usually be appreciated. Do not bring local food, however, as this is your host's responsibility and honor. Show your appreciation for the food and eat a lot. Avoid political or religion discussion.

3. After dinner at one of Shanghai's famous restaurants with your Chinese host, how can you show your appreciation to the waiter?
    a. Leave a good tip.
    b. Give him your company's lapel pin.
    c. Ask him to join you for a drink.
    d. Give him your business card.

A company lapel pin (b) would be a nice memory of your visit. A tip would also be appreciated (a). There is no need to leave your business card in this kind of social environment and certainly no invitation to drink.

4. After dinner, you want to present your hosts with gifts, so you:
   a. Give one to your group leader.
   b. Give a gift to everyone.
   c. Hand the gift to the leader when he is alone.
   d. Give the leader the gift at your hotel.

It is expected that equally valued gifts will be handed to every participating member of the team (b). It's not a bad idea to hand the leader a more expensive gift later (c) in further appreciation of his extra effort.

5. A Chinese person burps loudly after a meal. This is an indication that:
   a. The food was too rich.
   b. He appreciates the meal.
   c. You should burp, too.
   d. He needs a glass of water.

Burping is a show of appreciation (b) for the meal and drink, along with your hospitality. Don't be offended by what your culture might perceive as rudeness; it is, in fact, a way of thanking you.

6. The Chinese signal the end of a meal by:
   a. Offering a fish course.
   b. Putting their chopsticks next to the dish.
   c. Passing a hot towel.
   d. Any of the above.

All of these (d) indicate the end of the meal course. No more food will follow.

Keep in mind the following social etiquette when dealing with the Chinese:

- You must offer gifts of equal value to a Chinese manager and staff.
- If the Chinese person doesn't open your gift immediately, that does not mean that person is not interested in your offer.
- Do not wrap gifts in black or white paper (a sign of death).
- The first dinner toast should be offered before the first course.
- Foreigners' spouses are welcome at social occasions and are considered equal in rank to the businessperson.
- If you must turn down an invitation to a Chinese person's home, explain why.

- If you accept an invitation, bring a gift.
- Eat a lot—show your enjoyment of the food. Reply to apologies with compliments. Don't leave immediately after the meal.
- Don't give clocks, cut flowers, green hats, or extravagant gifts.
- Gifts are commonly offered at the end of meetings.
- Red color indicates success.
- Keep your guests' plates full of food.
- When you are full, leave some food on your plate. Enormous quantities of food on the table demonstrate the host's generosity.
- If a Chinese person asks, "Have you eaten?" they are only asking about your well being.
- Slouching in a chair and pointing with anything but the hands is considered crude.
- Most Chinese expect gifts to come in pairs and money in even numbers.

Summary

Many foreign firms might be attracted to the Chinese market because of its market size. The Chinese, however, will usually only allow these foreign firms to come in under specific joint venture agreements. To the Chinese, joint venture means that foreign firms bring in their technology and money and the Chinese authority will provide the land, the labor, and the promise of a potential market.

Some foreign suppliers may be lucky if they sell more than one factory or go beyond licensing new technology. The Chinese will usually follow with their own brand name and sell through their own distribution channel in the Chinese market. Under these conditions, one must assure that a strong relationship does exist between him, his firm, and the Chinese partner and government.

You will never be a Chinese person but you can learn from them. Maintain and enhance the established relationship. If you do not know something, just ask a mentor or a close friend and you will end up on the correct cultural path. Keep in mind all the Chinese norms presented concerning personal introductions, written communication, the conduction of meetings and negotiations, and social taboos. This will put you ahead of your competitors. Compare what you have learned about dealing with the Chinese to what you learned about dealing with other cultures in the previous chapters and you will sail smoothly through China and discover what is behind the Chinese facade.

Epilogue

Going global is a reality of today's business environment. The tools provided by the Internet and e-commerce have created new technology to communicate faster than ever imagined, but speed is not enough to compete globally. It is your cultural competency that will give you a competitive edge in the global market.

In this book, we have examined and interacted with various Eastern and Western cultures. Prior to traveling abroad or coming in contact with someone from another culture, you might be unaware of your own cultural assumptions. In today's business world, this is a dangerous oversight because of the increasing number of joint ventures and the diversity of each company's workforce. It is necessary to discover your core cultural values. For some people, these cultural assumptions become painfully clear during an important business meeting or discussing a possible sale of your product to a foreign corporation. This book has given you the opportunity to look at your own cultural values and compare those to cultures from all over the world.

This cultural awareness is a necessity in business, as seen in the various tables, charts, examples, quizzes, and stories. You have discovered your own personal values and how different or similar they are to other cultural values you come in contact with. Each person you meet will have their own unique values that have been rewarded by their family, community, business, and nation. It is now your job to create a synergy between your own cultural assumptions, what you have learned, and your understanding of other cultures. Applying this new awareness will give you the opportunity to create a new culture between you and your client. However, it is crucial to remember not to push your cultural values on anyone else. Creating a balance between you and your colleagues will build a lasting business relationship. This advantage over your competitors will be well rewarded if you keep learning about other cultures and apply that knowledge to your next venture.

We only covered some of the world's cultures, but, through the nine chapters presented, you have built the skills necessary to be culturally competent, so that you may be better prepared to deal with a variety of cultures in the future. Don't assume that your title, business card, product, or price will open the door. You have enhanced your cultural competency, which will supplement your product and price to give you an advantage over your competitors. When you embark on your journey and enter a new culture, you are there to learn from that culture. Do not make many assumptions, because that is how you will lose business. Simply ask how and why things are done a certain way in America, Japan, China, Saudi Arabia, Germany, or wherever. If you ask and show an interest in learning more, someone will be happy to help you better understand their culture.

Whether you read this book before you start a journey or if you are currently doing business globally, I hope that you will learn from my mistakes and accomplishments, so that you may enhance your own experiences. It is your cultural competency that will be the most important value to successfully compete globally.

F.E.

Recommended Reading

Abdullah, A. *Going Global: Cultural Dimensions in Malaysian Management.* Kuala Lumpur: Malaysian Institute of Management, 1996.

Althen, G. *American Ways: A Guide for Foreigners in the United States.* Yarmouth, ME: Intercultural Press, 1988.

Andres, T. D. *Team Building and Creating Effective Work Systems.* Quezon City: New Day Publishers, 1992.

Andres, T. D. *Negotiating by Filipino Values.* Manila: Divine Word Publications, 1988.

Andres, T. D. *Understanding Filipino Values: A Management Approach.* Quezon City: New Day Publishers, 1981.

Axtel, R. *Gestures: The Do's and Taboos of Body Language Around the World.* New York, NY: Wiley & Sons, 1991.

Barnett, A. *How to Understand Our Relationship with Korea.* Sacramento, CA: The American Intercultural Consultation Group, 1988.

Bedi, H. *Understanding the Asian Manager.* North Sydney, Australia: Allen & Unwin, 1991.

Bennett, M. E. and Stewart, E. C. American *Cultural Patterns: A Cross-Cultural Perspective.* Yarmouth, ME: Intercultural Press, 1991.

Black, J. S., et al. *Global Assignments: Successfully Expatriating and Repatriating International Managers.* San Francisco, CA: Jossey-Bass, 1992.

Bosrock, M. M. *Put Your Best Foot Forward Europe: A Fearless Guide to Intercultural Communication and Behavior.* St. Paul, MN: International Education Systems, 1994.

Brake, T.; Walker, D. M.; Walker, T. *Doing Business Internationally: The Guide to Cross Cultural Success.* Princeton, NJ: Training Management Co., 1995.

Brannen, C. *Going to Japan on Business.* Berkeley, CA: Stone Bridge Press, 1991.

Brislin, R. W.; Petersen, P. B.; Weeks, W. H. *A Manual of Structured Experiences for Cross-Cultural Learning.* Yarmouth, ME: Intercultural Press, 1985.

Brussow, H. I., and Kohls, L. R. *Training Know-How for Cross-Cultural and Diversity Trainers.* Yarmouth, ME: Intercultural Press/Adult Learning Systems, 1995.

Bucknall, K. B. *Kevin B. Bucknall's Cultural Guide to Doing Business in China.* Oxford, UK: Butterworth-Heinemann Ltd., 1994.

Business Week, *Preparing Your Business for the Global Economy.* New York, NY: McGraw-Hill, 1996.

Casse, P. and Deol, S. *Managing Intercultural Negotiations: Guidelines for Trainers and Negotiators.* Washington, DC: SIETAR International, 1985.

Casse, P. *Training for the Multicultural Manager.* Washington, DC: SIETAR International, 1982.

Chia, A. and Putti, J. M. *Culture and Management: A Casebook.* Singapore: McGraw-Hill, 1990.

Conway, W. A.; Douress, J. I.; and Morrison T. *Dun & Bradstreet's Guide to Doing Business Around the World.* Englewood, NJ: Prentice Hall PTR, 1997.

Cooper, N. and Cooper R. *Culture Shock Thailand.* Singapore: Times Books International, 1986.

Cooper R. *Thais Mean Business: The Foreign Businessman's Guide to Doing Business in Thailand.* Singapore: Times Books International, 1992.

Covey, S. R. *The 7 Habits of Highly Effective People: Powerful Lessons in Personal Change.* New York, NY: Simon & Schuster, 1989.

Crane, P. S. *Korean Patterns.* Seoul, Korea: Kwangjin Publishing Co., 1978.

Crowther, G.; Else, D.; Finlay, H.; Fitzpatrick, M.; Greenway, P.; Humphreys, A.; Jousiffe, A.; Linzee Gordon, F.; Murray J.; Roddis, M.; Singh, S.; Swaney, D.; Talbot, D.; Willett, D.; Williams, J. *Africa on a Shoestring.* Australia: Lonely Planet Publications, 1998.

De Mente, B. *Korean Etiquette & Ethics in Business: A penetrating analysis of the morals and values that shape the Korean business personality.* Lincolnwood, IL: NTC Business Books, 1991.

Draffen, A.; Jones, R.; McAsey, C.; Pinheiro, L.; Selby, N. *Brazil: From Amazon adventure to revelry in Rio.* Australia: Lonely Planet Publications, 1998.

Draine, C. and Hall, B. *Culture Shock: Indonesia.* Portland, OR: Graphic Arts Center Publishing Co., 1993.

Dyer, W. G. *Team Building: Issues and Alternatives.* Reading, MA: Addison Wesley Publishing Co., 1987.

Elashmawi, F. "Communicating Effectively with Your Arab Partner." *Trade & Culture*, Jan. 1996: 54–6.

Elashmawi, F. "Creating a Winning Corporate Culture: Experience Inside the Asian Telecommunications Industry." *European Business Review*, Vol. 12, no. 3 2000: 148–56.

Elashmawi, F. "Culture Clashes: Barriers to Business." *Directions*, Feb.–Mar. 1993: 33–5.

Elashmawi, F. "Dealing Successfully with the Americans." *Certified Management Digest*, July 1996, 20–1.

Elashmawi, F. "Dealing with Indonesians." *Trade & Culture*, Feb–Mar. 1997.

Elashmawi, F. "Doing Business with the Koreans: The Clash of the Cultures." *Certified Management Digest*, May 1996: 26–7.

Elashmawi, F. "Don't Let Yourself Be Misunderstood." *World Executive's Digest*, Oct. 1993: 50.

Elashmawi, F. "Hidden Messages in Intercultural Negotiations." *Directions*, June–July 1993: 50–2.

Elashmawi, F. "Improving Your Business in Korea." *Tokyo Business Today*, Feb. 1994: 38–41.

Elashmawi, F. "Intercultural Negotiation: New Skills for the Global Manager." *Directions*, Sep.–Oct. 1993: 48–51.

Elashmawi, F. "Japanese Culture Clash in Multicultural Management." *Tokyo Business Today*, Feb. 1990: 36–39.

Elashmawi, F. "Learn the Customs to Gain An Edge." *World Executive's Digest*, July 1993: 48–9.

Elashmawi, F. "Making the Shoe Fit." *World Executive's Digest*, June 1998: 56–7.

Elashmawi, F. "Management Multicultural' *Ejectivos de Finanzas,* Junio 1997: 49–51. (trans. into Spanish)

Elashmawi, F. "Managing Culture Conflict in the Arab World." *Trade & Culture*, Sept.–Oct. 1994: 48–9.

Elashmawi, F. "Managing Multicultural Human Resources." *Directions*, May 1994: 35–37.

Elashmawi, F. "Managing Successful Multicultural Joint Ventures—Part I." *Certified Management Digest*, Feb. 1998: 61–62.

Elashmawi, F. "Managing Successful Multicultural Joint Ventures—Part II." *Certified Management Digest*, Mar. 1998: 61–2.

Elashmawi, F. "Mr. Bell Goes to Arabia: A Cautionary Tale." *Trade & Culture*, Jan.–Feb. 1995: 43–4.

Elashmawi, F. "Multicultural Business Meetings and Presentations: Tips and Taboos." *Tokyo Business Today*, Nov. 1991: 66–68.

Elashmawi, F. "Multicultural Management and Negotiation: Dealing Successfully with Indonesians." *Certified Management Digest*, June 1996: 11–3.

Elashmawi, F. "Multicultural Management and Negotiation: Doing Business with the Japanese." *Certified Management Digest*, Apr. 1996: 26–7.

Elashmawi, F. "Multicultural Management: New Skills for Global Success." *Tokyo Business Today*, Feb. 1991: 54–6.

Elashmawi, F. "Negotiating Successfully with Koreans." *Directions*, Jan–Feb. 1994: 35–9.

Elashmawi, F. "Negotiating with Chinese: Cultural Dimensions." *Directions*, Jan. 1995: 72–76.

Elashmawi, F. "New Dimensions in Business Training." *International Journal of Human Resources*, Nov. 1994: 25–29.

Elashmawi, F. "Overcoming Multicultural Clashes in Global Joint Ventures." *European Business Review*, Vol. 98, no. 4 1998.

Elashmawi, F. "Overcoming Multicultural Clashes in Global Joint Ventures." *Trade & Culture*, May 1997: 43–5.

Elashmawi, F. "Sailing Across Cultures." *Certified Management Digest*, Mar. 1996: 23.

Elashmawi, F. "Succeeding in Business with Americans." *Directions*, July–Aug. 1996: 61–4.

Elashmawi, F. "Testing Your Intercultural Communication Skills: Interacting with Americans." *International Business Communication* 1(3), 1989: 16–19.

Elashmawi, F. "Testing Your Intercultural Communication Skills: Interacting with the Japanese." *International Business Communication* 1(2), 1989: 23–6.

Elashmawi, F. "The Many Faces of Chinese Business Culture" *Certified Management Digest*, June 1997: 53–5.

Elashmawi, F. "The Many Faces of Chinese Business Culture." *Trade & Culture*, Mar.–Apr. 1995: 30–1.

Elashmawi, F. "Turning Friction into Synergy." *World Executive's Digest*, Oct. 1997: 58–9.

Elashmawi, F. and Harris, P. R. *Multicultural Management: New Skills for Global Success*. Houston, TX: Gulf Publishing Co., 1993.

Elashmawi, F. and Harris, P. R. *Multicultural Management 2000: Essential Cultural Insights for Global Business Success*. Houston, TX: Gulf Publishing Co., 1998.

Fernandez, J. P. *Managing a Diverse Work Force: Regaining the Competitive Edge*. Lexington, MA: Lexington Books, 1991.

Fieg, J. P. and Mortlock, E. *A Common Core: Thais and Americans*. Yarmouth, ME: Intercultural Press, 1989.

Fisher, G. *International Negotiation: A Cross-Cultural Perspective*. Yarmouth, ME: Intercultural Press, 1980.

Fisher G. *Mindsets: The Role of Culture and Perception in International Relations*. Yarmouth, ME: Intercultural Press, 1991.

Foster, D. A. *Bargaining Across Borders: How to Negotiate Successfully Anywhere in the World*. New York, NY: McGraw-Hill, 1995.

Gochenour, T. *Considering Filipinos*. Yarmouth, ME: Intercultural Press, 1990.

Grove, C. L. and Wenzhong, H. *Encountering the Chinese: A Guide for Americans*. Yarmouth, ME: Intercultural Press, 1991.

Hall, E. T. and Hall, M. R. *Understanding Cultural Differences: Germans, French and Americans*. Yarmouth, ME: Intercultural Press, 1990.

Harris, P. R. and Moran, R. T. *Managing Cultural Differences: Leadership Strategies for a New World of Business*. Houston, TX: Gulf Publishing Co., 1996.

Harris, P. R. and Moran, R. T.; Stripp, W. G. *Developing the Global Organization: Strategies for Human Resource Professionals*. Houston, TX: Gulf Publishing Co., 1993.

Ihsan, Z. and Mittman, K. *Culture Shock: Pakistan*. Portland, OR: Graphic Arts Center Publishing Co., 1991.

James, D. L. *Doing Business in Asia: A Small Business Guide in the World's Most Dynamic Market*. Cincinnati, OH: Betterway Books, 1993.

Jandt, F. E. and Pedersen, P. B. *Constructive Conflict Management: Asia-Pacific Cases*. Thousand Oaks, CA: Sage Publications, 1996.

Johnson, M. J. and Moran, R. T. *Robert T. Moran's Cultural Guide to Europe.* Oxford, UK: Butterworth-Heineman, 1992.

Kelly, C. and Meyers, J. *The Cross-Cultural Adaptability Inventory.* Yarmouth, ME: Intercultural Press/NCS Assessment Inc., 1997.

Kohls, L. R. *Developing Intercultural Awareness.* Washington, DC: SIETAR International, 1981.

Leppert, P. *Doing Business with the Chinese: A Taiwan Handbook for Executives.* Sebastopol, CA: Patton Pacific Press, 1990.

Leppert, P. *Doing Business with the Thais: A Handbook for Executives.* Sebastopol, CA: Patton Pacific Press, 1992.

Leppert, P. *Doing Business with the Koreans: A Handbook for Executives.* Sebastopol, CA: Patton Pacific Press, 1991.

Mann, R. I. *Expats in Malaysia: A Guide to Business, Working, and Living Conditions.* Toronto, Canada: Gateway Books, 1989.

Mann, R. I. *The Culture of Business in Indonesia.* Toronto, Canada: Gateway Books, 1996.

Meriwether Craig, J. *Culture Shock: Singapore.* Portland, OR: Graphic Arts Center Publishing Co., 1994.

Metcalf, G. and Wallach, J. *Working with Americans: A Practical Guide for Asians on How to Succeed with U.S. Managers.* New York, NY: McGraw-Hill, 1995.

Moran, R. T. and Stripp, W. G. *Dynamics of Successful International Business Negotiations.* Houston, TX: Gulf Publishing Co., 1985.

Moran, R. T. and Stripp, W. G. *Successful International Business Negotiations.* Houston, TX: Gulf Publishing Co., 1991.

Munana, Heidi. *Culture Shock: Malaysia.* Portland, OR: Graphic Arts Center Publishing Co., 1991.

Nydell, M. K. *Understanding Arabs: A Guide for Westerners.* Yarmouth, ME: Intercultural Press, 1987.

Putti, J. M. and Chia-Chan, A. *Culture and Management: A Casebook.* Singapore: McGraw-Hill, 1990.

Rissik, D. *Culture Shock: South Africa.* Portland, OR: Graphic Arts Center Publishing Co., 1994.

Roces, A. and Roces, G. *Culture Shock: Philippines.* Portland, OR: Graphic Arts Center Publishing Co., 1992.

Rowland, D. *Japanese Business Etiquette: A Practical Guide to Success with the Japanese.* New York, NY: Warner Books, 1985.

Saccone, R. *The Business of Korean Culture*. Elizabeth, NJ: Hollym, 1994.

Schneiter, F. *Getting Along with the Chinese: For Fun and Profit*. Hong Kong: Asia 2000, 1992.

Seligman, S. D. *Chinese Business Etiquette: A Guide to Protocol, Manners, and Culture in the People's Republic of China*. New York, NY: Warner Books, 1999.

Stewart, E. C. *American Cultural Patterns: A Cross-Cultural Perspective*. Yarmouth, ME: Intercultural Press, 1985.

Tan, R. *Chinese Etiquette: A Matter of Course*. Singapore: Landmark Books Pte Ltd: 1992.

Tan, R. *Indian & Malay Etiquette: A Matter of Course*. Singapore: Landmark Books Pte Ltd: 1992.

Tawfik, H. *Saudi Arabia: A Personal Experience*. San Jose, CA: Windmill Publishing Co., 1991.

Trompenaars, Fons. *Riding the Waves of Culture: Understanding Cultural Diversity in Business*. London, UK: The Economist Books, 1993.

Yang, S. M. *Korean Customs and Etiquette*. Seoul, Korea: Moon Yang Gak, 1993.

Zimmerman, M. A. *Dealing with the Japanese*. London: Unwin Paperbacks, 1985.

Index